B134

PELICAN BOOKS
A 407
EARLY MUSLIM ARCHITECTURE
K. A. C. CRESWELL

A
SHORT ACCOUNT
OF EARLY MUSLIM
ARCHITECTURE

*

K. A. C. Creswell

PENGUIN BOOKS

Penguin Books Ltd, Harmondsworth, Middlesex

U.S.A.: Penguin Books Inc., 3300 Clipper Mill Road, Baltimore 11, Md

AUSTRALIA: Penguin Books Pty Ltd, 762 Whitehorse Road,
Mitcham, Victoria

—

First published 1958

—

Made and printed in Great Britain
by Richard Clay & Company, Ltd, Bungay, Suffolk
Collogravure plates by Harrison & Sons Ltd

CONTENTS

CONTENTS

LIST OF PLATES

vii

LIST OF TEXT FIGURES

EDITORIAL FOREWORD

BY

M. E. L. MALLOWAN
Professor of Western Asiatic Archaeology,
University of London.

THE astonishing development of Muslim architecture a generation after the Arabs had begun to move fanwise across Syria and Iraq is a story which must appeal to all who are interested in the origins of those religious and artistic notions which have had a profound effect upon a large part of mankind. The simple tribesmen who had lived under tent or behind the mud walls of Arabia, with unconscious genius, made us of the technical and artistic ability which they found in the great cities of the time, in Jerusalem, Damascus, and elsewhere, and thus initiated the growth of wondrous buildings as places of worship, and as residences for their princes. This was the architecture of Islam, steeped in the traditions of the past, but created anew for the spread of a faith which soon attracted to it the best of contemporary skill for the adornment of its monuments.

Professor K. A. C. Creswell, the author of this book, has spent a lifetime in the study of Islamic architecture, and his great volumes published at Oxford in 1932–40 are monuments in themselves. These earlier tomes, however, are not easily accessible to the general reader, and it is therefore fortunate that the author has found himself able to condense that material, and add new comment in this Pelican book, which indeed does not replace but supplements his earlier writings. Here we have in fact a guide-book to this early architecture, indispensable for any who would follow the spread of Islam into Syria and Iraq, Palestine, North Africa, and Spain.

Architecture has a language of its own. It is the visible expression of the thoughts, beliefs, and aspirations of man. In Islam we find ideas, emotions, and a sense of poetry vividly evoked by the beauty of its buildings. Professor Creswell with his acute powers of observation, his gift for logical deduction and geometric calculation expounds for us with singular clarity many remarkable intricacies of construction. He holds strong opinions and boldly goes into battle against what he conceives to be false or slipshod theory. With ingenious learning he is often able to explain problems which have eluded others, and a relentless pursuit of detail adds to the fascination of his subject. Lastly it is well to remember that the author has himself often been present when repairs to famous buildings have exposed long forgotten evidence, has initiated excavations at important sites, and has more than once predicted what such exposures would reveal. Not the least important result of this book should be a further stimulus to Islamic art and archaeology which still have so much to reveal of their ancient accomplishments.

PART ONE

The Umayyad Dynasty

*

CHAPTER I

PRIMITIVE ISLAM

ARABIA, at the rise of Islam, does not appear to have possessed anything worthy of the name of architecture. Only a small proportion of the population was settled, and these lived in dwellings which were scarcely more than hovels. Those who lived in mud-brick houses were called *ahl al-madar*, and the Bedawīn, from their tents of camel's-hair cloth, *ahl al-wabar*.

The sanctuary at Mekka, in the time of Muhammad, merely consisted of a small roofless enclosure, oblong in shape, formed by four walls a little higher than a man, according to Ibn Hishām, or about 9 cubits (say 4½ m.; 15 ft) according to Azraqī, built of rough stone laid dry. It was oblong in shape, the following being the measurements of its sides, according to Azraqī: north-east 32 cubits, north-west 22, south-west 31, south-east 20. Within this enclosure was the sacred well of Zemzem. This little sanctuary, known as the Ka'ba, lay at the bottom of a valley surrounded by the houses of Mekka, *which came close up to it*, and we are expressly told that when Umar wanted to surround it by an open space, large enough to contain the Faithful, he had to demolish many houses.[1]

The Rebuilding of the Ka'ba

The Ka'ba, being in a bad state, was demolished and reconstructed by the Quaraysh, when Muhámmad was in his thirty-fifth year, i.e. in A.D. 608. The Quraysh took the wood of a ship which had been wrecked, and employed a carpenter and builder named Bāqūm, who had been on the ship, to help them in the rebuilding. Azraqī[2] says that the new Ka'ba was built with a course of stone alternating with a course of wood up to the roof, there being sixteen courses of stone and fifteen of wood, that is to say there were thirty-one courses,

1. Balādhurī, *Futūḥ*, p. 46.
2. Wüstenfeld's ed., *Chroniken der Stadt Mekka*, I, 110, last line, p. 112, l. 12.

beginning and ending with a course of stone. Azraqī's statement that Bāqūm was a builder and carpenter now becomes understandable – to erect such a structure a man would need to be both. The walls were probably covered with a coating of stucco, because it would appear, from Azraqī's account of the burning of the Ka'ba in A.D. 683, that it was only then that the people discovered, apparently with surprise, that its walls were partly constructed of wood. The door, which had previously been at ground level, was now placed with its sill 4 cubits and a span from the ground. The roof rested on six pillars (*sawārī*, plural of *sāriya*) arranged in two rows of three each. Total height of structure: 18 cubits, from which it follows that each course was roughly 31 cm. high. Azraqī says that on the ceiling, walls, and columns were pictures (*suwar*) of the Prophets, trees, and angels. On the column nearest the door was a picture of Abraham, and another of Mary with Jesus on her knee. This statement is so little known, and so remarkable, that I think it advisable to mention that Azraqī, who died in A.D. 858, is the oldest historian of Mekka. His history is mainly based on material collected by his grandfather before the end of the eighth century.

Architectural Origins

Where can this remarkable style of building, with alternate courses of stone and wood, have come from? Certainly not from a country like Arabia, where timber is scarce; it can only have been evolved in a country where wood was plentiful, and it is precisely in such a country – Abyssinia – that many examples of this extraordinary technique are to be found, e.g. the churches of Debra Damo, Debra Libanos, Imrahanna Kristos (Imraha), and Asmara.[1] Unfortunately the oldest of these churches does not go back beyond the ninth century; nevertheless it can be proved that this technique was employed in Abyssinia at a much earlier date, that is to say at the time when the great monolithic *stelae* of Aksum were carved. They are of oblong cross-section and are carved to resemble houses of many storeys, and the technique just described is counterfeited on the stone. The largest, now fallen and broken, measured 33·3 m. (109 ft) in height, tapered

1. '*Altere Denkmäler Nordabessiniens*' (*Deutsche Aksum Expedition*, Bd. II), pp. 168–94; and Buxton in *Archaeologia*, XCII, pp. 6–13.

upward, and ended in a crescent-shape which was the symbol of Mahrem, the Abyssinian God of War. As King Ēzānā, the Abyssinian Constantine, was converted to Christianity in the fourth century and made it the State religion, it follows that the latest possible date for these stelae is the fourth century.

We are therefore fully justified in asserting that the peculiar technique employed in building the Ka'ba came from Abyssinia, and even more than that, for Dr Enno Littmann tells me that Bāqūm is probably an abbreviation of Enbāqōm, the Abyssinian form of Habakkuk, so the 'carpenter and builder' employed was most probably an Abyssinian.[1]

The Migration (Hijra) to Madīna and Construction of Muhammad's House

When Muhammad, as a result of the hostility of the unbelieving Mekkans, migrated to Madīna in 622, he built a house for himself and his family. It consisted of an enclosure of mud-brick about 100 cubits (c. 56 yd) square, with walls 7 cubits high and a portico on the south side made of palm-trunks used as columns to support a roof of palm-leaves and mud. Against the outer side of the east wall were built small huts (hujra) for the Prophet's wives. All opened into the courtyard. We have a description of these huts preserved in Ibn Sa'd,[2] due to a man named 'Abd Allāh ibn Yazīd, who saw them just before they were demolished by order of al-Walīd in A.D. 707.

There were four houses of mud brick, with apartments partitioned off by palm branches plastered with mud, and five houses made of palm branches plastered with mud and not divided into rooms. Over the doors were curtains of black hair-cloth. Each curtain measured 3 by 3 cubits. One could touch the roof with the hand.

In the south-west corner of the courtyard was a primitive shelter similar to the portico on the north side, serving as a home for the poorest of those who had followed Muhammad from Mekka, who for this reason came to be known as the People of the Portico.

1. See my 'Ka'ba in A.D. 608', in *Archaeologia*, XCIV (1951), pp. 97–102.
2. *Tabaqāt*, I₂, p. 180.

Such was the house of the leader of the community at Madīna. Nor did Muhammad wish to alter these conditions; he was entirely without architectural ambitions, and Ibn Sa'd records the following saying of his: 'The most unprofitable thing that eateth up the wealth of a Believer is building.' [1] At this time Ṭā'if was the only town in the Hijāz that possessed a wall. When Madīna was attacked in 5 H. (627) it had no wall, so Muhammad had a ditch dug to defend it; the idea is said to have been due to a Persian slave named Salmān, and it created a great sensation, for nobody had ever heard of such a thing before. The word *Khandaq* given to it is Persian. Madīna was first surrounded by a wall in 63 H. (682–3).[2]

The Qibla, or Direction of Prayer

At first Muhammad prayed towards Jerusalem, probably because of the immense veneration in which he saw it was held by the Jews, who at this time formed the leading community in Madīna. To enable Islam to expand there, it was obvious that an agreement would have to be reached with them, either to convert them or to oblige them to leave the place; their adhesion to Islam would be a great triumph, whereas their enmity would be the greatest danger to his ambitions. To the conversion of the Jews he therefore attached a special value; to them he made large concessions and put forth his warmest appeal. They, on the contrary, showed themselves irrevocably hostile to all his efforts, and intercourse with them became more and more strained in the second year of the Hijra, and at last he decided to break with them.

The first manifestation of this decision was the changing of the *qibla*, the abandonment of the idea of Jerusalem as the centre of the world, and the substitution of the Ka'ba in its place. The change came quite suddenly; Muhammad was in the *Musallā* (or praying place) outside Madīna, and had just made the second prostration towards Jerusalem, when he received an inspiration to pray in future towards Mekka, and immediately recited the revelation recorded in the second Sūra of the Qurān. He then turned towards the south, and the whole

1. *Op. cit.*, I_2, p. 181, ll. 7–8; also VIII, p. 120, ll. 7–8.
2. Mas'udi, *Tanbīh*, p. 305, l. 4.

congregation did likewise.[1] The Musallā was henceforth known as the 'Mosque of the two Qiblas'.

Arnold regards this event as of fundamental importance:

This change of direction during prayer has a deeper significance than might at first sight appear. It was really the beginning of the National Life of Islam: it established the Ka'bah at Mecca as a religious centre for all the Muslim people, just as from time immemorial it had been a place of pilgrimage for all the tribes of Arabia. Of similar importance was the incorporation of the ancient Arab custom of pilgrimage to Mecca into the circle of the religious ordinances of Islam, a duty that was to be performed by every Muslim at least once in his lifetime.[2]

Minarets

In the time of Muhammad no such thing as a minaret was known, and when he and his followers first came to Madīna they prayed, according to Ibn Hishām, without any preliminary call to prayer. But having heard that the Jews used a horn (shofār) and the Christians a nāqūs or clapper, they wanted something similar for their own use. Muhammad therefore ordered Bilāl to give the call to prayer, which he was accustomed to do from the highest roof in the neighbourhood.

Death of Muhammad

No further change had taken place in Muhammad's house at the time of his death on 8 June 632. He was buried in the room which he had occupied in his lifetime. His house had not yet become a mosque and its transformation to such was by no means a rapid process. It apparently remained a house long after his death, for Abū Bakr, on being elected Khalif, or Successor, made use of it in the same way as Muhammad himself. It was still a house in A.D. 655, when the Khalif Uthmān was murdered there, in the room next to that in which the Prophet lay buried. Caetani considers that the fundamental change took place when 'Alī transferred the seat of government to Kūfa in 657 and Madīna sank back to the status of a provincial town. It was

1. Ibn Hishām, I, p. 427; Ibn Sa'd, I, pp. 3-5; Bukhārī, Bk VIII, c. 31-2; Tabarī, I, p. 1279-81, etc.

2. *The Preaching of Islam*, p. 22.

then that the memories of the Prophet, with which it was so intimately associated, raised it to the grade of sanctuary, as the place where more than half the Qurān had been revealed, the place which had been his home for ten years, and finally his grave.[1] In any case the transformation to a mosque was completed by A.D. 674, when the Feast of the Pilgrimage was celebrated there instead of at the Musallā, which was henceforth abandoned.

Election of Abū Bakr

Abū Bakr was then elected Khalif, or Successor. It must be clearly borne in mind that up till now there had been no foreign conquests, and a whole year had to be spent in putting down revolts before campaigns outside Arabia could begin. But clashes with Arab tribes on the borders of Syria and 'Irāq soon led to great expeditions against the Byzantine Empire on the one hand, and the Sasanian on the other. By the end of A.D. 637 the whole of Syria and 'Irāq was in the hands of the Arabs, and the conquest of Egypt was to follow.

To understand how Muslim architecture was born and to explain its early evolution and duality we must study the circumstances of the Arab conquest. The Arab advance was fanwise. At first they followed approximately the line taken by the present Hijāz Railway; then one detachment turned left at the level of Jerusalem, a second at the level of Damascus, whilst a third turned 45° to the right to the conquest of 'Irāq, and reached the Euphrates at the place where Basra was founded.

Now the men who formed these armies were mainly Bedawīn, but even those who came from permanent settlements, such as Mekka and Madīna, knew nothing of art or architecture. They soon found themselves in two totally different cultural environments. Those who had entered Syria found themselves in a region which had been under Hellenistic influence for nearly a thousand years, i.e. from the time of Alexander down to the Arab Conquest in A.D. 637–8. Those who entered 'Irāq (and Persia shortly after) found themselves in a region which had been under Persian influence for even longer.

And not only were the cultural conditions different, the material conditions were different also. Syria was a country of splendid build-

1. *Annali dell' Islam*, I, p. 442.

ing materials. Syrian limestone was the best of its kind, resisting weathering and acquiring a beautiful amber tint on exposure, and cedarwood was plentiful, for the Lebanon had not yet been deforested. So the seventh-century invaders found themselves in a country of splendid buildings – churches of cut stone, some of ashlar in courses 90 cm. (3 ft) high, with arcades on marble columns, gable roofs of cedarwood and large surfaces decorated with panelling of quartered marble, and coloured glass mosaics on a glistening gold background.

In the other cultural sphere they met with buildings of brick, sometimes only of mud brick, sometimes vaulted, and sometimes with flat roofs of palm-trunks, palm-leaves, and mud.

Conversion of Churches into Mosques

In these early days, the Muslims, when they conquered a town in Syria, usually took one of the churches and used it as a mosque, or merely *divided* one of the churches if the town had surrendered without resistance. At Homs, for example, they took a fourth part of the Church of St John. At Aleppo, according to Balādhurī, they took half the churches. How was a church converted into a mosque? One can easily guess. In Syria the qibla (direction of Mekka) is due south, whereas churches are turned towards the east. Under these circumstances it was only necessary to close the western entrance (or three entrances), pierce new entrances in the north wall, and pray across the aisles. That this is exactly what happened can be verified in the Great Mosque of Hamā, where the west front of the Kanīsat al-'Uzma (Great Church), which was converted into a mosque in A.D. 636–7, now forms the west end of the sanctuary. Its three western doors have been converted into windows and it is now entered from the north.

The Situation in Persia and 'Irāq

In Persia the Muslims apparently utilized existing buildings also, for Muqaddasī says: 'The Friday Mosque at Istakhr (Persepolis) ... is constructed after the fashion of the congregational mosques of Syria with round columns; on the top of each column is a cow. They say that it was formerly a Temple of Fire.' [1] From the reference to bull-

1. p. 436, ll. 3–5.

headed capitals I conclude that it was originally an *apadāna*, or hypo-style hall of the Persian kings, with a flat roof resting on columns with double bull-headed capitals (Figure 1).

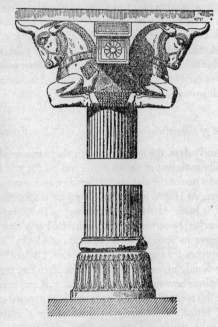

Figure 1. Persepolitan column and capital

At Qasvīn the first Friday Mosque, built by Muhammad the son of Hajjāj (d. 710), was known as the 'Bull Mosque'. This again suggests the use of ancient Persian columns, perhaps even the actual conversion of an *apadāna*.

But the situation was different in 'Irāq, for here the Arabs founded new towns (which they did not do in Syria),[1] so pre-existing build-ings could not be employed, and they had to construct some sort of place for themselves, and although none of these primitive mosques

1. With the exception of Ramla, founded by the Khalif Sulaymān.

has survived to the present day, descriptions of several have come down to us. What manner of buildings were the first mosques of the earliest towns in Islam?

At Basra, founded about A.D. 635, the first mosque, according to Balādhurī,[1] was simply marked out (*ikhtatta*), and the people prayed there without any building. According to another version, also given by Balādhurī,[2] it was enclosed by a fence of reeds. At Kūfa, founded in A.D. 638, the first mosque was equally primitive. Its boundaries were fixed by a man who threw an arrow towards the *qibla*, then another towards the north, another to the west, and a fourth to the east.[3] A square with each side two arrow-casts in length was thus formed. This area was not enclosed by walls but by a ditch only, and the sole architectural feature was a covered colonnade (*zulla*), 200 cubits long, which ran the whole length of the south side.

The columns were of marble, taken from some buildings of the Lakhmid Princes at Hīra, about 4 miles away. This *zulla* was open on all sides, so that, in the words of Tabarī (I, p. 2494), a man praying in it could see the convent known as Dayr Hind and the gate of the town known as Bāb Jisr.

On the *qibla* side, and only separated from the praying place by a narrow street, was built an official residence (Dār al-Imāra) for Sa'd, the Commander-in-Chief. Included in it was the public treasury (Bayt al-Māl). One night some thieves made a hole in the wall and stole the money, whereupon Sa'd wrote to the Khalif 'Umar informing him of the fact and describing the topography of the spot. 'Umar replied ordering him to shift the mosque so that it was in contact with his residence, 'for the mosque has people in it day and night; they are the best safeguard for their treasure'.[4]

It is important to observe that already at this early date we have a group – a square mosque with a Governor's residence built against its *qibla* side – which we shall see persisting for more than two centuries although derived from two trivial facts – viz. the marking out of the mosque by arrow-casts and a burglary.

1. *Futūh*, pp. 341, 342, and 346–7.
2. pp. 346 and 350.
3. Balādhuri, pp. 275–6; Tabarī, I, p. 2481, ll. 12–13.
4. Tabarī, I, p. 2491, l. 12 to p. 2492, l. 7.

The First Mosque at Jerusalem

None of the early Arabic historians, such as Balādhurī and Tabarī, speaks of the construction of a mosque when Jerusalem capitulated to 'Umar in 637, and the statements of Christian historians such as Theophanes, Elias of Nisibis, and Michael the Syrian that a mosque was built are accompanied by legendary details. However, there is no doubt that some primitive structure was erected at this time, for the early pilgrim Arculf, who visited Jerusalem *c.* A.D. 670, gives a description of it, saying:

But in that renowned place where once the Temple had been magnificently constructed, placed in the neighbourhood of the wall from the east, the Saracens now frequent a quadrangular place of prayer, which they have built rudely, constructing it by setting great beams on some remains of ruins; this house can, it is said, hold three thousand men at once.[1]

This may be called the First Aqsā Mosque. As for these ruins, they must have been those of the Royal Stoa of Herod, destroyed by the army of Titus in A.D. 70. According to the description of Josephus,[2] it consisted of a three-aisled portico which extended the whole length of the south side of the Temple area. It was like a basilica, of which the side aisles were 30 ft wide and 50 ft high and the central aisle half as wide again and twice as high, which certainly implies clerestory lighting. There were 162 columns of the Corinthian order, set in four rows, of which the southern were bonded into the outer wall, whereas the northern formed the façade on the court.

Eutychius tells a curious story in connexion with the capture of Jerusalem which shows that the early Muslims were not particular as to where they prayed. He says that 'Umar visited the Basilica of Constantine and prayed at the top of the flight of steps leading up to the entrance, after which he went to Bethlehem and prayed in the southern apse (*al-hanīya al-qiblīya*) of the Church of the Nativity. He adds that in his day (A.D. 939) the Muslims had taken possession of half the narthex of the Basilica of Constantine at Jerusalem.[3]

1. Tobler's ed., *Itinera Hierosolymitana*, I, p. 145.
2. *Antiquities of the Jews*, XV, 11, 5.
3. Pococke's ed., II, pp. 284–9; Cheikho's ed., pp. 17–19.

The First Mosque in Egypt

The conquest of Egypt took place in 640–41, and the Mosque of 'Amr was built at Fustāt in the winter of 641–2. Here again we have the testimony of an eye-witness, Abū Sa'īd Sulaf al-Himyarī (preserved in Maqrīzī, II, p. 247), who was present one day when 'Amr presided at the Friday prayer. It was small and primitive and measured only 50 by 30 cubits, say 29 by 17 metres (95 by 56 ft). It had two doors on every side except on the *qibla* side. The roof was very low and there was no interior court. The floor was not paved, but simply strewn with pebbles. Although small, it was too large to be spanned by single beams: we are not told how the roof was supported, but there can be little doubt that palm-trunks were used as columns to support beams of split palm-trunks and a thatching of palm-leaves and mud, exactly as in Muhammad's house at Madīna twenty years earlier. The walls were not even plastered and were doubtless of mud brick.

Introduction of the Maqsūra

According to Ibn Khaldūn,

the enclosure in which the Sultan stands during public prayers is an enclosure which includes the mihrāb (praying niche) and its neighbourhood. The first *maqsūra* was established by Mu'āwiya as a result of the attempt of the Kharijite who had struck him with a sword. According to another account it was [the Khalif] Marwān the son of al-Hākam (A.D. 683–5) who introduced the custom after having been stabbed by a Yemenite. ...[1]

This, the explanation usually accepted, has been contested by Lammens, who points out that the date 44 H. (664–5) given by Ya'qūbī [2] antedates the attempt on Mu'āwiya's life and puts Ibn Khaldūn's explanation out of court. Admitting this, the fact still remains that of the first four Khalifs, three were murdered, two in the very mosque itself, so Mu'āwiya already, before 664, had ample reasons for taking such a precaution. All existing *maqsūras* are open screens of *mashrabīya*, the oldest existing one being that of Qairawān (first half eleventh century).

1. 'Prolégomènes', de Slane's transl. in *Notices et Extraits*, XX$_{(1)}$, p. 71.
2. *History*, II, p. 265.

The Great Mosque of Basra, rebuilt A.D. 665

In Syria at this time we do not hear of any building activity, no doubt owing to the fact that in most towns the Muslims had either divided or taken complete possession of the principal church. In Mesopotamia, however, conditions were different, for two new towns, Basra and Kūfa, had been founded, and it is here apparently that Muslim architecture really began to make progress under Ziyād ibn Abīhī, who was appointed Governor of Basra in 665.

The mosque at this time, according to the expression of Wellhausen, was the forum of primitive Islam, the place of assembly, where decisions affecting Islamic society were taken. Thus we see Khalifs on the first day of their reign, and Governors arriving at the capital of their province, going directly to the mosque to meet their new subjects. Only after this ceremony of installation did they begin to exercise their new functions. If there were important despatches to be communicated, or if it were necessary to influence public opinion to get a measure adopted, a general assembly was called without waiting for Friday. Take the example of the trial of Khālid ibn al-Walīd at Homs. We read that the Khalif's representative summoned Khālid from Qinnasrīn, proclaimed an assembly in the Great Mosque and, standing in the pulpit, began the trial.

Ziyād, who was well acquainted with the turbulent spirit of the cities of 'Irāq, thoroughly realized the political importance of the mosque, that dominating position in which was concentrated at that time the political and social life of the Arab Empire. At the same time he felt that the *masjids* of the tribes were a danger to him, hence his anxiety to embellish and enlarge the Great Mosque, so that by its splendour and proportions it would eclipse the tribal *masjids* and attract all to it.

Balādhurī says that Ziyād greatly enlarged the mosque, using burnt brick and mortar, and roofed it with teak. The roof of the sanctuary rested on five rows of columns, the stone for which came from Jabal Ahwāz. Pebbles were spread on the ground, because when people prayed their hands became covered with dust, which they used to remove by clapping. This caused Ziyād to say: 'I am afraid that in the course of time the clapping of hands will be taken as part of the religious ceremony.'

At the same time Ziyād removed the official residence from the north-east to the *qibla* side of the mosque, saying: 'It is not fitting that the Imām should pass through the people.' [1]

The Great Mosque at Kūfa, rebuilt A.D. 670

Tabarī [2] says that Ziyād summoned masons 'of the Days of Ignorance' (i.e. non-Muslims), saying that he wished to erect a building that would be without equal. A man who had been one of the builders of Khusrau replied that that could only be accomplished by using columns from Jabal Ahwāz, the drums of which should be hollowed out, drilled, and fitted together by means of lead and dowels of iron. The roof should be 30 cubits (15 m.; 49 ft) high. He built it with sides (side porticoes?) and back (porticoes?). The height of the roof struck all observers. Ziyād then said: 'That is what I desired, but I could not express it.' Ibn Jubayr, who saw it in 1184, speaks of it as

a vast mosque, the *qibla* side has five aisles, whereas the rest have two only; the aisles are supported by columns like masts, composed of hard blocks of stone superimposed piece by piece, bedded on lead, and *not surmounted by arches*; extremely high, they go up to the ceiling of the mosque. I have nowhere seen a mosque of which the columns are so long or the ceiling so elevated.[3]

It is obvious that its roofing system resembled that of an *apadāna*, or Hall of Columns of the old Persian kings.

Enlargement of the Mosque of 'Amr and Introduction of the Minaret, A.D. 673

Thirty-two years after its foundation the people complained that the Mosque of 'Amr had become too small, so the Khalif Mu'āwiya ordered Maslama, the ninth Governor of Egypt, to enlarge it. al-Kindī expressly says that he pulled down what 'Amr had built.[4] He enlarged it towards the north-east and north-west, adding an open court in the latter direction. He also plastered the walls and spread matting on the floor in place of the pebbles which were formerly strewn there.

1. Balādhurī, pp. 347 and 348. 2. 1, p. 2492, ll. 8–15.
3. de Goeje's ed., p. 211. 4. Guest's ed., p. 38, ll. 15–16.

Maqrīzī says that the Khalif Muʻāwiya ordered Maslama 'to build sawāmiʻ (plural of saumaʻa) for the call to prayer. So Maslama constructed four sawāmiʻ for the mosque at its four corners. He was the first to construct them in it, there having been none there before his time'.[1] This is our first reference to a minaret.

What were these four sawāmiʻ? Now the Khalif who gave this order ruled from Damascus, where the Muslims at that time prayed in what had been the temenos, or sacred enclosure, of a Syrian temple. The temenos in question was, of course, the enclosure which is now the Great Umayyad Mosque (see below, pp. 44–81). At the time of the Arab conquest it had four square towers of no great height, one at each corner; these towers became the first minarets, for Ibn al-Faqīh (A.D. 903) refers to them as such,[2] although he knew that they were older than Islam, and Masʻūdī says that when al-Walīd built the Great Mosque 'the sawāmiʻ in it were not changed, they serve for the call to prayer at the present day'.[3] There is therefore every reason for believing that the four sawāmiʻ of Maslama were suggested by the four towers at the corners of the temenos at Damascus.

Three words have been employed in Arabic to denote minarets: midhana, saumaʻa, and manāra. The first is derived from adhān, the call to prayer, and simply means the place where the call to prayer is pronounced. The second appears to have been the name given by the Arabs to hermits' towers. All Syrian church towers and minarets built before the thirteenth century are square, and in this connexion it is specially interesting to find that this word is employed throughout North Africa, where minarets are nearly always of this type. It was carried into Spain by the Arabs and has been incorporated into the Spanish language as zoma. The third term, manāra, literally means 'a place where fire (nār) burns'. For this reason it was applied to the Pharos, at the top of which a fire burnt at night, then to lighthouses generally, and then, by analogy, to mosque towers, our word 'minaret' being derived from it.

Death of Muʻāwiya, A.D. 680

Before his death Muʻāwiya warned his son Yazīd against Husayn and ʻAbdallāh ibn az-Zubayr, a warning that turned out to be fully justi-

1. *Khitat*, II, p. 270, ll. 21–4.   2. p. 108.   3. *Prairies*, IV, pp. 90–1.

fied, for a few months later the former set out for Kūfa, intending to set himself up as Khalif. He was stopped at Kerbalā, and a few days later met his death under very tragic circumstances. This produced a reaction in favour of the House of 'Alī, a reaction which grew rapidly and ultimately brought about the fall of the Umayyad Dynasty in 750. Its immediate consequence was that Ibn az-Zubayr set himself up as rival Khalif at Mekka, whereupon Yazīd dispatched a force which took and sacked Madīna in 683 and then marched on Mekka. After a siege of two months the Ka'ba caught fire (we have seen above that it was built of alternate courses of stone and wood), and was destroyed. Shortly after Yazīd died the siege was raised, and Ibn az-Zubayr was left in possession as rival Khalif.

Rebuilding of the Ka'ba, A.D. 684

Ibn az-Zubayr demolished what was left of the Ka'ba in 684 and built a new one with walls 2 cubits thick entirely of stone.[1] Mas'ūdī says that glass mosaics were taken from a church at San'ā' in the Yemen which had been built by Abraha the Abyssinian during the invasion in the middle of the sixth century.[2] This is the earliest instance of the use of mosaics in Islam, for it antedates those of the Dome of the Rock by seven years. Persians were employed, for the *Kitāb al-Aghānī*[3] mentions 'the Persians singing in Persian when they were building the Ka'ba for Ibn az-Zubayr'.

Summary

It would appear that the pre-Islamic Arabs had but the crudest notions of building, that their principal sanctuary before 608 was nothing more than four walls the height of a man enclosing the sacred well Zemzem, and that in the early days of Islam they brought nothing architectural to the conquered countries beyond what would serve their simple ritual requirements. At this time nine-tenths of the population were nomads, for whom the finest architecture is the tent of camel's-hair. It is clear, as Richmond has expressed it, that their architectural resources, before they 'started on their career of conquest,

1. Azraqī, pp. 140–5.   2. *Prairies*, v, pp. 192–3.
3. III, p. 85, l. 4.

were barely enough to give the rudest expression to their needs'.[1] In other words, Arabia constituted an almost perfect architectural vacuum, and the term 'Arab' should never be used to designate the architecture of Islam. The first mosques in the great *hīras*, or half-nomadic encampments of the conquest, such as Basra, Kūfa, and Fustāt, were primitive in the extreme, and in Syria the first mosques were churches that had been converted or merely divided; in fact there is no reason for believing *that any mosque was built as such in Syria until the time of al-Walīd* (705–15) or possibly 'Abd al-Malik (685–705). For over a generation the Arabs remained quite untouched by any architectural ambitions and showed not the slightest desire to make use of the developed architectural talent of the conquered peoples. When they did begin to feel such ambitions it was chiefly for political reasons. They then turned to Sasanian architects on the Mesopotamian front (e.g. at Kūfa) and to Syrian architects on the Syrian front. We shall now study the splendid buildings for which the latter must receive the credit.

1. *Moslem Architecture*, p. 9.

CHAPTER 2

THE DOME OF THE ROCK

HISTORY AND DESCRIPTION

Reason for its Construction

WE have just seen that Ibn az-Zubayr had been left as rival Khalif at Mekka. 'Abd al-Malik, wishing to prevent his influence from being disseminated through Syria by the crowds of returning pilgrims, some perhaps 'indoctrinated', decided to prevent further pilgrimages from Syria, and to substitute the Sakhrā, or Rock, for the Ka'ba.

The Sakhrā is an irregular mass of natural rock in the midst of the Temple Area at Jerusalem known to-day as the Haram ash-Sharīf; it actually forms the summit of Mt Moriah. It measures about 18 by 13 m. (60 by 14 ft) and its maximum height above the floor of the Dome of the Rock is about 1½ m. Beneath the Rock is a cave about 4½ m. (15 ft) square, with a hole in the roof about 1 m. (3 ft) in diameter. There is every reason for believing that the Rock is the *lapis pertusus* of the famous Bordeaux Pilgrim (A.D. 333) to which the Jews in his day came once a year 'to anoint with oil, weep, rend their garments, and depart',[1] and that it was the actual foundation of the Altar of Burnt Offering, the cave beneath being the 'hollow or pit which was under the altar', which received the blood of the victims, mixed with the water used for ablution.

Jerusalem had already come to be looked upon as the place whence Muhammad had made his famous night journey to heaven, and it is possible that the Sakhrā, being the highest point in the Temple Area, had come to be regarded as the actual spot. Ya'qūbī (874) records 'Abd al-Malik's order forbidding the pilgrimage to Mekka, and his statement that

this Rock, of which it is reported that upon it the Apostle of God set his foot when he ascended into heaven, shall be unto you in the place of the Ka'ba. Then 'Abd al-Malik built above the Rock a dome ... and the

1. In Geyer, *Itinera Hierosolymitana*, pp. 21–2.

people took the custom of circumambulating the Rock, even as they had paced round the Ka'ba.[1]

Muqaddasī, who wrote over a century later (985), gives another reason, which may well have been a factor in the case, although Ya'qūbī's explanation must have been the principal one, for it so perfectly fits the political situation of the time. Muqaddasī, who seems to have had an extremely modern mind, remarked one day to his uncle that it would have been better if the vast sums of money spent on mosques had been spent on roads and caravanserais and frontier fortresses. But his uncle replied that

Syria had long been occupied by the Christians and that it was full of beautiful churches still belonging to them, so enchantingly fair and so renowned for their splendour, such as the church of the Holy Sepulchre and the churches of Lydda and Edessa,

and that al-Walīd had built the Great Mosque at Damascus (below, pp. 44ff.) to prevent the Muslims regarding them. And he ends up by saying:

And in like manner the Khalif 'Abd al-Malik, noting the greatness of the Church of Holy Sepulchre and its magnificence, was moved lest it should dazzle the minds of the Muslims, and hence erected above the Rock the dome which is now to be seen there.[2]

Thus we may say that Ya'qūbī gives the political reasons for the erection of the Dome of the Rock, whereas Muqaddasī explains why in some respects it resembled the Church of the Holy Sepulchre as it was at that time.

Description

The Dome of the Rock being the earliest existing monument of Muslim architecture, an accurate knowledge of its original appearance is therefore of the greatest importance, and I shall now attempt to describe it as it was in the days of 'Abd al-Malik. It is an annular building (see Plates 1–10 and Figure 2), and consists in its ultimate analysis of a wooden dome 20·44 m. (about 67 ft) in diameter, set on a high drum, pierced with sixteen windows and resting on four piers and twelve columns, placed in a circle just large enough to surround the Rock, and so arranged that three columns alternate with each pier.

1. *History*, II, p. 311.   2. p. 159.

A central cylinder is thus formed, of height about equal to its diameter. This circle of supports is placed in the centre of a large octagon averaging about 20·60 m. (67½ ft) a side, formed by eight walls 9·50 m. (29½ ft) in height (excluding the parapet, which measures 2·60 m.; 8½ ft). Externally there are seven bays in each side, but those next the corners – that is to say the two bays at the end of each side, or sixteen in all – are treated as blind panels. The remainder are pierced in their

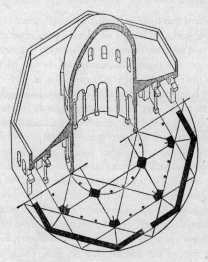

Figure 2. Jerusalem: Dome of the Rock

upper part by five windows. There is a door 2·60 m. (8½ ft) wide and 4·30 m. (14 ft) high in each of the four sides of the octagon which face the four cardinal points, and on these sides the central window above the door is consequently much smaller than the others. The space between the circle and the octagon being too great to be conveniently spanned by single beams, an intermediate octagon, consisting of twenty-four arches borne by eight piers and sixteen columns, so arranged that two columns alternate with each pier, has been placed between the two to provide the necessary support for the roof. The two concentric ambulatories (Plate 2) thus formed were, of course, intended for the *tawwāf*, or ceremonial circumambulation of the sacred object, the Rock. They are covered by a slightly sloping roof of wood sheathed with lead. The interior is lit by fifty-six windows arranged as follows: five in each face of the octagon = forty, and sixteen in the drum. The total – fifty-six – agrees with the number given by Ibn al-Faqīh in 903.

Setting Out of the Plan

It will be noted that there is a considerable difference in the width of the two ambulatories, although we should have expected the intermediate support to have been placed half-way between the inner circle and the outer octagon. This fact is explained by Mauss' theory,[1] and is one of the most striking confirmations of it. According to him the plan was engendered by two crossed squares inscribed in the circle formed by the outer edge of the central rotunda; the sides of these two squares, when prolonged, determine by their intersections the corners of the octagonal arcade (Figure 2). The sides of this octagon, when prolonged, form two other squares which may be circumscribed by a circle struck from the same centre as the central rotunda. An octagon, inscribed in this circle with sides parallel to the previous one, determines the exterior of the building. This process may, of course, be reversed. Being given the outer circle, an octagon may be inscribed within it; this will give the outer walls of the building. Two squares set crossways within the same circle will give, by their intersections, the sides of the intermediate octagon. The position of the four piers of the central ring may be found by joining up the corners of the octagon, as shown. But I believe that the other process was adopted because we shall see (below, p. 35) that there is no doubt that the diameter of the dome of the Holy Sepulchre was taken as the basis of the whole scheme.

I am convinced, however, that Mauss was not quite right in taking the *exterior* of the drum; if we take the centre line of the piers, which is almost but not quite the same thing, we get an even closer agreement. Adopting this, the differences between theory and the actual measurements of the building range from 1 in 366 to 1 in 980. This is conclusive proof that the actual dimensions were not chosen by chance.

1. In the *Revue Archéologique*, 3e série, t. XII, pp. 14–23.

It follows that every part of the building is related to every other part in some definite proportion, and the extraordinary harmony of its interior is the first thing to strike the observer. Hartmann describes it as 'ein Werk von vollendeter Harmonie';[1] Hayter Lewis says: 'There is an elegance of proportion which does not exist in any other building I am acquainted with',[2] and van Berchem was struck by 'its character of grandeur and majesty which it owes to its clear and simple plan, and to the harmonious lines of its architecture'.[3]

The Outer Walls

Part of these was exposed for a short period during the repairs of 1873-4 and again a few years ago. They are built of stone in courses

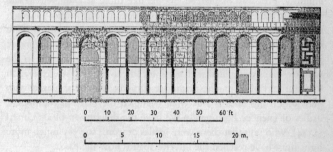

Figure 3. Jerusalem: Dome of the Rock, masonry of w. and s.w. façades, partly exposed in 1873-4

about 80 cm high. The seven tall, narrow, recessed panels on each face were found to be covered by semicircular arches, although subsequently disguised in 1552 by the coating of faience, and given a slightly pointed outline.

The Windows

These have double grilles: an outer set forming part of the faience facing and therefore dating from Sultan Sulaymān's work of 1552, and

1. *Der Felsendom*, p. 20.
2. *The Holy Places of Jerusalem*, pp. 26-7.
3. *Corpus Inscriptionum Arabicarum–Jérusalem*, II, p. 224.

an extremely beautiful inner set, also due to him (some, however, are later replacements). None of the original windows exists, but thanks to Richmond's careful researches, it is now possible to fix the position occupied by them in the thickness of the wall, and also the thickness of the window itself. The thickness of the wall is 1·30 m. (4¼ ft) and on the soffit of one of the window openings he found traces of the glass mosaics which originally covered the upper half of the outer walls (below, p. 31). This fragment was bordered on its inner edge by tesserae set in a straight line 23 cm. (9 in.) from the outer edge of the arch. This line marks the junction of the mosaics with the outer face of the original window. The marble panelling of the interior turns into the window opening for a distance of 92 cm. (3 ft) and stops 15 cm. (6 in.) from the line of mosaic. The original window, probably of pierced marble like those at Damascus (Plate 16), must therefore have been 15 cm. thick, at least round the edge, but not necessarily all over. Thus on the outside of the window there was a shallow reveal of 23 cm. covered with mosaic, and on the inside a reveal four times as deep lined with marble. The openings in the window-slabs were filled with glass, for Ibn al-Faqīh (903) says: '…in its walls and high in the drum are fifty-six windows, glazed with glass of various hues'.[1] But what occupied the place of the present grilles of faience? Fortunately we have the description of al-'Umarī (1344), who says that there were grilles of iron,[2] so very much more light must have reached the interior than is now the case.

The Parapet

Immediately above the course which runs above the arches of the panels is a salient string course, in which leaden gargoyles are set at regular intervals, there being six in each face.

It was revealed during the works of 1873-4 that the parapet on each side above this point was decorated with thirteen little semi-domed niches, which had been hidden since 1552 by Sultan Sulaymān's coating of faience. These little niches are expressly mentioned by al-'Umarī, who says: 'Above the spouts a wall 4 cubits high covered with mosaic in the same fashion [as the wall below]. On each side of

1. p. 101.
2. *Masālik al-Absār*, i, p. 140. ll. 7 and 11-12.

the octagon are represented thirteen mihrābs.'[1] These niches (ten, however, instead of thirteen) are also clearly shown in the drawing of Erhard Reuwich of Utrecht, who accompanied Felix Fabri and Brydenbach to Jerusalem in 1483.[2]

The Porches

Let us begin with the northern and eastern, which appear to have undergone least change. They both form salients, a little over 9 m. (29½ ft) wide, with a projection of 2·80 m. (9 ft). In the centre is a door from which a little tunnel-vault about 2½ m. (8¼ ft) wide runs back to the door in the main wall. To right and left is a little room, clearly not original, for the four columns which support the vault in the north porch are embedded in the walls. In the eastern porch the vault still retains its original decoration of gilt and coloured-glass mosaic. What did the vault rest on? On a massive wooden beam of about 42 cm. (16½ in.) square section, with a bearing of 1·77 m. (5¾ ft) from impost block to impost block.

There are only three columns here, embedded in the walls, the capitals being exposed, but in al-'Umarī's day there were four in the left half,[3] exact position not stated; if we assume that there were once four in the other half also, it seems probable that a pair on each side carried the beam on which the vault rested, and that another pair on each side carried another beam supporting a flat roof covered with lead, the porch therefore being completely open. I suggest that the little tunnel-vault in the centre was covered by a rather shallow gable roof like that to be seen at the southern porch. The western porch has been much altered, no columns remain, and an inscription under the hood over the door states that it was restored by 'Abd al-Hamīd [the First] in 1194 H. (1780), which is in perfect keeping with its style – the early Ottoman baroque of the second half of the eighteenth century.

1. *Masālik al-Absār*, 1, p. 140, l. 13.
2. Brydenbach, *Peregrinationes* (Mainz, 1486), Plate 8. Best consulted in H. W. Davies, *Bernhard von Brydenbach*, Plates 26 and 27.
3. *Masālik*, 1, p. 140.

The Four Doorways

The doorways measure 2·60 m. in width and 4·30 m. in height, and each one is spanned by a lintel with a stilted semi-circular arch above. Each lintel is decorated on its underside with sheet metal, either copper or bronze, worked *en repoussé* and exhibiting a variety of designs, chiefly vine-scrolls, vine-leaves, bunches of grapes, and acanthus (Plate 4). Nail-heads are visible here and there, so there must be massive wooden planks beneath the lintel for these nails to be driven into. The raised parts of the design are gilt, the background of the central part is painted black, and of the outer borders light green (green bice). The present plated doors date only from Sultan Sulaymān. In Muqaddasī's day (985) the doors were of wood finely worked in panels. He says that they had been presented by the mother of the Khalif al-Muqtadir (A.D. 908-32). They were therefore not the original doors, concerning which we have no information.

The Interior

On entering we behold an interior of extraordinary splendour, glittering with marble panelling, marble columns with gilt capitals, and mosaics – green, blue, gilt, and mother of pearl (Plates 2 and 3). Straight in front of us are the three arches of one side of the intermediate octagon, resting on two marble columns which come between the two marble-faced corner piers. Above their gilt capitals run massive tie-beams, their underside covered with metal plates worked *en repoussé*, and painted and gilt like those over the four doorways. The faces and soffits of the arches are decorated with glistening mosaics, and beyond is the inner circle of supports, through the arches of which we see the gorgeous decoration of the wooden dome, with designs and inscriptions picked out in gold. It is an experience never to be forgotten. If we turn round we notice that the walls, from top to bottom, are lined with panels of quartered marble and pierced by thirty-six beautiful windows.

The Octagonal Arcades

The columns of this arcade have capitals of varying type, some being Corinthian, others composite. The shafts vary in length, but this fact is concealed under the panelled marble boxes. The moulded bases seen above these boxes were not really bases at all, but merely marble collars clipped round the shaft and resting on the top of the box.

The arches of the octagon do not rest directly on the capitals of the columns. Each column is surmounted by a cubical impost-block of stone, resting on a wooden beam, or tie, which runs through each arcade. Each consists of two beams laid side by side, measuring together 76 cms. wide and 27 high (30 by 10½ in.), and these beams, which meet end on over each impost block, are dovetailed together as shown (Figure 4). The height of the underside of these beams from the floor is 6 m. (19½ ft). A course of stone blocks approximately equal in depth to the tie-beams has been placed upon them, the total thickness being 64 cm. (25 in). The springer blocks of the arches come directly over the junction of the tie-beams.

A beautiful decorated sheet-metal covering (copper or bronze) is applied to the under side and outer face of these beams. It is worked *en repoussé* with a great number of designs which vary considerably in decorative value (Plates 8*b*, 9). This covering is fixed to the beams by large nails, the heads of which can be seen here and there. There are twenty-four tie-beams, and one design, not the most beautiful, is repeated nine times; the remaining fifteen all bear different designs, thus making sixteen varieties in all. The raised parts of the design are gilt, the background of the central part is painted black, and of the outer border green bice, exactly as over the four entrances.

The most beautiful of all, in my opinion, is S_2 (Plate 9*b*), and the architect was perhaps of the same opinion, for he has placed it in the centre of the side facing Mekka. Here we have a vine-scroll rising out of a vase in the centre and forming loops to right and left, each containing one bunch of grapes and one five-pointed vine-leaf, a motif which we shall find again in the base-moulding at Mshattā, at Sāmarrā, on the ninth-century pulpit of Qairawān, in the Dayr as-Suryānī (A.D. 914), and at Nāyin. This band of ornament must be regarded as the archetype of one of the most important themes of early Muslim art. In another we have a tree in the centre, instead of a vase, and similarly filled loops alternating with another variety. In two others we see loops containing one element only: a bunch of grapes alternating with a vine-leaf. In N_3 we have a kind of chain formed by half palmettes with a bunch of grapes hanging from the junction of their tips (Plate 9*a*) and curious motives rising from their bases. That to the

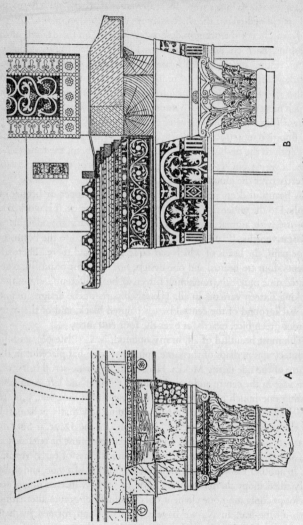

Figure 4: Jerusalem: Dome of the Rock, tie-beams and impost-block of intermediate octagon

left of the centre also occurs in the mosaics of the intermediate octagon (Plate 7, in spandrel to left of pier). It is a most important motive, for it occurs several times in the façade of Mshattā and also at Qaṣr aṭ-Ṭūba, and it is another piece of evidence pointing to an Umayyad date for them. The pine-cone occurs on another lintel, and this is a motive which, set radially, forms the centre of some of the rosettes on the soffits of the window-arches in the transept of the Great Mosque at Damascus, and also at Mshattā.

The inner side of these tie-beams differs from the outer, for it is treated like an extremely rich Corinthian entablature in wood, painted and gilt (Plate 5), which conceals the tie-beams and the stone course above them.

Now, although I have called these beams 'tie-beams' – which they certainly are, for they were intended to take a thrust, as is shown by the fact that their ends are dovetailed together – I must emphasize the fact that they are treated on their inner face as architraves, for the *emphasis is on the elaborate Corinthian cornice* and not on the arches above, which are treated as though they were relieving arches only.

In this connexion one cannot fail to be struck by the following passage in al-ʿUmarī: 'Height of column excluding the base, six and a half cubits, on which are *basāṭil*, plated with brass carved, and gilt over the carving. Above the *basāṭil* are arches covered with gilt tesserae.'[1] The word used by al-ʿUmarī for these beams shows that he fully realized the point made in the last paragraph, for the word *busṭul*, pl. *basāṭil*, although not to be found in dictionaries, is obviously derived from the Greek ἐπιστυλίον, which Liddell and Scott define as an 'entablature or architrave above a row of columns'.

The Inner Circle under the Dome

The arches of the inner circle have a breadth of 1·11 m. (3¾ ft), which is equal to the thickness of the drum they carry. They rest directly on the capitals of the columns, without the intervention of an impost block. They are very slightly pointed, a form due to the marble casing, which is probably due to Sultan an-Nāṣir Muhammad in 1318–19 (see below, p. 28). The tie-beams here are of wood 8–9 cm. (3–3½ in.) square (Plate 3).

1. *Masālik*, I, p. 141, ll. 11–12.

The Roof

The roofing of the inner ambulatory is composed of a series of king-post trusses with their outer principal rafters prolonged until they meet the drum. They are placed fanwise and set very close together. The rafters rest directly on the roof-principals, and are therefore parallel to the faces of the octagon. The ceiling beneath is a light covering of wood fastened to the under side of the roof-principals, and partly decorated with circular coffers, placed about half a diameter apart (Plate 2) and decorated with painted designs recalling Anatolian pottery of the eighteenth century. This ceiling, according to an inscription under the west porch, was reconstructed in 1194 H. (A.D. 1780) [1] and decorated with porcelain dishes, a few of which still remained in 1860, when they were seen by de Vogüé.

As the outer ambulatory is much narrower, its roof rests on simple beams only. Its ceiling is quite different and altogether superior to that just described (Plate 8b, above beam); there is no cornice, and its flat surface is divided into large rectangular and triangular fields decorated in relief, some with interlacing star patterns, others with great circular medallions of elaborate arabesque, executed in plaster and painted and gilt, no doubt on a backing of palm-fibre glued to the boards. The elements of which this arabesque is composed recall the present decoration of the interior of the dome, and also that of the dome of the Aqsā Mosque, which bears the name of Sultan an-Nāsir Muhammad and the date 728 H. (1327/8). I therefore cannot help believing that the ceiling of the outer ambulatory, or at least a considerable part of it, is also due to this Sultan, who carried out work here in A.D. 1318–19.

The Drum

This is 20·44 m. (about 67 ft) in diameter, and the height from the ground to the springing of the dome is almost exactly the same, viz. 20·40. It is strengthened by four buttresses which rise from the four piers of the inner circle, pass through the roof, and are visible externally. Their masonry is larger than that of the drum and breaks bond with it. Can they be a later addition or an afterthought? In the drum

1. Van Berchem, op. cit., II, pp. 343–6.

just above the roof-level, are sixteen windows. Some of these are the oldest in the mosque, for their symmetrical arabesque framework certainly belongs to the work of 1318–19.

The Wooden Dome

Ibn al-Faqīh, who saw the original dome in A.D. 903, says that it consisted 'of a dome over a dome (i.e. an inner and outer) on which are sheets of lead and plates of copper gilt'.[1] Ibn 'Abd Rabbīhi in 913 gives further details, saying that the dome was covered by 3,392 sheets of lead, over which were placed 10,210 plates of brass gilt.[2]

The present dome, the construction of which has been lucidly described by Richmond,[3] consists of two shells independent of each other; the ribs of the outer shell are braced to each other in their lower part by liernes and St Andrew's crosses, and the section of each is pointed. The height of the apex above mean floor-level is 35·30 m. (116 ft), and the finial measures 4·10 m. (13½ ft). There is a little door in the base of the dome which gives access to the space between the two shells. As the inner is pierced all round its base by openings between each rib, flanked by little turned columns, the passage which runs all round between the two shells forms a gallery, lit from the interior. The inner and outer domes are constructed with converging ribs. The ribs of the outer dome spring from a wall-plate laid along the outer edge of the drum; it is composed of pieces of timber scarfed together so as to form a continuous circular chain (Figure 5). The ribs of the inner dome spring from wall-plates 21 cm. (8¼ in.) square in section, sunk transversely in the wall and passing under the wall-plate of the outer dome. In length they measure more than the thickness of the wall and project 85 cm. (33½ in.) externally and 35 cm. (13¾ in.) internally, where their ends provide support for a bold wooden cornice; their outer ends provide support for the broad, lead-covered 'lip' which throws off the rain-water beyond the face of the drum. Between each inner rib is a bracing-piece. Each dome has thirty-two ribs, which meet at the summit in a circular plate, and each is built in three sections, one above the other, the ribs of the lower section of the outer dome being cross-braced. To the inner side of the inner dome is

1. p. 101.   2. al-'Iqd al-Farīd, III, p. 367.
3. The Dome of the Rock, pp. 11–13.

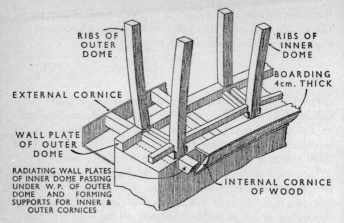

Figure 5. Jerusalem: Dome of the Rock, setting of double wooden dome on drum

nailed a wooden planking which carries the painted-and-gilded plaster decoration seen from within. The ribs of the outer dome are covered with planking on the outside, and to this is fixed the outer covering of lead. Some seventy years ago there were four inscriptions on the ribs of the dome (two no longer exist), evidently intended to face the four cardinal points, according to which the dome was built by the Fātimid Khalif az-Zāhir in 413 H (1022–3), the previous dome having fallen in 407 H. (1016–17). Why this long delay of six years? Probably because the first four years correspond with the period during which the Fātimid Khalif al-Hākim's madness took its most violent form, and repairs had to wait until az-Zāhir succeeded him.

The present dome has a finial of bronze (or brass) 4·10 m. (13½ ft) high, surmounted by a crescent, but it cannot be earlier than 1187, for the Arabic historians say that when Jerusalem was recovered from the Crusaders in that year, the dome was surmounted by a gilt cross which was immediately removed.

The Inner Lining of the Dome

This is decorated in slight relief with arabesques, executed in painted and gilded plaster on a backing of palm-fibre glued to the planking. Round the base, just above the open arcade of the gallery at the base of the dome, runs a great band of inscription between two parallel bands of ornament, linked together by eight loops forming medallions. Van Berchem, in a brilliant analysis,[1] has shown that these inscriptions have been tampered with, but there is no doubt that the splendid decoration of the vast dome surface above is due to Sultan an-Nāsir Muhammad in 1318–19.

The Decoration

The upper part of the outer walls and the drum also, although at present covered with panels of faience, were originally covered with gold and polychrome mosaics, which are mentioned by the Abbot Daniel (1106), John of Würzburg (1165), Theoderich (c. 1172), William of Tyre (1184), etc. It was only in 1552 that Sultan Sulaymān replaced it by its present coating of faience. This coating has been restored several times and varies in quality, and it has been suggested that the finest part is so good that it may go back to a period earlier than Sultan Sulaymān. It must therefore be emphasized that this is not the case, for Tschudi (1519) says:

… and the face of the walls externally round about are of costly mosaic work, even as S. Mark's Church at Venice, and the Church of the Holy Sepulchre, and the Church at Bethlehem are inside of the same work, but in the Temple of Solomon (i.e. the Dome of the Rock) there are no pictures except Cherubim (?winged motifs), and close by a palace (see the Damascus mosaics, Plates 18 and 19) and ciboria.[2]

Antonio de Aranda (1530) says: 'This edifice externally from the middle downwards is all faced with very rich marble; from the middle upwards it is worked in rich mosaics, foliage, and other beautiful frescoes.'[3] Finally Pantaleo d'Aveiro in 1552 describes it as 'from the ground up to the middle covered with large slabs all in a piece, polished, of finest marble: from the middle upwards to the first moulding of the top is all of the richest mosaic, with many designs of branches, roses, and other beautiful flowers'.[4]

In this year the outer walls were faced with faience, according to an

1. *Op. cit.*, II, pp. 289–98.
2. *Reiss und Bilgerfahrt zum Heyligen Grab*, pp. 226–7.
3. *Verdadera informaciõ d'la tierra santa*, fol. lxiii b.
4. *Itinerario da terra santa*, fol. 115 a.

inscription over the north door. The drum had already been faced in 1545–6. In 1586 Zuallart mentions this new coating, saying: '... decorated externally, in the upper part with slabs and coloured tiles after the Damascus fashion, and below with white marble. ...'[1]

We have seen that the vaults of all four entrance porches were doubtless decorated with mosaic. As for the inner face of the outer wall, it is faced from top to bottom with panels of quartered marble, and a band of ornament in black and gold, 50 cm. (19½ in.) wide, which runs all round at a height of 3·85 m. (12½ ft).

The four fan-lights over the door-lintels are variously filled; those over the east and west entrances are filled with stone grilles, consisting of a mesh of superimposed semicircles (imbrications), like so many Roman grilles, and are probably original; the other two are relatively late. The south and west lunettes are framed in borders, the decoration of which resembles that of the metal covering of the lintels below.

The eight piers of the octagon are faced with marble. The elaborate Corinthian cornice which decorates the inner sides of the tie-beams is continued round the inner face of the piers, forming a cornice (Plate 2 to left) above which everything is covered with mosaic. As the surface above the arcades consists of a series of more or less triangular spaces, the artist has composed his designs on the axis of each column. A sort of fantastic tree rises above each capital and spreads out to right and left as the surface widens, giving rise to what Strzygowski has called the candelabra motif (Plate 5). It is encrusted with jewels, necklaces, pendants, and sometimes even with bunches of grapes.

But at the end of each arcade, next to the pier, where the space left is only half that above the columns, another system has been adopted. The composition, instead of starting from below, begins at the top of the arch and descends towards the side of the pier; it generally consists of a cornucopia with a stalk emerging from it and coiling inwards. In one case (Plate 7, to left) it ends in a motif which we shall meet with again at Qasr at-Tūba (Plate 31a). All this decoration is crowned by a band of inscription in Kufic about 240 m. in length, which ends on the south outer face of the arcade with the date 72 H. (= A.D. 691).

The broad faces of the piers are decorated with pairs of acanthus stems, rising from an acanthus root and encrusted with necklaces,

1. *Il devotissimo viaggio di Gerusalemme*, p. 161.

pendants, etc. (Plates 6 and 7), but the narrower flanks are always decorated either with a naturalistic tree or a fanciful composition consisting of diverse elements superimposed (Plate 10b). Here is a curious fact: there are eight piers, and therefore sixteen flanks; eight consecutive ones are decorated with a tree, the other eight with a bizarre composition, from which I conclude that two schools of craftsmen with different principles divided the task. I cannot refrain from calling special attention to the beautiful composition on Plate 10a, where the wind-blown date-palm is so immeasurably superior to the miserable specimens in the mosaics of Ravenna. Note also the little tree below on either side of the trunk, for here we already have a basic principle of Muslim art – *the even covering of the field*.

The four dome-piers are also faced with marble on all four sides, but their flanks are decorated in addition with panels or medallions of gilt ornament. They are provided with slightly splayed cornices, decorated with acanthus scrolls (Plate 2), above which point (which is 6·90 m. from the floor) they are decorated with mosaic, as are the spandrels of the arches. The arches, however, are decorated with alternate slabs of black and white marble, presumably put there to hide damage suffered by the mosaics at the edges, for the pattern is cut short by it. It already existed in 1344 when it is mentioned by al-'Umarī, so it is probably due to Sultan an-Nāsir Muhammad in 1318–19.

The inner face of the drum is decorated as follows: first there is a facing of marble which covers the arches and their spandrels; this is crowned by a band of ornament matching that which forms the cornices of the dome piers, and above this is a great quarter-round moulding covered with mosaic (Plate 3). Above this is the drum proper, which is decorated by two great bands of mosaic separated by a great moulding. These two bands together measure 9·40 m. In the upper band are the sixteen windows, their sills resting on the great moulding. The upper band is crowned by a wooden cornice on which, at a height of 20·40 m. from the ground, rests the blind arcading at the base of the dome.

The Architect

The name of the architect of the Dome of the Rock is not known and there can be no doubt that the duties of Rajā ibn Haywā and Yazīd ibn Sallām, sometimes mentioned in this connexion, were confined to financial and administrative control. This is perfectly clear from the statement of Abu'l-Maʿālī al-Musharraf (thirteenth century), who speaks of a treasury being built to the east of the Dome of the Rock and put in charge of these two men. They cannot be regarded as architects any more than Geoffrey Chaucer can be called an architect because he held the office of Supervisor of Works in 1389.

ARCHITECTURAL ORIGINS

The Plan

With the solitary exception of the Marneion at Gaza, there does not appear to be any evidence for the existence, in Syria and Palestine, of a rotunda earlier than Constantine's Church of the Holy Sepulchre, finished about A.D. 335. But long before that there were a number of circular buildings in Greece, such as the Temple of Palaimon at Corinth, the Temple of Athena Pronaia at Delphi, the Tholos of Epidarus, the Tholos of Delphi, the Philippeion at Olympia, etc.

A circular domed structure became the most popular form of Roman mausoleum, whereas types entirely different prevailed in Syria. Of existing examples in Rome we have Hadrian's mighty Pantheon (A.D. 120–24), the Nymphaeum in the Licinian Gardens, known to-day as Minerva Medica (253–68), and the Mausoleum of St Helena (early fourth century). Concentric aisled rotundas occur as early as the fourth century, e.g. the Rotunda of Santa Costanza (324–6). The Church of the Holy Sepulchre built by Constantine seems to have been derived directly from the latter, which had been built by him a few years earlier, for it likewise consists of a central ring of supports carrying a dome, with an ambulatory between it and the outer circular wall. The dome of Santa Costanza rests on an inner ring of supports consisting of twelve pairs of columns arranged in a circle; a cruciform effect is produced by making the arches facing the four cardinal points wider than the rest (Figure 6). This same effect is produced in the Holy Sepulchre, which has an inner ring of supports consisting of twelve columns and eight piers so arranged that a pair of piers comes between every three columns. All these columns have

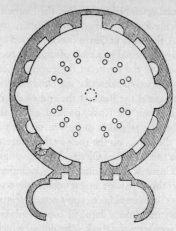

Figure 6. Rome: Mausoleum of Santa Costanza

long since been encased in masonry (one column much calcined was actually seen during repairs in 1867). Here again the arches on piers, which face the four cardinal points, are slightly wider than the rest. Thus we have: two piers, three columns, two piers, three columns, etc., and the arrangement in the Dome of the Rock is almost the same: we have one pier, three columns, one pier, three columns, etc. And Syria's part in this evolution included the system whereby the relationship between the outer circle and the inner ring was fixed by a system of triangulation (above, p. 20), a similar (but slightly different) system having also been employed, as Mauss has shown, for the Holy Sepulchre, whereas no such system was employed for Santa Costanza, for the outer wall is just twice the diameter of the dome.

We have seen (above, p. 18) that Muqaddasī says that the Dome of the Rock was built by 'Abd al-Malik to rival the Church of the Holy Sepulchre, and that the diameter of the dome in the former is 20.40 m. (about 67 ft) against 20·44 to 20·48 for the latter.[1] But this is

1. It is impossible to take a direct measurement across the floor, on account of the chapel in the middle containing the tomb of Christ, but Mr Wm. Harvey at my suggestion, during the works of 1934 when scaffolding was erected, was able to take direct measurements above it from pier to pier and found that the diameter varied from 20·44 to 20·48. Letter of 12.v.1934.

not all: the general resemblance between the Dome of the Rock and the Holy Sepulchre can be carried even farther, for, according to Eusebius (d. 340), the tomb of Christ (since covered by a little edifice) in these early days consisted of a mass of unhewn rock with a cavern inside it, rising out of the centre of the pavement under the dome, words which would exactly describe the Dome of the Rock before a palisade was put round the Rock at the end of the twelfth century. Similarly the marks on the Rock, pointed out as the footprints of Muhammad when he ascended to heaven on his famous midnight journey,[1] recall the marks on the rock in the centre of the Dome of the Ascension on the Mount of Olives, shown to pilgrims as the footprints made by Christ at the moment of His ascension.

In addition to this a passage in Eutychius[2] shows that the Khalif al-Walīd (705–15) was anxious to copy certain features of Christian churches, for he carried off a dome of copper gilt from a church at Baalbek, and placed it on the Rock. The dome, which of course cannot have been the dome of the church, was doubtless a hemispherical ciborium supported on columns, which covered the altar – a baldachin, in fact.

The Doorways

Provided with lintel and arched lunette, these are of a type completely Syrian. In the fourth century we have the Baptistery of Mār Ya'qūb at Nisibin, built A.D. 359. In the fifth century we have fine examples in the great church at Qal'at Simān, at Dayr Simān, and at Hāss. In the sixth century we find the same type of doorways with lunette above in the Church of St Stephen at Jūwānīya, built in 554, and also in the great church at Qalb Luzeh. But all these examples are decorated with Classical mouldings and ornament. The doorways which come closest to those of the Dome of the Rock are those of the Cathedral of Bosrā, 512–13, and the Church of St George at Ezra', 515–16. Here the doorways are practically identical with ours, for the masonry is absolutely plain, except that the arch of the lunette at Ezra' has a moulding. We shall meet with the same type of doorway at Qasr al-Hair (Plate 27a) and in the Great Mosque of Cordova

1. This tradition is very ancient, being found as early as 874 in Ya'qūbī.
2. Pococke's ed., II, pp. 372–3.

(Plate 40*b*). As for the porches of the Dome of the Rock as they must have been originally, it is clear from the holes in the masonry of the church of Qatb Luzeh that it was preceded by a similar gable-roofed porch.

The Wooden Dome

Hartmann's remark that a wooden dome is an astonishing feature in a country like Syria, which is poor in wood and rich in stone,[1] although applicable at the present day, does not hold good for the seventh century, when the Lebanon had not been deforested.

Several wooden domes are known, of which the earliest is that of the Marneion of Gaza, a temple built in the second century A.D. in honour of the fish-god Marnas, of which a description has come down to us.[2] The second was that of the Holy Sepulchre of Constantine, A.D. 335, burnt by the Persians and rebuilt by Modestus in 616–28. However, it must be admitted that the latter example, and perhaps the former also, were *cones*. The most imposing example of a wooden dome, before Islam, must have been the dome of the Church of St Simeon Stylites at Qal'at Simān (25 miles from Aleppo), built after his death in 459 but before 560, and most probably before 500. This church consists of four great basilicas radiating from a central octagon, 27 m. (88½ ft) in diameter. Owing to the absence of any signs of there having been a dome over the octagon, and especially the term ἀυλη ὑπαιθρίος used by Evagrius, who visited the church in 560, no one had ever supposed that it could have been covered by a dome. But a great controversy was started when Krencker, in 1933, carefully examined the fallen masonry on the floor of the octagon, block by block, and found voussoirs of which the radius was 2·20 m. (7¼ ft), belonging to the coupled windows which pierced the drum of the octagon. He continued his researches in 1938,[3] and found the voussoirs of several more windows, the remains of four squinches (of which there must have been eight to convert the octagon into a figure

1. *Felsendom*, p. 22.

2. Mark the Deacon, *Life of Porphyry, Bishop of Gaza*, ed. of Grégoire and Kugener, pp. 52–60.

3. *Abh. der Preussischen Akad. der Wissenschaften*, 1938, phil.-hist. Klasse, No. 4, pp. 15–20.

of sixteen sides), and several blocks of the moulded cornice which formed the summit of the octagon. Cut in the latter were transverse grooves, 27–31 cm. (10½–12¼ in.) wide and 22–27 cm. (8½–10½ in.) deep, made to receive the transverse wooden wall-plates of a wooden dome, *exactly as in the Dome of the Rock* (Figure 5), where, however, they measure 21 by 21 cm. (8¼ by 8¼ in) only, which is quite natural, for they belong to a dome 20·44 m. (67 ft) in diameter, against nearly 27 m. (88½ ft) at Qal'at Simān.

To reconcile the expression of Evagrius (ὑπαιθρίος = open to the sky) with the definite fact that provision was made for the setting of a dome, Krencker suggests that the famous earthquake of 526 at Antioch may have caused the dome to fall.

In any case, we are absolutely safe in saying that, whether the dome was actually erected or not, the architect *designed the church to have a wooden dome, and arranged to set it on the drum by the very same method employed two hundred years later at Jerusalem.*

The Decoration on the Cornices of the Dome-piers

The scrolls of acanthus, which form whorls with a little flower in the centre, decorating the cornices of the dome-piers, and likewise the great band which runs round the interior of the drum just below the mosaic, are merely the result of a development which had already begun in Syria a century or two before the Arab conquest. The first stage may be seen on the cornice of a pyramidal tomb (fifth to sixth century) at al-Bāra; here the scrolls are free-flowing and continuous (Figure 7). There is a strikingly similar frieze in the apse of the Church

Figure 7. Al-Bāra: Pyramidal tomb, detail of cornice

of St Simeon Stylites mentioned above. Other examples occur over a doorway at Mijlayyā, and at Jerusalem on the Golden Gate and the Double Gate. Our friezes may therefore be regarded as purely Syrian.

The External Coating of Mosaic

It may appear surprising that such a delicate form of decoration should be used externally. However, this feature was not new, for the old basilica of St Peter at Rome had its façade adorned with mosaic *c.* A.D. 450, and an example of the sixth century still exists in the basilica at Parenzo near Trieste.[1] But the Muslims probably got the idea from the Church of the Nativity at Bethlehem, the west front of which, at that time, was so adorned.[2] Another Syrian example may be cited – Ruṣāfa – where Yāqūt, quoting the Christian physician Ibn Butlān, says that there was 'a mighty church, the exterior of which is ornamented with gold mosaics, begun by order of Constantine, the son of Helena'.[3]

It is obvious from our analysis that the Dome of the Rock is a thoroughly Syrian building.

Superficial Influence of the Arab Conquest

The conclusion which we have arrived at is quite in keeping with what is found in other fields of human activity, e.g. the Government Secretariat and the Coinage. The Arabs, having brought no administrative machinery with them from Arabia, and having nothing resembling it, were only too glad to adopt the administration which they found in being in Syria and Persia. Thus it came about that the staff of the revenue offices in Syria continued to be composed of Christians, and in ʿIrāq and Persia of Persians. Balādhurī says that the language used for the Land Tax Register in ʿIrāq was Pahlavi, until Hajjāj decided that Arabic should be used instead.[4] In Syria, where Greek had been used, it was only in 700 that the Khalif ʿAbd al-Malik ordered the adoption of Arabic. In Egypt it was only in 706

1. Errard and Gayet, *L'Art Byzantin*, p. 32 and Plate II.
2. Clermont-Ganneau, *Receuil d'archéologie orientale*, II, pp. 129–30.
3. *Muʿjam*, II, p. 784. 4. *Futūh*, p. 193.

that the Governor ordered all administrative documents to be drawn up in Arabic instead of Greek. And even this order was not fully effective at once, for the Aphrodito papyri, which consist of letters from the Governor of Egypt to the people of the village of Aphrodito, written between 709 and 714, are still in Greek (see p. 43).

The same happened with the coinage. Before Islam, and during the lifetime of its founder, the Arabs had none of their own, the money circulating in Arabia being either Byzantine dinars or Sasanian dirhems, brought from Syria and 'Irāq by the profitable caravan trade. When the Arabs became masters of Syria, 'Irāq, and Persia they continued, for the first few years, to use a coinage with which they were familiar, and after that made only the slightest modifications.

In Persia the standard coin was the Sasanian dirhem, which bore on one side the portrait of the king wearing the tiara, and on the reverse two figures standing on either side of a fire altar; in the border, outside three milled circles, was a star and a crescent three or four times repeated. They adopted this coin, leaving everything intact, and contented themselves with merely adding *Bismillah* in Kufic, and using the Hijra reckoning for the date. This series continued until 'Abd al-Malik put an end to it about 693.

In Syria the first coins minted by the Arabs were struck at Damascus in 17 H. (638). One bears the effigy of Heraclius standing full-face, with all the symbols of Christianity: a cross surmounted by a diadem, a long cross supported by the right hand, a globe bearing the cross in the left hand, etc. But instead of the Indiction we have the date expressed according to the Hijra reckoning. Then the words *in the name of God* in Arabic are gradually introduced and the cross disappears. Later on Mu'āwiya (661–80), according to Maqrīzī, struck dinars on which he was represented girt with a sword. None of these coins is known today, but a number of similar coins bearing the name of 'Abd al-Malik have been preserved. Then came the introduction of a new type, purely Arabic, in 692.

THE GREAT MOSQUE OF WĀSIT

Until a few years ago the Great Mosque at Damascus (705–15) was the oldest congregational mosque known, and the Mosque at Qasr al-Hair (729) the second oldest, after which came the oldest part of the Great Mosque at Harrān (744–50). No 'Irāqī mosque of the Umayyad period has survived. But about eighteen years ago I was asked by the Department of Antiquities to suggest two Muslim sites likely to repay excavation. I suggested Wāsit and Kūfa, pointing out that the former was founded by the Governor of 'Irāq, Hajjāj ibn Yūsuf, on virgin ground in 703–4, and that he was known to have built a mosque there, measuring 200 cubits (a little over 100 m.; 330 ft) each way, placed back to back, as was the custom in early Islam, with a Dār al-Imāra 400 cubits square.[1]

Wāsit to-day is a deserted site, about 25 miles from Qūt al-Amāra, without any population. It is called Manāra because there is an old thirteenth-century building there with the entrance flanked by two minarets. An examination of the site revealed what looked like a sunken tennis-court; this on excavation turned out to be the *sahn* of a mosque 102.8 m. (337¼ ft; roughly 200 cubits) square. After the excavations were well advanced they were extended to the back or *qibla* side of the mosque, but to my great disappointment no Dār al-Imāra was found.

Some time after, the excavations were continued in depth and a very interesting discovery was made, viz. that the mosque first discovered rested on another mosque which faced south-west, instead of being properly oriented towards Mekka, the difference being about 33°. This mosque, which was also a little over 100 m. (330 ft) square (from 103·50 to 104·30 m.), rested on the virgin soil. It had five rows of eighteen columns on the *qibla* side, but one row only on the three other sides. The excavators were a little worried because there was no concave niche in the centre of the *qibla* wall,[2] until I pointed out that this was exactly as it ought to be, for the concave mihrāb was introduced for the first time when al-Walīd rebuilt and enlarged the mosque at Madīna in 707–9 (below, p. 44). A number of sandstone drums were found during the excavations, which had presumably been used in the second mosque, but the Sasanian-like decoration carved on a number of them (some were plain) left no doubt that they had been taken from the first mosque. The columns, therefore,

1. Balādhurī, *Futūh*, p. 290.

2. Fuad Safar, *Wāsit* (1945), p. 20, expressly says so, although a rectangular mihrāb is shown in his reconstructed plan, Fig. 11.

had been built up with circular drums about half a metre high, super-imposed and connected by an iron rod which ran through a hole in the centre of each, exactly as in Ibn Jubayr's description of the columns of the second Great Mosque at Kūfa (above, p. 13). This rod was set in lead, for traces of both metals remained. The columns varied in diameter from 90 to 110 cm. (35 to 43 in.).

The walls and foundations were of kiln-baked bricks and reddish gypsum, the bricks varying from 30 by 30 by 6 cm. (12 by 12 by 2⅓ in.) to 23 by 23 by 5 (9 by 9 by 2 in.). The thickness of the walls was 2·26 m. (7½ ft) and the foundations projected 16 cm. (6¼ in.) within and 10 (4 in.) without. On the walls were pilasters corresponding to each row of columns. The colonnades had continuous foundations 1·50 m. (5 ft) wide, running in both directions and forming a grid, the spaces between usually measuring 3·80 by 3·50 m. (12½ by 11½ ft). The first pavement consisted of soft red bricks, set in rows parallel to the sides of the building.

We now have what is the *oldest mosque in Islam of which remains have come down to us*, a mosque which we are justified in calling the '*Irāqī type*, for it conforms exactly with what we have reconstructed at Basra (665) and Kūfa (670), and which we shall see was repeated at Baghdād in 765 (below, pp. 179–82).

After this discovery I suggested that a fresh attempt should be made to find the Dār al-Imāra, by excavating behind the *qibla* wall. This was done, and it was found that the back wall of the mosque continued to right and left and ended in a three-quarter round tower on a plinth 8·20 m. (27 ft) square, the total length being 208·8 m. (685 ft; 400 cubits). Part of the foundations and column bases were found of a triple colonnade which apparently stopped abruptly at each end when it reached a point corresponding with the sides of the mosque. The excavations, unfortunately, have not been continued, but we know from the sources that the Dār al-Imāra had four (?three) main entrances, each opening on to a street 80 cubits wide,[1] and that it had a green dome, probably placed in the centre of the building, which could be seen from a long way away, and which caused the palace to be known as al-Qubbat al-Khadrā = the Green Dome.

1. Bahshāl's MS. *History of Wāsit*, quoted by Fuad Safar, *op. cit.*, p. 2.

CHAPTER 3

THE WORKS OF AL-WALĪD

The Second Aqsā Mosque

WHEN was the First Aqsā Mosque, the mean structure seen by Arculf, replaced? If we are to believe some of the Arabic authors who deal with this question, it was 'Abd al-Malik who was the first to build an Aqsā Mosque worthy of the name, whereas others attribute it to al-Walīd. Fortunately we now possess a better authority than any of the above, the earliest of whom wrote over two centuries after the event. I am referring to the contemporary Aphrodito papyri, the official correspondence (in Greek) of Qurra ibn Sharīk, Governor of Egypt from 709 to 714, with the Prefect of the District of Aphrodito in Upper Egypt. No. 1403 refers to 'the maintenance of labourers and skilled workmen employed on the Mosque of Jerusalem, ... 3 persons for 12 months'; [1] likewise Nos 1414 and 1435, which is dated Hathyr 20, 14 Indiction, year 97 (= A.D. 715–16).[2] Thus there cannot be any doubt that it was al-Walīd and not 'Abd al-Malik, who built the Second Aqsā Mosque. We shall see that it is just possible that the arcades on marble columns, to right and left of the dome, may go back to this period (below, p. 112 and Plate 24).

al-Walīd rebuilds the Mosque of Madīna, 88–90 H. (707–9)

Balādhurī says that al-Walīd wrote to his Governor at Madīna ordering him to pull down the mosque and rebuild it, at the same time sending him eighty Greek and Coptic artisans, inhabitants of Syria

1. Bell (H. I.), Greek Papyri in the British Museum, IV. The Aphrodito Papyri, pp. 75–6.

2. Ibid., III, p. 137, and IV, pp. 93 and 95. This dispatch of workmen from Egypt to Jerusalem was no new thing, for we learn from Leontius of Neapolis (wrote A.D. 645) that Modestus, about A.D. 629, sent thousands of Egyptians to Jerusalem to assist in rebuilding the churches which had been destroyed by the Persians in 614; see his Life of John, Archbishop of Alexandria, Gelzer's ed., p. 37, and notes on pp. 137–8.

and Egypt.[1] Ya'qūbī says that the little huts (*hujra*) of the wives of the Prophet, which opened into the east side of the mosque (above, p. 3), were pulled down and the area so obtained added to the mosque.[2] Samhūdī, quoting Wāqidī (d. 823), says: 'The Copts erected the sanctuary and the Greeks (Rūm) have worked at the sides and back of the mosque.'[3] Muqaddasī says that the mosque was built of cut stone. Tabarī gives the final measurement as 200 by 200 cubits. Ibn Jubayr, who saw the mosque in 1183, describes the supports as consisting of very tall columns composed of drums connected by iron rods set in lead, exactly as at Kūfa and Wāsit, and without arches resting on them.[4] The new mosque was decorated with marble panelling and polychrome mosaic (*fusaifisā*), and had four minarets, one at each corner.

A most important innovation was made at this time, for Ibn Duqmāq and Maqrīzī [5] (the latter quoting Wāqidī, who died in 823) say that the first who made a mihrāb in the form of a niche was 'Umar ibn 'Abd al-'Azīz when he rebuilt the Mosque of Madīna by order of al-Walīd. The passage from Samhūdī, cited above, helps us to explain this innovation, for it appeared in the part constructed by the Copts, and at once suggests a Coptic origin. Lammens in fact quotes a passage from a work by as-Suyūṭī (fifteenth century) as follows: 'At the beginning of the second century (Hijra, therefore shortly after A.D. 715) it was forbidden according to the Traditions, to make use of it, as it was a feature of churches.'[6] In 710–12 the Mosque of 'Amr was rebuilt and enlarged, and on this occasion it was given a mihrāb in the form of a niche, this being the second example in Islam.

THE GREAT MOSQUE OF DAMASCUS

By the time of al-Walīd the Muslim population had increased to such an extent by immigration and conversion that one of his first acts was the provision of a congregational mosque, not only of adequate size, but one which, in splendour and magnificence, would rival the finest

1. *Futūh*, p. 7.   2. *History*, II, p. 339.   3. *Khulāsa*, Mekka, ed., p. 131.
4. Wright's ed., p. 195.   5. II, p. 247.
6. In the *Rivista degli studi orientali*, IV, p. 246, n. 1.

churches in Syria. Muqaddasī has made this quite clear (above, p. 18).

He therefore proceeded, as Muqaddasī says, to collect craftsmen for the purpose. This is confirmed, as regards Egypt, by the Aphrodito papyri, one of which reads: 'Pay for the wages of a sawyer for work on the mosque at Damascus for six months in the present 8th Indiction 4 nominal *solidi* only. Written the 7th Hathyr, 8th Indiction' (= 3 November 709). Another reads: 'For part of the maintenance of 40 skilled workmen for the construction of the mosque of Damascus. ...' [1]

Although the foundation inscription no longer exists, its text has been preserved by Masʿūdī, who saw it in 944. It stated that the order to build it was given by al-Walīd in 87 H. (706).[2] Ibn Shākir says that the work was finished in 96 H. (714–15), i.e. the year in which al-Walīd died.

The Ancient Temenos

The statements of the Arabic authors that the Great Umayyad Mosque was originally a pagan temple have been abundantly confirmed by the discovery of a considerable part of the inner, and traces of the outer *temenos* (or sacred enclosure), although the temple has entirely disappeared. An accurate knowledge of this *temenos* is essential if we are to attempt to decide how much of the present mosque is due to al-Walīd, and to explain its form.

The outer *temenos* was an immense, slightly trapezoidal enclosure measuring about 385 m. (421 yd.) from east to west and 305 m. (334 yd.) from north to south. A bazaar, sheltered by a portico, ran all round the interior, and in the centre rose the walls of the temple area proper, a great oblong enclosure with pilastered walls, $157\frac{1}{2}$ m. ($516\frac{3}{4}$ ft) from east to west and nearly 100 m. (328 ft) from north to south. There was a square tower at each corner, but only the south-western remains intact. This enclosure, of which the west side has been completely preserved together with considerable portions of the south and east walls and about 21 m. (69 ft) of the north, is of fine masonry, the courses being about 85 cm. ($33\frac{1}{2}$ in.) in height, decorated with simple pilasters.

1. Bell (H. I.), *op. cit.*, p. 80; and in *Der Islam*, III, p. 373.
2. *Prairies*, v, pp. 362–3.

The west side is intact with eighteen pilasters (Plate 11); they project 17–18 cm. (6¾–7 in.), average 1·64 m. (5⅓ ft) in width and the interspaces 3·57 (11¾ ft). Their height from the podium to the necking of the capitals is 10·62 m. (35 ft). The latter measure 59 cm. (23¼ in.), and above them are three more courses of stone. This system of pilasters runs round the corners at each end and continues along the north and south sides, the upper part turning inwards at the third pilaster in each case. This turning in only applies to the capital of the pilaster in question, for the lower part of the wall continued onwards, reduced in height and with shorter pilasters, exactly as at Palmyra. At the corner is a nearly square tower (12 by 11 m.; 39 by 36 ft) which rises to a height of 9·55 m. (31¼ ft) above the capitals (Plate 11). The southern half of the east wall has been rebuilt, but the northern half shows that this wall must have resembled the western.

The lower part of the south wall is unfortunately hidden by the shops of the bazaar to a height of 7 or 8 m. (about 25 ft) (Plate 12), but Dickie, a few years after the great fire of 1893, was able to make a number of observations. A little to the right of the centre is the famous triple entrance (Figure 8). Dickie examined the inner face of this wall and found that the south-eastern transept pier overlapped the opening of the central doorway by 76 cm. (2½ ft). We shall see the importance of this later on (below, pp. 60–61). Ibn Shākir states, and Dickie was able to confirm, that the mihrāb is fitted into the opening of the western doorway.

The wall to the east of this triple entrance is decorated with pilasters, much the same in width and spacing as those of the western wall, but much less in height (about 7·30 m.; 24 ft). Moreover, they lack capitals, and the wall terminates in an inverted ogee moulding 13 cm. (5 in.) in depth, which is carried round the pilasters and runs along continuously 3·16 m. (10½ ft) below the window-sills. Most of the western part of this wall was rebuilt in 1328.

Let us now endeavour to determine its original height. There are two limiting factors: (1) the level of the top of the relieving arch over the central doorway, and (2) the return of the pilaster capital below the south-west tower. Now, the minimum level required to clear the relieving arch of the central doorway, and the maximum possible if the capital of the angle-pilaster of the tower is to be kept clear, is precisely the level of the window-sills of the two wings. I therefore

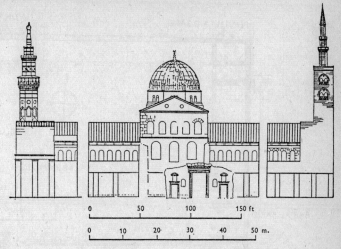

Figure 8. Damascus: Great Mosque, south side

assume that it represents the original top of the *temenos* wall on this side, and that we have here *the very factor which determined the level of the window-sills of the mosque.*

In addition to the triple entrance on the south side, there were three others, one in each face, the chief one obviously being that on the east side, now known as the Bāb Jairūn, where a great central doorway and two smaller side ones were placed under an enormous colonnaded portico over 16 m. (52½ ft) deep and nearly 28 m. (92 ft) wide, preceded by a broad flight of steps.

The Date of the Temenos

Germer Durand in 1900 discovered an inscription, dated 327, referring to the construction of the north-east corner tower,[1] and Hanauer discovered another on the outer face of the east wall of the outer *temenos* dated 349.[2] At first it was assumed that these dates belonged to the era of Pompey (began 63 B.C.), in which case they

1. *Revue Biblique*, 1900, pp. 92–3 and 307.
2. *Palestine Expl. Fund, Q. St.*, 1912, p. 40.

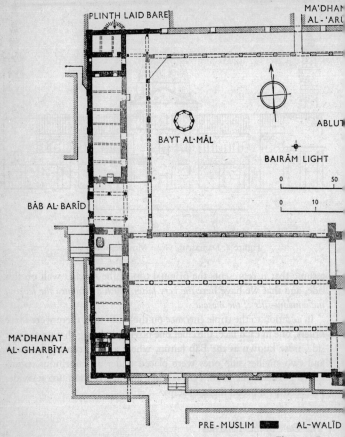

Figure 9. Damas

correspond to A.D. 264–5 and 285–6 respectively. As a result there
was a complete divergence between the date arrived at on stylistic
grounds and that given by epigraphy. Seyrig, however, has pointed
out that the Seleucid era (began 312 B.C.) is admittedly used for the
coinage of Damascus and that it is unreasonable to suppose that another era was employed for inscriptions on public buildings; the dates

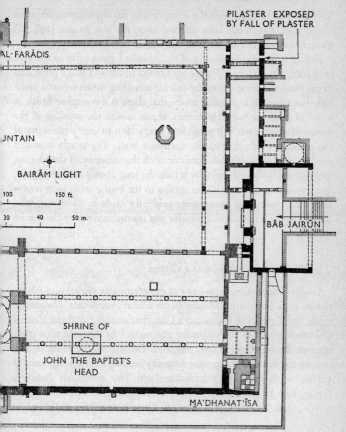

AL-FARĀDIS

PILASTER EXPOSED
BY FALL OF PLASTER

~UNTAIN

BAIRĀM LIGHT

100   150 ft.

30   40   50 m.

BĀB JAIRŪN

SHRINE OF
JOHN THE BAPTIST'S
HEAD

MA'DHANAT 'ĪSĀ

~ALIK SHĀH ▨   LATER OR INDETERMINATE ▨

~t Mosque, plan

of these two inscriptions must consequently correspond to A.D. 15–16 and 37–8.[1] As the Egyptian gorge, so popular at Petra and Madā'in Sālih, is used in Syria as late as the first century A.D., we may now say that there is no longer a conflict as to the date of the *temenos* on stylistic grounds and epigraphy. We may therefore safely place it in

1. 'Sur les ères de quelques villes de Syrie', in *Syria*, XXVIII, pp. 34–7.

the first century A.D., with the exception of the triple entrance in the sound wall, which has been inserted later, for it is 70 cm. (27½ in.) thicker than the rest of the wall and breaks bond with it.

Before leaving the question of the *temenos* I must refer to the two long rooms at each end (Figure 9). Thanks to the fact that a great deal of the plaster coating above the marble panelling in the western vestibule has fallen, it is possible to see that there is a complete break in bond in both the western corners. If we mount the staircase in the south-western tower it is possible at every turn to verify the unity of the masonry with that of the enclosure wall. The north-west and south-west towers are therefore one with the masonry of the *temenos*, whereas the L-shaped walls, by which the long rooms are formed, are not. No doubt this conclusion applies to the two eastern long rooms also. These two long rooms were evidently made by al-Walīd, who wished to get a rectangular interior not encroached on by the corner towers.

The Temple transformed into a Church

Under Theodosius (379–95) Pagan ceremonies ceased and Christianity took possession. Malalas (sixth century) says that Theodosius made the Temple at Damascus a Christian church,[1] and the Paschal Chronicle (c. 640) makes a similar statement.[2] At the same time three inscriptions were carved over the triple entrance in the south façade, that on the lintel of the central doorway reading: 'Thy Kingdom, O Christ, is an everlasting Kingdom, and Thy dominion endureth throughout all generations', which is the Septuagint version of Psalm CXIV, with XC for Christ inserted. These inscriptions still exist.

The Mosque Proper

Let us now study the interior of the ancient *temenos*, to-day a mosque. Within is a court (*sahn*), an oblong rectangle measuring about 122½ m. (402 ft) from east to west and 50 m. (164 ft) on the east, tapering to 47·87 (157 ft) at the west end (Plate 13 and Figure 9). On the south side is the sanctuary nearly 136 m. (446 ft) in length and a

1. 'Chronographia', in *Corpus Scriptor. hist. byz.*, VIII, pp. 344–5.
2. In the *Corpus Scriptor. hist. byz.*, IX, p. 561.

little over 37 m. (121 ft) in depth, formed by three arcades running parallel to the south wall. A broad transept, running from north to south, cuts these arcades into two nearly equal halves, each half consisting of eleven arches. The arches next the court spring from piers, but the inner rows spring from marble columns, standing on cubic pedestals. The inner rows were entirely rebuilt after the great fire of 1893. Of the arcades demolished, Sir Charles Wilson, who saw them in 1865, says: 'In the eastern half there is a variety of capitals; two at the south-east corner are Ionic; ... and many of the Corinthian capitals, which have been taken from other buildings, are too small for the columns on which they stand.'[1] Above these arcades was a second tier of smaller arches springing from piers,[2] there being two of these small arches to every one of the main arches below.

The arched openings, which form the upper tier next the court (Plate 14), were filled (before the fire) with stucco lattices, and must be regarded as windows, and in the back wall of the sanctuary is a similar row, forty-four in all (excluding the six at the end of the transept). Their sills are 10·33 m. (34 ft) above the floor, and they correspond in size and position with the openings over the three rows of arcades. Each aisle is covered by a gable roof resting directly on the upper tier of arches.

The Transept

The transept, which is set slightly askew, is entered from the court by a triple arch, resting on two marble columns; above are three windows, and the whole is very slightly set back in a great arched frame, slightly pointed and very slightly stilted. To right and left is a great buttress to take the thrust of the transept arches (Plate 14). The façade of the transept rises just over 10 m. (33 ft) above the façade on either side, its cornice being 25·67 m. (84¼ ft) above the pavement. Its north and south ends terminate in a shallow stone gable, behind which is a steeper one of brick, showing that the roof has been made steeper than it was originally.

The flanks of the transept are lit by windows, three in each bay,

1. In the *Palestine Expl. Fund*, Q. St., 1897, p. 299.
2. The piers were replaced after the fire by dwarf columns during the atrocious restoration of Apéry.

looking on to the roofs of the side aisles, but the latter having also been made steeper than they were originally, it will be seen from Plates 13, 14 that the central window in each bay has been blocked up, and the two side windows partly so.

The central bay is covered by a stone dome on squinches, but the present arrangement is not the original one, for the fire of 1893 revealed that there is a straight vertical joint between the part of the piers carrying the transept arches and the part carrying the transverse arches under the dome, and that the horizontal beds of the masonry were not in the same line. That is to the transept, as first built, was bounded to east and west by three great arches resting on piers *c*. 3·24 by 1·55 m. (10½ by 5 ft) and that at some subsequent date, piers *c*. 3·24 by 2·50 m. (10½ by 8¼ ft) were built against the four piers of the middle bay without being bonded into them. Before this, the central bay, like the other two, must have been oblong. The object of these additions was, of course, to make it square, so as to take a dome.

This work took place in 1082–3 when Malik Shāh restored the mosque after the fire of 1069, for four practically identical Kufic inscriptions, which were to be seen affixed to these piers before the fire of 1893, recorded the construction 'of this dome and these arches and these piers in the year 475' (= 1082/3).[1]

The Dome

Nevertheless there was a dome here previously, for one is expressly mentioned by Nābigha ash-Shaibānī, a poet of al-Walīd's court, and by Muqaddasī (985), who says that at its apex was an orange surmounted by a pomegranate, both being of gold.[2] On what did it rest? Presumably it was of wood and rested on great cross-beams, in much the same way as does Lājīn's dome in the Mosque of Ibn Tūlūn.

The dome erected by Malik Shāh was also of wood, and Ibn Jubayr's description of it, when he saw it in 1184, shows that it must have closely resembled that of the Dome of the Rock at Jerusalem. It was known as the Qubbat an-Nisr = the Dome of the Eagle. Ibn Jubayr says:

1. Van Berchem, 'Notes d'archéologie arabe', *Journal Asiatique*, 8e série, t. XVII, pp. 420–23, and XIX, pp. 394–6.   2. pp. 157–8.

And the people have likened it to a flying eagle – the dome itself being as the head, the aisle below being the breast, and half of the wall of the right aisle, and the half to the left, being the two wings of the eagle. The width of this main aisle leading towards the court is thirty paces. The people are wont to name this part of the mosque *an-Nisr* – 'The Eagle' – on account of this likeness.[1]

This is only a pretty story invented to explain a designation that was not understood. The real explanation is that the Greek word ἀετός, 'eagle', is also used in a technical sense for 'gable', and this word, in its correct technical signification – 'gable' – was evidently used by the Greek-speaking Syrian workmen employed by al-Walīd. But some Arabs who had acquired a superficial knowledge of Greek, instead of translating it as *qubbat al-jamalūn*, or Dome of the Gable, translated ἀετός by its ordinary meaning, and so arrived at the term 'Dome of the Eagle'. Then people, later on, to explain this term invented the fable related by Ibn Jubayr.

The Mihrābs

In the back wall of the sanctuary are four mihrābs: one in the eastern half called the mihrāb of the Companions of the Prophet, the great mihrāb at the end of the transept, and a third for the sake of symmetry in the western half. Ibn Shākir says that the mihrāb of the Companions of the Prophet did not have the form of a niche until the time of al-Walīd.[2] It then became the third niche-formed mihrāb in Islam. The fourth mihrāb at the western end must be quite modern.

The Arcades round the Sahn

These are built in two tiers similar to the arcades of the sanctuary. Above them is a wooden roof, sloping slightly towards the *sahn* and covered with sheets of lead; its eaves are 15·35 m. (50⅓ ft) from the pavement. The lower tier consists of nine arches on the east and west sides (Plate 13) and twenty-four on the north; the arched openings above these correspond in size and level with those of the sanctuary, except that in many cases they are coupled together with a column between them. No doubt all were once in this state. Nearly all the

1. Wright's ed., p. 265. 2. In Quatremère, *Sultans Mamlouks*, II(1), p. 263.

arches of the lower tier on the north side rest on piers (Plate 13), but to east and west the piers alternate with a couple of columns. I believe that this scheme once obtained on the north side also, although it has been almost entirely rebuilt on piers; in fact Ibn 'Asākir [1] and al-'Umarī [2] make one of al-Walīd's masons say: '... we will place a pier between every two columns'. This would give the following numbers:

	Piers	Columns
East side	2	6
North-east corner	1	0
North-west corner	1	0
West side	2	6
North side	7	16
East portico	0	2
West portico	0	4
	13	34 = 47 supports in all

Now Ibn Jubayr says: 'All round three sides of the court is an aisle. On the eastern, western, and northern sides its breadth is 10 paces. The number of its supports is 47, of which 14 are piers and the remainder (47−14 = 33) are columns.' In other words, he found one pier more and one column less than my theoretical figure, from which we may conclude that only one column had been replaced by a pier at the time of his visit, since which date the process has continued until the present figure is twenty-one columns and twenty-six piers, the total remaining forty-seven, as before.

The foregoing leads one to ask: Did the façade of the sanctuary once rest in a similar manner, on piers alternating with columns, which have since been replaced, or merely walled-up? Let us return to Ibn Jubayr's account:

The aisles of the mosque adjoin the southern side of the *sahn*, and are three in number, running from east to west ... and they rest on 68 supports. Of these 54 are columns, while 8 are piers and 2 are marbled and set into the wall which divides the aisles from the *sahn*. The remaining 4 piers are of most exquisite marble. ...[3]

1. Damascus MS, 1, fol. 155a, l. 29.
2. *Masālik al-Absār*, 1, p.181, ll. 10–13.
3. Wright's ed., pp. 264–5.

We have, therefore, 68 supports: 54 columns, 8 piers, and 2 + 4 of marble = 68. Now the number of supports in the present sanctuary is as follows:

	Columns	Piers
Two inner arcades (4 rows of 10 columns each)	40	0
Under dome	0	4
Front of transept	2	2
	42	6
Left over for rest of façade (20 supports in all)	12	8

A glance at the plan shows 10 supports on the façade on either side of the transept = 20, the required number. Of these the south-eastern and south-western corner piers must always have been piers, for they have to take the thrust of the side arcades. This leaves 18. If we start at the corner pier we should have: angle pier : 2 columns : 1 pier : 2 columns : 1 pier : 2 columns : 1 pier, and then one more arch only instead of two, and we are up against the outer transept pier. This grouping is confirmed by the fact that the piers marked as original on my plan can be distinguished (1) by the height of their courses, whereas those which according to my theory are built-up columns are of much smaller masonry, and (2) by the greater width between the springing of the arches resting on them.

The Form of the Arches

Two types are employed. The arches of the sanctuary were of slightly horse-shoe form before the fire of 1893.[1] Very slightly pointed arches also occur, e.g. the great arched frame at the north end of the transept, where the separation of the two centres is about one-tenth to one-eleventh of the span.

[1] See *Extracts from the Diary of Captain (now Major-General Sir Charles) Wilson, in 1865*; Palest. Expl. Fd., Q. St., 1897, p. 299.

The Marble Grilles

Six beautiful grilles, 1·77 m. (5¾ ft) high and 1·14 (3¾ ft) wide, formed of marble slabs about 12 cm. (4¾ in.) in thickness, are to be seen in the mosque. Four of them, placed with their sills at a level of 4·90 m. (16 ft) above the raised floor of the western portico, give light to the north-western long room; the remaining two are to be seen to right and left of the vestibule (Plate 16). There are four different geometrical patterns, all very simple. The original windows of the Dome of the Rock must have been of this type (see above, p. 22).

The Original Decoration

All accounts agree that the decoration was of the most splendid kind. The whole area was paved with white marble and the walls were panelled with the same material. From the description of Muqaddasī, who speaks of 'the wonderful setting of the various coloured marbles and how the veining in each follows from that of its neighbour',[1] it would appear that the slabs were quartered and set with the veining arranged in a manner that may still be seen in the eastern vestibule, next the southern lateral door (Plate 17). To the right of the pilaster is a fine intact example of twelve pieces, but to the left only two slabs remain in position, next to the base of the pilaster. This, I am convinced, is a fragment of the original decoration because quartered marble panelling, although such a beautiful and effective treatment, is never found, so far as my knowledge goes, in any Muslim monument after the Umayyad period.

We also have here a clue to the original scheme of decoration, for the attractive little pilasters, which are 1·77 m. (5¾ ft) in height and 4·88 (16 ft) from the ground, correspond exactly in height and level with the two marble grilles in the western vestibule. Thus we are justified in believing that a band of quartered marble panelling 1·77 m. (5¾ ft) broad, with pilasters and marble grilles at intervals, ran all round. The existing remains in the eastern vestibule show that below this band were more panels of quartered marble, but whether they extended right down to the ground, or whether there was a plain dado, say a couple of metres high, it is not possible to decide.

1. p. 158.

Directly above this panelling – that is to say at a height of 6·65 m. (21¾ ft) – began the coating of mosaic, as may be seen under the east portico, where it is well preserved (Plate 17). This extended up to the roof, which is about 15 m. (50 ft) from the ground, so it must have been over 7 m. (23 ft) broad.

As regards the decoration of the sanctuary, we are told that marble panelling ran all round to twice the height of a man; at this point ran the famous golden vine (*karma*) mentioned by Ibn 'Asākir,[1] in which we must recognize a frieze decorated with a long, undulating vine-stem gilt, or an acanthus scroll carrying grapes, after the pattern of some of those in the Dome of the Rock. This is confirmed by a photograph taken before the fire and published by Baron von Oppenheim,[2] which shows that a band with pilasters similar to those in the eastern vestibule ran along the southern end of the transept. Immediately above is a band consisting, not of a true vine-stalk, but of an acanthus scroll carrying bunches of grapes here and there, as in some of the fantastic plant ornament of the Dome of the Rock; it can only be the *karma* mentioned by Ibn 'Asākir. But as the windows are 10·35 m. (34 ft) from the floor, they must have cut into the mosaic, instead of coming between the pilasters, as they do in the western vestibule.

The capitals of the columns were gilt, and Muqaddasī says that even the cresting was faced on both sides with mosaic.

To-day all the marble panelling in the sanctuary dates from after the fire of 1893, likewise all that in the western vestibule. A large surface of mosaic has been preserved in good condition on the north outer face of the transept, under the gable, where trees and little pavilions appear on a background of gold (Plates 20 *a*, *b*). Some also exists on the arcades of the west portico (Plate 14) and on the arches of the vestibule, but the most splendid piece is the panorama of the Baradā River, 34½ m. (113 ft) long and over 7 m. (23 ft) high, uncovered by de Lorey, on the back wall of this portico (Plates 18, 19). The left extremity is shown on Plate 18.

When completed by al-Walīd there must have been a greater surface of mosaic than ever existed in any other building.

1. Damascus MS., 1, fol. 158 *a*, ll. 5–6 and 10–11.
2. *Vom Mittelmeer zum Persischen Golf*, 1, plate facing p. 54.

The Minarets

The four square towers at the four corners of the *temenos* served as minarets, the first in Islam. As Ibn al-Faqīh (903) says: 'The minarets which are in the Damascus mosque were originally watch towers in the Greek days ... when al-Walīd turned the whole area into a mosque, he left these in their old condition';[1] and Mas'ūdī says: 'Then came Christianity and it became a church; then came Islam and it became a mosque, al-Walīd built it solidly and the *sawāmi* (i.e. the four corner towers) were not changed, they serve for the call to prayer at the present day.'[2] Of these only the south-western tower remains intact to-day, and it is surmounted by a minaret built by Sultan Qāyt-Bāy in 1488. The north-western and north-eastern towers have disappeared and also the south-eastern. In its place has been built a minaret, apparently about 1340. Alongside the northern entrance is a third minaret dating from the end of the twelfth century, but there was an earlier minaret at this point dating from before 985, for it is mentioned by Muqaddasī.

The Domed Edifices in the Sahn

There are three little edifices in the *sahn*, of which only the western one concerns us, the other two being comparatively modern. It consists of a tall octagonal chamber, of courses of stone and brick alternately, resting on eight columns with Corinthian capitals, surmounted by a classical entablature (Plate 13). The area surrounded by the columns is treated as a basin with a little parapet all round, and in the centre is a hole, no doubt intended for the jet of a fountain. The octagonal chamber is surmounted by a lead-covered dome, and its entrance is a rectangular opening in the north-west side which can only be reached by a ladder. It measures 4·63 m. (15 ft) from the pavement to the architrave and 9·95 m. (32½ ft) to the eaves of the dome.

Muqaddasī says: 'On the right [i.e. the west] side of the *sahn* is a treasure house raised on eight columns. It is finely ornamented and its walls are covered with mosaic.'[3] Ibn Jubayr says: 'It stands as tall as a tower on eight columns of marble, ornamented with polychrome

1. p. 108.   2. *Prairies*, IV, pp. 90–91.   3. p. 157.

mosaic as beautiful as a garden, and it is surmounted by a dome made of lead. They say that it was originally the treasury of the mosque.'[1] Abu'l-Baqā says that it was constructed by al-Walīd.

The Part played by al-Walīd

Although the Arabic authors are unanimous in asserting that al-Walīd destroyed the Church of St John the Baptist and built the mosque as it stands to-day, with the exception of the walls of the *temenos*, and although Phené Spiers, who was the first to make a detailed study of the problem, accepted this view, Dussaud, Diehl, Strzygowski, Watzinger and Wulzinger, and Lammens have attempted to prove that the present sanctuary, with the exception of its dome, is none other than the church in question.

Before discussing these theories, it would perhaps be just as well to give a synopsis of the accounts of Ibn Jubayr (1184), al-'Umarī (*c.* 1340), and Ibn Shākir (*d.* 1362) concerning the capture of Damascus. The latter claims to be quoting Ibn 'Asākir (*d.* 1176), but we shall see that this is scarcely correct.

It is said that the Arabs had two main bodies besieging Damascus, one under Khālid ibn al-Walīd on the western, the other under Abū 'Ubayda on the eastern side. These two forces entered the town simultaneously, that of Khālid under the terms of a treaty whereby the Arabs were to leave the Christians fourteen churches, but to take that of St John, whereas Abū 'Ubayda had at that very moment stormed the East Gate. The two forces advancing met in the centre of the town or, according to Ibn Jubayr, in the centre of the church. After a long discussion it was agreed that half the town should be considered as having been taken by assault, the other half as having been occupied by treaty.[2] The Arabs therefore took the eastern part of the Church of St John, which they turned into a mosque. Ibn Shākir adds that the Muslims prayed where is now the mihrāb known as the mihrāb of the Companions of the Prophet, leaving the western half to the Christians, and that the Muslims and the Christians entered by the same gateway, that of the original temple, placed on the south

1. Wright's ed., p. 268.
2. We have seen above (p. 7) that when a city surrendered by capitulation the fate of the churches was better than when it had been taken by storm.

side, where is now the great mihrāb; then the Christians turned to the west to go to their church, and the Muslims turned to the right to go to their mosque.[1]

Things remained thus until November 705, when al-Walīd, having become Khalif, wanted to take the part left to the Christians and convert the whole into one mosque. Then followed the bargaining with the Christians, and eventually the demolition of the church, until there remained nothing more than a rectangular enclosure, which must mean the four walls of the *temenos* with the four towers at the corners.

The Theory of Watzinger and Wulzinger

Watzinger and Wulzinger suggested that the temple of the Syrian god, called Jupiter Damascenus by the Romans, stood in the middle (but a little to the west of the centre) of the *temenos*, and that it was merely converted into a church by Theodosius (379–95), that a new church was built by Heraclius about 629, that this church is the present sanctuary of the mosque, and that al-Walīd's work was confined to the addition of the dome.[2] Having decided that the present sanctuary was built as a church, what prevents them from attributing its erection to Theodosius? Obviously the insuperable difficulty created by the fact that the south-eastern pier of the transept partly overlaps and obstructs the middle door of the triple entrance, and it is inconceivable that the Emperor who carved the invocation over the doorway would, at the same time, partly block it up! We shall see that Dussaud is influenced by this fact also (below, pp. 61–2). They therefore suggest that the earthquake of 602 and the Persian invasion of 613 resulted in the ruin of the converted temple, and that Heraclius, after his victorious campaign, which resulted in the recovery of the 'True Cross' from the Persians, began a new church on his return journey. This theory is unsupported by any text, which is all the more remarkable, for we possess accounts of the works of Heraclius at Jerusalem, and even at distant Diyārbakr. It is indeed surprising that the sources

---

1. Quatremère's transl. *Sultans Mamlouks*, II(1), pp. 262–5.
2. *Damascus, I: Die antike Stadt*, pp. 96–7. Their final dictum is that 'the plan and elevation of the Byzantine Church of St John have remained almost unaltered', I, p. 93.

should mention his works in these two cities and yet remain silent regarding such an immense structure – it would have been the biggest church in Christendom [1] – as the sanctuary of the Great Mosque at Damascus, had it really been due to him. As it is, it is only after the middle of the seventeenth century that we find statements connecting the name of Heraclius with this building.[2] Moreover we are not even justified in assuming that the Persians gave themselves up to the destruction of churches here, for no less than fourteen, in addition to the church of St John, are spoken of shortly after the Arab Conquest.

Dussaud's Theory

Dussaud agrees with Watzinger and Wulzinger in believing that the work of al-Walīd was confined to the addition of a dome, and also assumes that there were two stages in the work, different, however, from those of Watzinger and Wulzinger. He agrees as to the position of the temple, but insists that it cannot have been converted into a church, not only on account of the smallness of its *naos*, but also because it must have been turned towards the west, the opposite to what is required by Christian ritual.[3] He therefore comes to the conclusion that Theodosius destroyed the temple and built a church along the south side of the *temenos*, that it was entered by the triple entrance which received the Greek inscriptions, and that it is none other than the present sanctuary. Baulked, however, like Watzinger and Wulzinger, by the fact that the central doorway is partly obstructed by one of the transept piers, he is obliged to assume that the church lacked the transept! His plan of the church of Theodosius shows the sanctuary with a wall next the *sahn*, and he remarks: 'It is to be presumed that the church only had a secondary entrance on this court which participated in the anathema pronounced against the ancient temple.' He then assumes that 'the utilization of the triple south doorway as principal entrance was inconvenient',[4] that the transept was built in the fifth century to reduce the awkward shape of the church, and that 'henceforth the entrance was made in the north façade of the

1. Old St Peter's at Rome, excluding the atrium, was only 380 ft in length against 446 for the sanctuary of the Great Mosque.
2. Bremond (1652), *Viaggi*, p. 246; Thevenot (1658), *Voyage*, p. 436, etc.
3. *Syria*, III, p. 235.   4. *Ibid.*, p. 235.

transept', and that only the western bay of the south triple entrance was left open. At this point his drawings fail to agree with his text, for the plan he gives of the church after the alteration shows an open arcade in place of the north wall of the previous plan. As he speaks of an entrance being opened in the north façade, one must conclude that the wall remained. No sources mention additions of the fifth century, nor does he produce evidence that the transept dates from the fifth century, but he is forced, like Watzinger and Wulzinger, to divide the work into two stages because of the existence of the Christian Greek inscription over a doorway which is partly obstructed by one of the transept piers.

Now these two theories are alike remarkable for the complete disregard which they exhibit for the evidence not only of the Muslim and Christian sources, but for the architectural facts as well. Let us deal with the latter point first.

The Architectural Evidence

How scholars and archaeologists can bring themselves to believe that a church of such an extraordinary type, over 136 m. long with one flank entirely open to the courtyard, ever existed, really is amazing. There is no mystery about the pre-Muhammadan churches of Syria; the type is well known, thanks to the fact that they have been preserved, literally by dozens, in Northern Syria. For any given period they are wonderfully true to type, and nothing the least resembling the sanctuary of the Damascus mosque is known, notwithstanding the startling assertion of Dussaud that 'the plan of the basilica, even after the addition of a transept, which gave it a monumental façade, remained quite simple and *enfermé dans les anciennes formules*'. How it could be so, both with and without the transept, is difficult to understand. No one hitherto has been able to cite a church in the least resembling it.

To begin with the question of proportion, Butler found that the earliest Syrian churches – those belonging to the fourth century – when measured within their walls, conform to the same proportions as the Classical buildings, length to breadth being as 3 : 2, the central nave being usually double the width of the side aisles. These proportions held good for five out of six basilicas, the sixth presenting the proportion of 5 : 3. Those of the fifth century present a new scheme, viz. 4 : 3. Seven out of eight conform to this proportion, in the eighth it was 5 : 3, like the previous variant. In the sixth century only two retain the old basilican plan with arcades on columns and semi-circular apse, but these also observe the proportion 4 : 3.[1]

Contrast this with the proportions of the sanctuary of the mosque – $3\frac{1}{4}$: 1. But there are many other objections. Where is a church to be found either with three aisles of equal width and height, or cut through its centre by such a transept?

Even if we suppose that a church with such proportions did exist, it can scarcely have had its flank open to the courtyard. Such a thing is inconceivable; even Dussaud, in his proposed reconstruction of the church of Theodosius, shows a wall next the court, but apparently fails to see the logical consequences of this admission, viz.: that the present façade must be due to al-Walīd, for it is not a wall in which a number of openings have been cut, but an open arcade on columns and piers, and must have been built as such. This admitted – and there is no way out of it – we must admit that the arcades on the other sides of the *sahn*, since they match it, are also the work of al-Walīd.

We now come to the question of the two arcades which divide the interior into three aisles of equal height and almost exactly equal width. Here again are two features unknown in Syria, where the central aisle is always very much wider than the side aisles, in fact generally double their width and greater in height also. Evidently we must admit that al-Walīd pulled down the old arcades, if indeed they stood here, and rebuilt them on a new alignment. There remains the transept. As the position of the four middle piers is governed by the alignment of the arcades just discussed, it follows that their attribution stands or falls by the same argument. This leaves us with the four walls of the enclosure which are admittedly antique.

The Mosque of Diyārbakr

It would appear that Watzinger and Wulzinger, as well as Dussaud, must have felt some uneasiness in asserting that such a structure as the Great Umayyad Mosque can have been a church, without parent

1. H. C. Butler, *Architecture and other Arts*, pp. 35–6; see also his *Early Churches in Syria*, p. 183.

among the churches of Syria and, to get over the difficulty, they are led to an extraordinary procedure. They point to the sanctuary of the Great Mosque of Diyārbakr and suggest, on the strength of a legend, that it also was once a church, corresponding both in date and type to the Church of St John the Baptist at Damascus.

The term legend is a mild one: it is based on the statement of Wāqidī that when Diyārbakr was taken by the Arabs, the principal church was divided, the Arabs taking two-thirds and the Christians one-third.[1] Yet we learn from Christian sources that the principal church of the town was that built by Heraclius in 629, and we also learn that this church – still a church, be it noted – was restored in 770.[2] We are therefore in difficulties at once. When we come to examine the sanctuary itself, which, like the mosque at Damascus, also consists of three aisles cut through the centre by a transept, we find that the façade on the *sahn* bears two inscriptions, one to the right dated 484 H. (1091–2) in the name of Malik Shāh, and another to the left dated 550 H. (1155–6). Moreover, the arcade next the *sahn* is composed of pointed arches of pronounced form, instead of semi-circular ones, so it can hardly have been built in the Christian period. Nor can it have been a church, for all three aisles are equal in height and nearly equal in width.[3] And we are quite justified in taking the inscription to mean that Malik Shāh *did* build the sanctuary, for the Great Mosque as described by Nāsir-i-Khusrau in 1046 does not correspond with the present building. Moreover, if we attribute it to Malik Shāh, its resemblance to that of the Great Mosque of Damascus would be easy to explain, for we have already seen (above, p. 52) that this famous Sultan had carried out extensive works there nine years previously.

We have now seen that all the architectural facts are against a Christian attribution for the sanctuary of the Great Mosque, and that these facts have been completely ignored in the discussion. We shall now see that the evidence of the sources, which has been ignored also, is equally emphatic against such an attribution, for every Arabic author who mentions this mosque attributes it to al-Walīd, and they all

1. Niebuhr-Mordtmann's transl., p. 108.

2. Dionysius of Tell Mahrē, Chabot's text, pp. 6 and 114; transl., pp. 5 and 96.

3. See Gertrude Bell's plan, *Ukhaidir*, Plate 90.

speak of the enormous sums spent on it. In addition to this there is the statement of Masʿūdī, a really early authority, that al-Walīd took magnificent columns of white marble from the Church of Mary at Antioch, and had them transported to Damascus for the Great Mosque,[1] a statement worthy of belief, for a variety of columns and capitals were to be observed in the sanctuary before the great fire of 1893 (above, p. 51).

The Alleged Partition of the Church of St John

De Goeje,[2] and von Kremer before him, have pointed out an anomaly, for the account of Ibn ʿAsākir says that the Muslims took the eastern half of the Church of St John and the Christians the western half, the reason being that the Arabs had entered the eastern part of the town by storm and the western by capitulation. How explain that it is precisely the eastern part of the present town which is occupied by Christians and Jews, the contrary to what we would have expected had this account been true? Secondly, there is the fact that Wāqidī (748–823), who claims to have actually seen the treaty itself, explicitly states that there was *no mention in it of the division of churches or houses*. He says:

I have read the treaty which Khālid ibn al-Walīd concluded with the people of Damascus, and I have found no mention in it regarding the sharing of houses or churches; tradition asserts it, but I do not know how the idea arose. The fact is that, after the surrender, a number of the inhabitants quitted the town and took refuge with Heraclius who was at Antioch; there were thus many empty houses, occupied later by the Muslims.[3]

In view of the complete confusion which admittedly reigns in all the accounts of the siege which have come down to us, this *original document* is of supreme importance, and justifies us in rejecting the legend forthwith, although western authors, until recently, have clung to it with extraordinary tenacity.

Miednokov has pointed out another difficulty. How, he asks, could the Christians carry on their services in the western part of the

1. *Prairies*, III, pp. 407–8.
2. *Mémoire sur la conquête de la Syrie*, pp. 96–7.
3. His statement has come down to us in Balādhurī, p. 123; Hitti's transl., p. 189.

church, for their altar must have been in the eastern half. If we amend the text and twist things round, supposing that the Arabs had the western half, this conflicts with the position of the traditional mihrāb of the Companions of the Prophet, which is in the eastern half. Thus whichever way the church is divided, there is a difficulty to be faced. He therefore concludes that Christians and Muslims never prayed in a divided church, and Caetani[1] agrees with him, adding that the evidence of Arculf, who visited Damascus about 670, shows that the church was intact. He speaks of the city 'in which the King of the Saracens reigns, having seized the government, and in which a large church has been built in honour of St John the Baptist. And in that same city has also been built a certain church of unbelieving Saracens, which they frequent'.[2] They were therefore two distinct buildings.

The Evidence of the Earliest Sources

Now the account of Ibn 'Asākir, which has been such an obstacle to a correct understanding of the history of the Great Mosque, is a relatively late text, which has been in everyone's hand thanks to the fortuitous advertisement given it over a century ago when Quatremère translated Ibn Shākir's version of it in the Appendix to his *Sultans Mamlouks*.

(1) The earliest document of all is the inscription of al-Walīd himself, which Mas'ūdī says was 'near the roof and next the minaret'. It ran: 'The Khalif al-Walīd hath ordered the building of this Mosque and the demolition of the church which was inside it.'[3]

(2) The next document is likewise contemporary, viz. verses of praise addressed to al-Walīd by the poet Nābigha ash-Shaibānī, in which he says: 'Thou hast torn their church from the middle of our mosque, pulled up its foundations out of the entrails of the earth, etc.'[4]

(3) Theophanes (d. 818), under the Year of the World 6199 (= A.D. 707), says that al-Walīd took away the most holy Catholic church of Damascus from the Christians. There is no mention of half a church.

1. *Annali*, III, p. 350.
2. Tobler and Molinier, *Itinera Hierosolymitana*, I, p. 186.
3. *Prairies*, V, pp. 362–3.
4. 'Dīwān', quoted by Lammens, *Bull. de l'Inst. français*, Le Caire, XXVI, p. 27.
5. Bonn ed., p. 575.

(4) Balādhurī (868) says that Mu'āwiya 'wanted to add the Church of St John to the Mosque' (in other words, the church was still intact) and that finally al-Walīd demolished it, and that it was included in the mosque.[1]

(5) Ibn Qutayba (d. 889) says: 'When al-Walīd *pulled down* the church of Damascus, etc.'[2]

(6) Ibn al-Fakīh (c. 903) says: 'When the Khalif al-Walīd had the intention of rebuilding the mosque at Damascus, he sent for the Christians and said to them: "We purpose to add your church to our mosque, but we will give you a place for a church elsewhere, and wheresoever you will."'[3] He goes on to say that al-Walīd destroyed the church and turned the whole area into a mosque.

(7) Tabarī (915), quoting al-Madā'ini says: 'al-Walīd desired to build the mosque of Damascus, and there was a church in it ... and they demolished the church and he built it up as a mosque.'[4]

(8) Eutychius (939) says that the Church of St John the Baptist was at the side of the congregational Mosque.[5]

(9) Mas'ūdī (944) says: 'The Mosque of Damascus, before Christianity, was a great temple. Then came Christianity and it became a church, then came Islam and it became a mosque. al-Walīd built it strongly and the *sawāmi'* [the corner towers] in it were not changed, they serve for the call to prayer at the present day.'[6]

(10) Agapius of Manbij (end of tenth century) says: 'In the first year of his [al-Walīd's] reign he destroyed the churches of Damascus, and especially the great church, he demolished it and constructed in its place a great mosque.'[7]

(11) Michael the Syrian (Jacobite Patriarch, 1166–99) says: 'This Walīd detested the Christians and he demolished churches. First of all he pulled down the great church of Damascus and built a mosque on its site.'[8]

We now come to Ibn 'Asākir (d. 1176), whose account, until recently, has only been known from the garbled version given by Ibn

---

1. p. 125.
2. '*Uyūn al-Akhbar*, Brockelmann's ed., p. 240.
3. pp. 106 and 108.   4. II, p. 1275, ll. 5–6 and 9–10.
5. Pococke's ed., p. 365.   6. *Prairies*, IV, p. 90.
7. 'Kitāb al-'Unwān', Vasiliev's ed., in the *Patrologia Orientalis*, VIII, p. 498.
8. Chabot's text, II, p. 451; transl., II, p. 481.

Shākir (d. 1363).[1] He is not nearly so explicit as the latter pretends, for Ibn 'Asākir does not express opinions. He was the author of a vast collection of *Hadīth*, or Traditions, on the history of Damascus. But he does not adopt a version, choose a school, or select from the vast mass of material collected by him. For example, in his account of the Khalif Mu'āwiya he piles up Umayyad and anti-Umayyad versions without it being possible to guess to which he gives the preference. This is the system he has adopted in his account of the Great Mosque. He tells us in one place[2] that Khālid ibn al-Walīd entered by force and Abū 'Ubayda by capitulation, and that half the church belonged to the Muslims and half to the Christians, which is merely the legend demolished by Wāqidī four centuries earlier (above, p. 65). But elsewhere he gives other accounts, saying that al-Walīd gave to the Christians, in place *of the church which was in the mosque*, the church known as ...;[3] that al-Walīd said to the Christians, 'We wish to enlarge our mosque by the addition of your church';[4] and again: 'al-Walīd wished to incorporate their church in the mosque.'[5] There is no mention of half a church, and the fact that the church remained inviolate is expressly stated in so many words: 'As for the church of Yuhanna (= John) it remained in the hands of the Christians, *as a church*, until al-Walīd took it from them as has been said.'[6] He also gives four more Traditions, according to which this church was demolished by al-Walīd,[7] and adds: 'al-Walīd built all that is in the interior of the mosque',[8] that is to say, everything in the *temenos*.

Thus Ibn 'Asākir, in spite of what Ibn Shākir says about him, is really a witness *in favour* of the theory that the church was never divided, that it was pulled down by al-Walīd, and that the mosque was entirely his work.

Our next authority in chronological order is Ibn Jubayr, who visited Damascus in 1184. He was a great admirer of Ibn 'Asākir, for he praises his work, and Lammens has shown that a number of historical details on Muslim shrines at Damascus given by him are bor-

---

1. Translated as an Appendix to the second volume of Quatremère's *Sultans Mamlouks.*   2. Damascus MS., I, fol. 155 *b*, l. 23 ff.
3. *Ibid.*, I, folio 155 *a*, ll. 10–11.   4. I, fol. 155 *a*, ll. 31–2.
5. I, fol. 155 *b*, l. 21.   6. *Ibid.*, I. fol. 155 *b*, ll. 31–2.
7. I, fol. 154 *b*, ll. 31–2; fol. 155 *a*, ll. 4–6; fol. 155 *b*, ll. 3–15, and fol. 156 *a*, ll. 3–6.   8. I, fol. 156 *b*, ll. 20–21.

rowed from it. But out of the varying versions just cited he selected the division story and ignored all the other incompatible accounts,[1] which is just what Ibn Shākir did two centuries later.

It is easy to understand how the expression 'in the mosque was a church', and Abu'l-Mahāsin's expression 'half of it had been occupied by a church',[2] could be corrupted into 'half the church became a mosque'.

The evidence of the sources, therefore, conclusively shows that we have to deal with two distinct edifices, viz.: a mosque and a church, *both of which occupied part of the present mosque area.*

The Site of the Church

Thiersch, Watzinger and Wulzinger, and Dussaud all agree that the temple must have stood in the middle of the *temenos,* and that it opened towards the east, for the eastern entrance of the *temenos,* unlike the western, was provided with an elaborate porch. Thiersch and Dussaud conclude that its axis was that of the *temenos,* and that there was a colonnade running all round the interior of the enclosure, as at Baalbek and Palmyra.

Thiersch, as well as Watzinger and Wulzinger, believe that the temple, on the victory of Christianity, was converted into a church, which conversion would have been quite possible even if it was turned towards the west. Dussaud describes this as an *impossibilité absolue,* because the Pagan temple was oriented in a direction just the very opposite of a church.[3] Far from being an *impossibilité absolue,* it does not present any difficulty at all, for many early churches were so oriented, and here are some examples in support of my contention.

(1) *Rome.* The first church of St John Lateran, begun in 313, had its altar at the west end.[4]

(2) *Rome.* The first great basilica of St Peter, A.D. 324–30, had its altar at the west end.[5]

(3) *Jerusalem.* Constantine's buildings at the Holy Sepulchre consisted of a basilica entered from the east, with an apse at the west end,

---

1. Wright's ed., pp. 263–4.   2. I, p. 237, ll. 7–8.

3. *Loc. cit.,* p. 235.   4. Rohault de Fleury, *Le Latran au moyen âge,* pl. IV.

5. Plan, made by Alfarano before its demolition in the sixteenth century, published by Bunsen, *Die Basiliken des christlichen Roms,* Taf. I.

behind which was a court with the Church of the Holy Sepulchre on the west side.[1]

(4) *Rome*. San Lorenzo fuori le mura, as built by Constantine in 335, had the altar at the west end.[2]

(5) *Constantinople*. The Church of the Apostles, built by Constantine in 337.[3]

(6) *Tyre*. Church of Constantine. Eusebius describes the triple entrance under a portico which opened towards the rising sun.[4]

(7) *Antioch*. Church begun by Constantine in 331, and finished by his son.[5] Socrates the ecclesiastical historian, in his chapter on the anomalies of his day (*d.* 440), says that at Antioch 'the church has a reversed direction, the altar is not at the east, but at the west'.[6]

(8) *Baalbek*. This is the most important of all for our purpose, for here we have a basilica built by Theodosius himself in the same country – Syria, and in the same conditions – in a *temenos*. Its remains have been exposed by the German expedition. It was entered from the east and had three apses at the west end. Later a great apse was built at the east end, and a new entrance cut in the original main apse.[7]

(9) *Rome*. San Paulo fuori le mura, finished by Honorius (393–423).[8]

(10) *Nola*. Paulinus of Nola, speaking of the basilica which he built about 400, expressly says: 'Prospectus vero basilicae non, ut usitatior mos est, orientem spectat.' [9]

Rivoira claims that the Basilica Ursiana, 370–96, at Ravenna, was the earliest example of a church with the apse at the east end,[10] and Funk says that the practice only became general in the following century,[11] a statement borne out by the remarks of Socrates, just quoted.

1. Vincent and Abel, *Jérusalem*, II, Chap. VI.

2. Cattaneo, *Architecture in Italy from the Sixth to the Eleventh Century*, pp. 46 ff. and Fig. 9.

3. Lethaby and Swainson, *Sancta Sophia*, p. 18.

4. *Life of Constantine*, Schwartz' ed., II(2), p. 874.

5. Malalas, *Chronicles*, pp. 318, 324, and 325; Theophanes, Bonn ed., p. 55.

6. Bk. V, cap. 22; in Migne, *Patrologia, Series Graeca*, LXVII, cols. 640–41.

7. Krencker, von Lüpke, and Winnefeld, *Baalbek*, II, pp. 130–43, 149–50, and Taf. 69.   8. Nicolai (N. M.), *Della basilica di S. Paulo*, p. 7.

9. Holtzinger, in the *Zeitschrift für bildende Kunst*, XX, p. 137.

10. *Lombardic Architecture*, I, p. 8, and II, p. 125.

11. His article 'Orientirung', in Krauss, *Real-Encyklopädie der christlichen Alterthümer*, II, pp. 559–60.

Dussaud's objection therefore falls to the ground. Nevertheless, it may have been that the temple did not lend itself to conversion and that it was pulled down by Theodosius and a new church erected. If so there can be no doubt that the new church rose on the site of the temple, for two reasons: (i) the well-known 'persistence of sites', and (ii) the analogy of Baalbek, for, as we have just seen, we have there a church, built by the *same* Emperor – Theodosius, in the *same* country – Syria, in the *same* conditions – in a *temenos*.

This then was 'the church which was in the mosque', or the Inner Church (*ad-dākhila*) of Ibn 'Asākir [1] and al-'Umarī.[2]

Now the much-quoted Ibn Shākir tells us that, after the capture of Damascus, the Muslims and Christians 'entered by the same doorway, which was that of the original temple, placed on the south side where is now the great mihrāb. Then the Christians turned to the west towards their church (this fits the above theory perfectly), and the Muslims to the right to reach their mosque'.[3]

Where? Opposite the traditional mihrāb of the Companions of the Prophet, i.e., under that part of the colonnade on the south side of the *temenos*, which lay to the east of the triple entrance. Moreover under this arrangement there would be no mutual interference. We have seen that the early Muslims were not particular where they prayed, e.g., in the *dihlīz* of the Basilica of Constantine at Jerusalem and in the church of the Nativity at Bethlehem (above, p. 10).

I therefore maintain that the position at this time was as shown in Figure 10, and this is supported by a remarkable passage in al-'Umarī (*c.* 1340): 'This church was surrounded by *riwāqs* (= colonnaded or arcaded porticoes) on all four sides.'[4] This provides another argument against those who believe that the church was built against the south side of the *temenos*.

If it be objected that Arculf's words – '... has also been built a certain church of unbelieving Saracens' – implies constructional work, I would suggest that the part of the colonnade used was perhaps enclosed by walls of mud brick, as deserving of the verdict 'vili fabricati sunt opere', as was the first Aqsā mosque (above, p. 10).

1. Damascus MS., I, fol. 154, *b*, l. 29.
2. *Masālik al-Absār*, I, p. 181, ll. 1–4.
3. In Quatremère, *Sultans Mamlouks*, II(1), p. 263.
4. *Op. cit.*, I, p. 189, ll. 7–11.

This accommodation remained adequate for some time, but when al-Walīd became Khalif the number of Muslims had very much increased; the provision of further space had, therefore, become imperative, and to obtain possession of the whole area he entered into the famous bargaining with the Christians.

Having obtained possession, he proceeded to pull down the church and the colonnades round the *temenos*, and, when nothing was left but

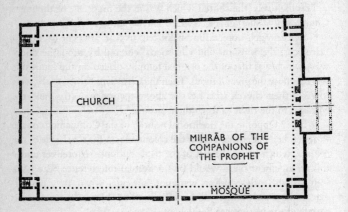

Figure 10. Damascus: state of the *Temenos* and Church from A.D. 635 to 705. The Muslims and Christians 'entered by the same doorway, which was that of the original temple, placed on the south side where is now the great mihrāb. Then the Christians turned to the west towards their church, and the Muslims to the right to reach their mosque' – Ibn Shākir

the four enclosing walls and the four corner towers, he began the construction of the sanctuary and the arcades round the *sahn*.

Thus every text is reconciled, even the greater part of Ibn 'Asākir and Ibn Jubayr. In fact it is only necessary to substitute *temenos* for church and the reconciliation is complete, for, under the scheme shown in Figure 10, it may fairly be said that of the *temenos* (not church) the Muslims took the eastern half and the Christians retained the western, which suited them perfectly, because it left them in possession of their church for seventy years, until al-Walīd took over the whole enclosure. Moreover the terms of the treaty seen by Wāqidī, whereby the Christians were guaranteed the possession of all their churches, were not violated.

But we can well imagine how easily the 'partition of a church' theory can have risen out of such a peculiar situation, for the whole *temenos* became the Great Mosque, and part of its area had been occupied by a church.

ARCHITECTURAL ORIGINS OF THE GREAT MOSQUE

Origin of Design

In 'Irāq, as we have already seen, the Muslims settled on unoccupied sites and founded new cities (e.g. Basra and Kūfa), which involved the foundation of mosques also (above, pp. 8–9). But in Syria they appropriated churches (or divided them) and used them as mosques, and there is every reason for believing that, with the possible exception of the Second Aqsā Mosque, sometimes attributed to 'Abd al-Malik (above, p. 43), the Great Mosque at Damascus was the first erected in Syria. Hence its fundamental importance. We have seen that it does not resemble any church in Syria; whence, therefore, did al-Walīd get his design?

First of all I believe that he chose a sanctuary three aisles deep because the Muslims of Syria, in converting churches into mosques, had thereby become familiar with a sanctuary of that type. But what of the transept and the façade?

Thiersch has attempted to connect this building with the Chalke, or Vestibule of the Palace of the Augusteion at Constantinople.[1] He bases his theory on the description of Procopius,[2] but neither Thiersch, Richter, Heisenberg, nor Strzygowski agree on the interpretation of the Greek text. Nevertheless, if we reject the enigmatic description of Procopius, and base ourselves on a pictorial representation of a building copied from the Chalke, we shall see that the façade of the latter and of the Umayyad mosque are closely related to each other. The Chalke, of course, has long since disappeared, but the Palace of Theodoric at Ravenna was supposed to have been copied from it, and a fine mosaic picture of it still exists in the Church of Sant'Apollinare Nuovo (built c. 519) in that city (Plate 20c). Here we see a building

1. *Pharos*, pp. 214–17.   2. *De Aedificiis*, I, 10.

with an open façade, composed of two tiers of arches. The upper openings are smaller than those below, being nearly but not quite twice as numerous. The arches are closed with curtains, just as Ibn Shākir [1] says those of al-Walīd's mosque were. There is, moreover, a transept with a triple-arched façade and gable roof, and the wings have gable roofs also. The façade is decorated with mosaic, just as that of the mosque once was. The resemblance throughout is really striking, the main difference being that the transept does not dominate the wings to the same extent as at Damascus.

As for the alternation of two columns with one pier, this scheme had already been adopted nearly two centuries previously for three sides of the atrium of Sancta Sophia, of which unfortunately nothing remains today. However, we have the plan of Salzenberg (1854) showing two of the columns on the south side still *in situ*,[2] and a photograph published by Wulff, showing one bay.[3] This fragment disappeared shortly after 1873.

There is therefore considerable evidence for saying: (1) that the façade of the sanctuary of al-Walīd's mosque was probably derived from a palace façade, or rather the courtyard façade of a palace at Constantinople, perhaps the Chalke; (2) that the three-aisled sanctuary was a result of the Arab's familiarity with sanctuaries of this type, so many Syrian mosques at that time being merely converted churches used laterally; and (3) that everything else – the shape and dimensions of the mosque and the position of the entrances – were fixed beforehand by the ancient *temenos*, and that even the level of the window-sills (above, pp. 46–7) was fixed by the top of the south wall.

The Round Horse-shoe Arch

Ignoring rock-cut examples, the earliest example of a round horse-shoe arch occurs in the Baptistery of Mār Ya'qūb at Nisibin built, according to a Greek inscription, 'by Volagesos the Bishop in 671' (of the Seleucid era = A.D. 359).[4] All the doorways have lintels with horse-shoe relieving arches above.

1. In Quatremère, *Sultans Mamlouks*, $II_{(1)}$, p. 273.

2. *Alt-christliche Baudenkmale von Constantinopel*, Blatt VI; see also Blatt X.

3. *Altchristliche und byzantinische Kunst*, II, Abb. 327.

4. Sarre and Herzfeld, *Archäologische Reise*, II, pp. 336–45 and Taf. CXXXVIII–CXXXIX.

Texier in 1840 saw and measured an example with a span of 4 m., the apse-arch of a church at Danā in North Syria. The circle of the arch, which no longer exists, was carried through 215°.[1] The church bore a date equivalent to A.D. 483. The fifth-century church at Khoja Kalesi in Asia Minor has an apse with a horse-shoe frontal arch of 4 m. span.[2] The sixth-century church of the West Monastery at Dayr Sim'ān also has an apse with frontal arch of horse-shoe form.[3]

The true home of the horse-shoe arch in Muslim times is Spain and North Africa.

The Geometrical Window-grilles

Geometrical ornament was known in Roman times, but its use was restricted and the designs generally show a poverty of imagination; its full development belongs to the art of Islam. An early Roman example (a pavement) has been preserved in the Domus Augustana on the Palatine, the greater part of which was built by Domitian (A.D. 81–96). This pattern may be drawn as follows: on a base line A–B (Figure 11) mark out a series of equal divisions; from these points draw a series of lines at 60° with a set-square, then turn over the set-square and repeat the performance. Then draw a series of lines parallel to the base line, so as to pass through the intersections of the two previous sets. We now have a mesh of equilateral triangles; these triangles may be grouped by sixes into regular hexagons. In our Roman pavement they are grouped so as to form hexagons which are not in contact.

Let us now try to analyse one of our window-grilles. Once more the same network solves the problem; we group our equilateral triangles by sixes, so as to obtain hexagons in contact at their corners, and then take their corners as centres from which to strike intersecting circles (Figure 12). We shall find that precisely the same network of hexagons forms the basis of one of the windows in the Mosque of Ibn Tūlūn (Plate 72b).

Now these patterns, and many others, belong to a group which

1. *Byzantine Architecture*, pp. 173–4 and Plate LIX.

2. Headlam, *Ecclesiastical Sites in Isauria*, Plate II₃ and Fig. 7.

3. Butler, H. C., *Ancient Architecture in Syria, Sect. B: Northern Syria*, p. 273 and Illus. 291–2.

Figure 11. Rome: Domus Augustana, geometrical pavement

may be called the hexagon group, or the 60° group because the mesh on which they are drawn is composed mainly of lines drawn at 60°.

But an octagon group was known at an early date; in some examples the octagons have equal sides, in others the sides are long and short alternately. As the latter are the result of crude and primitive methods of setting out, I shall give them first, although they are far from being the oldest. Excellent examples of this type have been revealed by the excavations at Jerash. The crudest type (Figure 13, left) occurs in the Church of Procopius, completed A.D. 526,[1] and in the Church of St George, 529–30. Why are the sides of the octagon alternately long and short? It is because of the crude method of setting out, a piece of paper ruled with squares being employed and the octagons obtained, as shown, by drawing lines following the side and diagonal of a square alternately.

Another example in which the octagons are very much better, but not perfect, occurs in three of the churches at Jerash (Figure 13, right). The octagons now have equal sides, but they are all slightly askew, as may be seen at once by turning the illustration round slightly. And here is the reason why. The sides of the octagons

1. Crowfoot, *Churches at Jerash*, British School of Archaeology in Jerusalem, Suppl. Papers, 3, pp. 33.

are formed, not of sides and diagonals as before, but of the diagonals of pairs of squares. This gives equal sides all round, but the octagon has a twist to one side, an askew form.

Here, however, is an example, very much earlier, of regular octagons (Figure 14). It is carved on the monolithic ceiling of the *cella* of the Great Temple at Palmyra, about A.D. 36, the only difference being that the octagons are treated as coffers. And this is the method by which it has been set out. Draw nine squares, add the diagonals and draw a circle in each touching all four sides. Then draw in the octagons and form the little squares by joining up the re-entrant angles of the stars. Twelve hundred years later we have the same pattern employed in Cairo for the coffered ceiling of Sultan Qalā'ūn's

Figure 12. Damascus: Great Mosque, analysis of marble window-grille

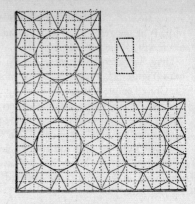

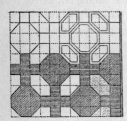

Figure 13. Jerash: two types of octagonal patterns

Mausoleum, the only difference being that the space between the octagons is occupied by a little octagon instead of by a tiny square. It looks so typically Muslim that it is difficult to believe that its pedigree goes back through twelve centuries.

The other window grille is composed of a simple combination of squares, with large interlacing circles struck from the centres of alternate squares, and small circles struck from the centres of the remaining squares (Figure 15).

The Dome of the Treasury

I cannot help thinking that the Dome of the Treasury has some connexion with the *phiale*, or fountain, which sometimes stood in the atriums of Byzantine churches, e.g. Sancta Sophia, 'a bubbling stream leaping into the air from a bronze pipe'.[1] It is not certain that this *phiale* had a canopy, for the only author who writes as though it had is an anonymous one, probably of the tenth century. But a canopied *phiale* still exists in St Demetrius at Salonika.[2]

However, the combination of a domed treasury with a fountain seems to have been an innovation, and a popular one too, for Istakhrī

---

1. Paul the Silentiary, quoted by Lethaby, *Sancta Sophia*, p. 189.

2. Diehl, Le Tourneau, and Saladin, *Les Monuments chrétiens de Salonique*, pp. 67–70 and figs. 28–9.

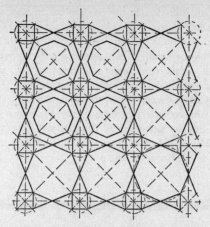

Figure 14. Palmyra: Great Temple, analysis of
coffered ceiling of *cella*

Figure 15. Damascus: Great Mosque, analysis of another
marble window-grille

(951) says: 'In Adharbayjān they deposit the treasure in the Great Mosque in a little structure called *bayt māl*, covered with a leaden roof, closed by an iron door, and supported on nine [? eight] columns.'[1] Muqaddasī (985), speaking of the customs peculiar to Syria, confirms this, saying: 'In the chief town of every province, in the Great Mosque, is a treasure chamber supported upon pillars.'[2]

Several of these structures may be cited: the Bayt al-Māl in the Mosque of 'Amr at Fustāt, built in 99 H. (717–18), which was a domed chamber resting on ten columns. Another still exists in the Great Mosque of Hamā, and others were seen by Ibn Jubayr in 1184 in the Great Mosque of Harrān (below, p. 152).

INFLUENCE OF THE GREAT MOSQUE

The influencé of the Great Mosque of Damascus, which was regarded by the medieval Muslims as one of the Wonders of the World, was naturally considerable. For example, the Great Mosque at Aleppo, built by the Khalif Sulaymān, the son of 'Abd al-Malik, was apparently copied from it.[3] The mosque at Qasr al-Hair (pp. 115–18), although much smaller, has clearly been modelled on it, for it has a sanctuary three aisles deep, a transept and clerestory, and columns alternate with piers in the arcades round the *sahn*, and this was the case in the oldest part of east *riwāq* of the Great Mosque at Hamā. In the Great Mosque of Cordova I believe that the present arcades round the *sahn*, in which two columns alternate with every pier, although late, represent a previous scheme, also derived from Damascus (below, p. 227).

The specific features which had a lasting influence were the following: (1) the three axial entrances, (2) the transept, (3) the alternation of piers and columns, and (4) the sanctuary three aisles deep.

(1) *The Three Axial Entrances*. It is practically certain that there were three axial entrances in the Great Mosque at Qasr al-Hair (below pp. 115–17) and Harrān and probably in the Great Mosque of Hamā, in the early days. A large number of examples of this feature occur in

1. p. 174.
2. p. 182.
3. Ibn ash-Shihnā, p. 62; Sauvaget's transl., *Les Perles choisis*, pp. 56–7.

Cairo, e.g. the Mosque of al-Hākim (A.D. 990–1013),[1] Mosque of as-Sālih Talā'i' (1160), Mosque of Baybars I (1266–9), Mosque of al-Baqlī (end of thirteenth century), Mosque of al-Māridānī (1339–40), Mosque of Zayn ad-Dīn at Būlāq (1448–9), and the Mosque of Ezbek (1475).[2]

(2) *The Transept*. A similar transept occurs in the Great Mosque at Qasr al-Hair (729), in the Great Mosque at Diyārbakr (end of the eleventh century), at Dera'ā, date uncertain, and at Ephesus. It first appears in Egypt in the Mosque of al-Azhar (970–72), then in the Mosque of al-Hākim (990–1013) and of Baybars (1266–9).

(3) *Alternation of Piers and Columns*. This feature occurs in the Mosques at Qasr al-Hair (729), Hamā, and Cordova. Also apparently in the Haram ash-Sharīf at Jerusalem before 985, for Muqaddasī says: 'In the court of the [Aqsā] mosque on the right-hand side (i.e. along the west side of the enclosure) are porticoes supported by marble columns and piers. ...'[3]

(4) *Sanctuaries Three Aisles Deep*. This feature, like the three already mentioned, occurs in the Mosque of Qasr al-Hair, in the Mosque at Qusayr al-Hallābāt, at Raqqa, in the mosque outside the walls at Bālis (1071), at Diyārbakr (end of eleventh century), and in the mosque of uncertain date at Dera'ā.

1. See my *Muslim Architecture of Egypt*, I.
2. Demolished in 1869. Plan in the *Comité de Conservation, Exercice 1894*, pl. I.
3. p. 168.

CHAPTER 4

THE WORKS OF AL-WALĪD
(CONTINUED)

THE PALACE AT MINYA ON LAKE TIBERIAS

THIS palace, which is close to the north-eastern shore of the lake, and less than a mile to the west of Tabgha, was first investigated by E. A. Mader, who began its excavation in 1932. Further work was carried out by A. M. Schneider in 1936, and by Schneider and Puttrich-Reignard in 1937–9.

It is a rectangular enclosure which, as Schneider remarks, externally resembles the *castra* of the Roman frontier in Transjordan. It has a round tower at each corner and a half-round tower, 4 m. (13 ft) in diameter, in the centre of each side except the east, where there is a curious gateway tower 16½ m. (54 ft) wide. The walls, which are 1·40 m. (4½ ft) thick, are carefully built of local limestone on a socle of basalt 40 cm. (15¾ in.) high. They are still preserved in some places to a height of 4½ m. (14¾ ft), and they must have had a cresting of stepped and undercut crenellations, for one was found intact among the débris.

The gateway consists of a room about 6 m. (19½ ft) square, set between two quarter-round towers. There is a semicircular recess to right and left, and above was a dome decorated with a cornice [1] and beautifully carved rosettes; it doubtless rested on spherical-triangle pendentives. On the inner side was an arched doorway, 3·75 m. (12⅓ ft) wide, opening into a hall, about 7 m. (23 ft) wide and 11½ m. (38 ft) long, which led directly into the central court. Excavation has revealed that a portico ran all round this court, resting on four L-shaped corner piers and six columns on each side (Figure 116).

In the south-west corner was a mosque, 13·10 m. (43 ft) wide and 19·42 deep (proportions almost exactly as 3 : 2), the mihrāb of which was laid bare in 1937. It could be entered from the corner of the central court, and also directly from the exterior by a postern gate, exactly as in Qasr al-Hair ash-Sharqī (below, p. 116).

1. Almost all the blocks of this cornice were found in the débris.

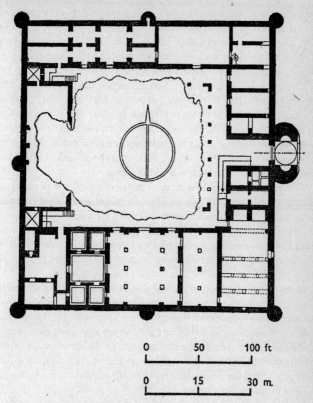

Figure 16. Minya: plan of al-Walīd's palace

The central part of the south side is occupied by a group of rooms, 19·42 m. (63¾ ft) deep (like the mosque) and 42·20 m. (138½ ft) in width. They must have been intended for ceremonial purposes, for the decoration was of great magnificence. The central part consists of a great hall, nearly 20 m. (65½ ft) square, which was entered from the court by three doors, and divided into a wide central aisle and two narrow ones by two rows of supports, of which the four wall-piers existed, but only the base of one column. Its position showed that there must have been three in each row. The floor and walls were originally lined with marble slabs, remains of which were found *in situ* all round the base of the walls. This panelling only rose to a certain height, above which the walls must have been decorated with mosaic, for the floor was covered with glass tesserae, some coloured, others white overlaid with gold leaf.

This great hall is flanked by two rectangles, the same in size and shape (19·42 m. (63¾ ft) in depth and 9·70 (31¾ ft) and 9·81 (32¼ ft) in width), which were each entered from it by three doors; they cannot be entered directly from the court. The eastern rectangle was divided into two aisles by a row of three columns down the centre. Only two column-bases were found *in situ*. A door near the back wall of this room opened into the back aisle of the mosque.

The rectangle on the western side consists of a group of five rooms: a large central one, with two small rooms to north and south opening into it. The floors of these rooms were all paved with mosaics in an extraordinary state of preservation, all the patterns being geometrical. That in the south-eastern room recalls a carpet, with a border of circles alternating with rhomboids. Equally uninjured were the mosaics of the door-sills.

Now it must be expressly noted that in the planning of this rectangle a system has been adopted which we shall meet with again at Mshattā in its fully developed form, viz.: *the successive, symmetrical subdivision into three*. Here the first subdivision into three gives us the main hall and its two flanking rectangles; by the second subdivision we get the basilical hall and, to the west of it, the large room flanked by a pair of smaller ones to north and south. At Mshattā this system is carried much farther (Figure 23).

In the masonry of the restored part of the gateway tower, Schneider found part of a marble slab with a Kufic inscription in the name of al-Walīd, built in upside down. The date, unfortunately, was missing.

QUSAYR ʿAMRA

Qusayr ʿAmra (the little palace of ʿAmra) stands in the desert on the edge of the Wādī Butm, about 50 miles east of ʿAmmān. It was discovered by Musil in 1898. He spent a fortnight there in 1901, accompanied by the Austrian artist Mielich, who copied some of the paintings.

It is a comparatively small building (Plate 21*a*) and has been well defined by van Berchem as a 'pavillon de chasse doublé d'un bain'. It is built of hard reddish limestone from the neighbouring hills, and is composed of two principal elements: (1) a rectangular audience hall, *A*, measuring roughly 8½ by 7½ m. (28 by 24½ ft), with an alcove, *B*, opening on the south side, flanked by two rooms, *C* and *C¹*, apsidal in form and without windows, and (2) a bath, consisting of three

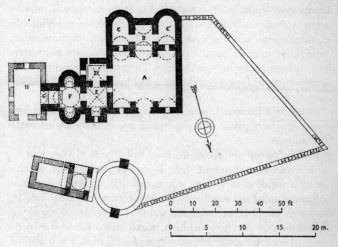

Figure 17. Qusayr 'Amra: plan

little rooms, *D*, *E*, and *F*, the first tunnel-vaulted, the second cross-vaulted, and the third covered by a dome (Figure 17). On the east side of the latter is a tunnel-vaulted passage, *G*, at present blocked-up, leading to an unroofed enclosure, *H*. The exterior corresponds exactly with the interior, and no attempt has been made to conceal the extrados of the vaults by raising the exterior walls, or otherwise.

On entering, the first thing to strike one is the curious vaulting system, the nearly square interior being divided by two transverse arches into three bays of almost equal width, on which rest three tunnel-vaults (Plate 21*b*). The transverse arches spring from low pilasters, and are remarkable for being slightly pointed, one of the earliest examples of this feature in Muslim architecture. They have been struck from two centres one tenth of the span apart.[1] There is a set-back of about 5 cm. (2 in.) at the springing, no doubt intended to support the centering.

At the back of the central bay is an alcove, B, which, although square-ended, resembles an apse; it is covered by a tunnel-vault, the crown of which is about $2\frac{1}{2}$ m. (8 ft) lower than the transverse vaults. There is a small window, placed as high as possible, at each end of the three tunnel-vaults, and two more high up in the eastern wall, making eight in all. A small door to right and left in the alcove opens into the flanking rooms, which are each roofed with a tunnel-vault ending in a semi-dome over the apsidal part. They lack windows and receive their light, such as it is, from the door. These two chambers were evidently intended for repose, the main hall being intended for official receptions.

Musil, and likewise Jaussen and Savignac,[2] found that these little rooms had been paved with glass mosaic representing conventionalized foliage.

A door on the east side of the main hall (Figure 7) leads into the little tunnel-vaulted room D (2·83 by 2·30 m.; $9\frac{1}{4}$ by $7\frac{1}{2}$ ft), which is lit by a window on the east side placed high up under the vault. Against the east and south walls is a little plastered bench 30 cm. (12 in.) high. Musil excavated in this and the two following rooms and found piers 70 cm. ($27\frac{1}{2}$ in.) high, which must have supported the original floor, the space between serving for the passage of heated air. The hypocausts in the Baths of Caracalla are constructed in this way. A door on the north side leads into a cross-vaulted room, 2·83 m. ($9\frac{1}{4}$ ft) square, with a little tunnel-vaulted alcove on the far side. At about 2 m. ($6\frac{1}{2}$ ft) above the floor the walls overhang 12 cm. ($4\frac{3}{4}$ in.), and in each corner beneath this projection are four clay water-pipes, about 7 cm. ($2\frac{3}{4}$ in.) in diameter, leading from the roof. The water was conducted along the roof in cemented channels.

A door on our right leads into F, a room quite different from any of the preceding. It consists of a central square practically the same in size as E, with a deep apsidal recess to north and south, both covered

1. I have verified this with a pair of compasses, on a wide-angle photograph taken on the axis of the arch.
2. *Les Châteaux arabes*, p. 81.

by tunnel-vaults terminating in semi-domes. The central part is covered by a dome, resting on spherical-triangle pendentives, between which and the dome is a stone cornice 30 cm. high, decorated with a triple chevron. The dome is pierced with four small windows which rest on this cornice.

The walls of these three rooms are all pitted with holes intended to provide a hold for a panelling of marble. The upper parts of the walls overhang as in the previous room, in each corner is a water-pipe, and under the floor are remains of hypocausts. At the far end of *G*, partly above and partly below ground level, is what appears to have been the furnace.

Purpose of the Building

A comparison with two little bath-houses at 'Abda and Ruhayba to the south of Beersheba suffices to show that the annexe on the east side of the main hall, *A*, was a bath. The first room, *D*, with its two benches but no pipes, must have served as the *apodyterium*, the second room, *E*, with its water-pipes and hypocausts under the floor, was the *tepidarium*, and the domed chamber next the furnace the *calidarium*.

The Decoration: the famous Fresco Paintings

We have seen that the little rooms flanking the alcove had mosaic floors, which were still in good condition in Musil's day. The other rooms were formerly paved with marble slabs 3 cm. (1¼ in.) thick, remains of which also existed at the time of his visits. All the rooms once had marble dadoes, and at the time of Musil's second visit the panelling of the eastern wall of the main hall was still intact; it rose to a point 80 cm. above the débris. Above this the walls are plastered and decorated with the now-famous paintings, the importance of which may be realized when one remembers that 'no such extensive decoration in fresco is known to have survived in any other secular building earlier than the Romanesque period'.[1] The colours are directly applied to a mortar facing about 3 cm. (1¼ in.) in thickness and, according to the Austrian chemists, Pollak and Wenzel, are to be regarded as fresco and not as tempera, for no trace of size was found.

1. Dalton, *Byzantine Art*, p. 281.

The range of colours was obtained as follows:

Bright blue – natural ultramarine.

Deep brown – a red, apparently produced from oxide of iron overlaid with a thin coat of ultramarine.

Light brown – ochreous compositions containing iron.

Dull yellow – the same, mixed with chalk.

Bluish-green – yellow which has received a light coating of ultramarine.

The paintings in the audience hall have suffered far more than those
in the small rooms. We are therefore almost entirely dependent on
the paintings of Mielich for our knowledge of them, which is all the
more to be regretted, for those paintings of his which can be checked,
viz.: those of the three rooms of the bath, are seen to be travesties of
the originals. This is due to the fact that his paintings are not copies
completed on the spot, but reconstructions worked up months later
in his studio, from his tracings, notes, copies of the colours, and from
two or three which were detached from the walls and taken away.[1] I
will now describe the principal paintings.

The Alcove

The walls from above the place occupied by the marble dado to
about half their height were painted to imitate hanging drapery. At
the back of the alcove was a throned monarch with a halo, under a
baldachin resting on two spirally decorated columns, on the arched
front edge of which was painted a Kufic inscription in white on a blue
background, invoking a blessing on some person whose name no
longer remains. To the right of the throne was a man waving a
flabellum. There can be no doubt that this alcove, directly opposite
the entrance, was intended for the throne recess.

Between the alcove and the south-west corner, according to Musil,
was the figure of a woman, above which to the right was the word
NIKH – Victory.[2] This figure, as has already been pointed out, must

1. See the remarks of Müller, the editor, in *Kusejr 'Amra*, pp. iv–vii, and of
Wickhoff, *ibid.*, p. 203; also van Berchem, *Journal des savants*, 1909, p. 308.

2. Tracing in Jaussen and Savignac, *op. cit.*, pl. LV₃. I was unable to distinguish this word.

surely have a direct connexion with the famous picture of the defeated enemies of Islam alongside (Plate 23a), at the south end of the
west wall. This consisted [1] of six richly dressed figures, three being
placed in the foreground with their hands open in sign of homage or
submission, and three placed behind them. Above the first four were
fragments of superscriptions in Arabic and Greek; it is on the interpretation of these superscriptions that the dating of the building rests,
so we shall return to this picture again. To the right of this was a
bathing scene, and to the right again a group of men practising gym-
nastic exercises.

On the north wall were traces of a hunting scene, the continuation
of which, better preserved, is to be seen on the east half of the south
wall. Above, to the right of the window under the vault, is a woman
with remains of the word ΠΟΙΗϹ[ΙϹ] (Poesy) painted alongside.
Facing her on the other side of the window are the remains of two
other figures with the words ΙϹΤΟΡΙ[Α] and ϹΚΨΗ(Σκέψις) (History
and Philosophy) written above them.

The Transverse Arches

Here the decoration is better preserved. On the southern half of the
eastern arch is a seated musician playing a long-handled stringed instrument. Above him, and reaching to the apex of the arch, is a
woman wearing nothing but a tight-fitting skirt, with her arms above
her head. The part above her hands had gone even when Musil saw it,
but I suggest that she is holding up a portrait medallion, as at Palmyra,
where very similar narrow slip compositions occur in a rock-tomb
known as Maghārat al-Jadīda.[2] On the southern half of the western
arch is a nude dancer making sinuous and undulating movements with
her arms and body.

The Apodyterium (D)

This contains the best-preserved paintings in the building. In the
tympanum over the door from the main hall is a Cupid with wings

1. It has since suffered so much that it is almost impossible to distinguish
anything.

2. Strzygowski, *Orient oder Rom*, pp. 11-12 and Taf. I; Chabot, *Choix
d'inscriptions de Palmyre*, pp. 96-105 and pls XIV, XV, and XVII.

spread, holding out his hands over two figures lying on the ground. In the centre of the tympanum opposite is a window, to the left (north) of which is a woman sitting with her chin resting on her hand (good) and looking towards a man (faded [1]) on the other side of the window.[2]

The tunnel-vault is divided up by bands, decorated with leaves, into seventeen lozenges, the outer points of which touch the edges, thereby forming twelve triangles. These lozenges and triangles are each filled by one subject, either a man, a woman, an animal, or a bird. On the north side (Plate 22) we have:

Row 1. Disappeared.

Row 2. Stork, gazelle, another gazelle.

Row 3. Man in Roman tunic playing a flute, female dancer wearing a long white skirt with a broad red border, above it a sleeveless tunic gathered in at the waist by a white girdle.

Row 4. Heron(?), an animal (perhaps a wild ass), another animal.

The apex of the vault is occupied by a row of three busts, one of a white-haired man. Wickhoff suggests that they are intended to represent the three ages of man.[3]

On the south side we have:

Row 1. A small animal, a snake coiled up ready to strike, a small animal like a cat watching its prey.

Row 2. A stork, a wild ass, a deer, a crested bird.

Row 3. Monkey or bear sitting on a footstool and playing a stringed instrument, a monkey standing on its hind legs and clapping its fore-paws, like Arabs at a *fantasia*, a man in a short tunic.

Row 4. Another stork, gazelle, trotting camel, crane(?).

The Tepidarium

The painting on the south tympanum of the cross-vault is the best preserved. To the left is a half-reclining woman, in the centre a figure holding a little child in its arms. To the right, at the door, another woman enters. All the figures are nude, which suggests the idea of a hot bath.

1. Now (1956) entirely gone.
2. See Jaussen and Savignac, *op. cit.*, pl. XLV–XLVII.
3. In Musil, *op. cit.*, pp. 206 and 212.

The Calidarium

The dome resembling the vault of heaven, it was evidently intended
to be painted as such, for the chief constellations of the northern hemi-
sphere are depicted there, together with the signs of the Zodiac. In the
centre are the Great Bear and the Little Bear, separated by the tail of
the Dragon. To the right, a person with arms extended was recognized by Jaussen and Savignac as Andromeda, with Cassiopeia at her
feet.

The Zodiac of Qusayr 'Amra is of the greatest importance, for it is
the earliest existing attempt to portray the vault of heaven on a *hemispherical, instead of a flat surface*, but the artist must have copied a drawing on a table in front of him, and in doing so has transposed everything from right to left.[1]

The Date of Qusayr 'Amra

The dating is based on the interpretation of the fragments of bi-
lingual superscriptions still preserved above the group of figures at the
south end of the west wall. They consist of four Greek and four
Arabic words, forming four doublets above the first four personages
from the left. Beginning from the left Nöldeke read Kaisar; then,
combining the mutilated Greek and Arabic over the third figure, he
obtained Chosdrois (for Chosroes, the Greek form of Khusrau). On
the head of this figure, moreover, is a crown of the same type as those
which appear on the coins of the later Sasanians, such as Khusrau II
(A.D. 590–629). After that he read the Arabic word over the fourth
figure as Najāshī. This reading has since been rendered certain by
Jaussen and Savignac's discovery of the corresponding Greek word
Nigos. Nöldeke showed his results to Littmann, who then read the
inscription over the second figure as Rōdorīkos.[2]

The four personages thus designated are of course the Byzantine
Emperor, the Visigothic king of Spain, the Sasanian Emperor, and the
Negus of Abyssinia, that is to say, sovereigns whom the rising Arab
power had overcome, or robbed of part of their territory.

1. See the brilliant study by the late Fritz Saxl and Dr Arthur Beer, contri-
buted in 1932 to my *Early Muslim Architecture*, I, pp. 289–303.
2. *Zeitschr. der Deutschen Morgenländischen Gesell.*, LXI, pp. 222–8.

The Byzantine Emperor is clad in his imperial robes with a tiara on his head; the Sasanian Emperor, beardless, with thick curly hair, wears a purple cloak and purple shoes and the Sasanian crown on his head, and the Negus is wearing a light-coloured garment with a dark-coloured stole.

Nöldeke points out that as Rōdorīk came to power in 710 and was killed in the battle of the Guadalete on 19 July 711, it follows that the painting must have been executed after his death in that year, and in any case not later than the fall of the Umayyad dynasty in 750.

Can the date be fixed still more closely? Van Berchem has brilliantly attempted to do so. He points out that the six personages in the group form a composition obeying definite rules, three being in the foreground and three being intercalated between and behind them, as shown in the diagram. Of these the first four are identified by inscriptions as follows:

1. Kaisar (the Byzantine Emperor).
2. Rōdorīk (the Visigothic King of Spain).
3. Chosroes (the Emperor of Persia).
4. Negus (the King of Abyssinia).

From this he deduces (1) that the personages in the foreground are sovereigns of great empires, whilst those in the background represent the rulers of simple kingdoms, and (2) that in each row the arrangement of the personages from left to right corresponds to their geographical situation from west to east. If these conclusions are correct number 5 must be intended for a great sovereign to the east of Persia, and number 6 for a ruler of the second order residing to the east of Abyssinia.

Now it was at the beginning of the eighth century that Qutayba recommenced against the Turkish races of Central Asia the campaign which had been abandoned during the civil war between 'Alī and Mu'āwiya, and two notable victories were gained, one in 707 between Merv and Bukhārā, the other in 712 under the walls of Samarqand. He points out that the Emperor of China at that time was regarded as the suzerain of all Central Asia, and it was he whom all the rulers of Turkish race called to their aid against the Arabs. Number 5 may therefore be intended for the Emperor of China, in

which case number 6 could represent one of the Turkish kings involved in the campaigns of Qutayba, or the Hindu King Dāhir, killed
in Sind in 712. Van Berchem continues:

If one reflects on these curious synchronisms; if one bears in mind that
all these victories, which carried the fortune of the Umayyads to its
highest point, followed each other, one after the other, during the reign
of Walīd I; that the latter was a great builder and resided in the Belqa
(Transjordan), it becomes very tempting to attribute 'Amra to him, in
which case this picture would be a monument to his victories. The
Kaisar would be one of the feeble Byzantine Emperors defeated by al-
Walīd's general Maslama in Asia Minor, the painting of Chosroes
would represent not Yazdagird himself, but one of his descendants who
attempted at the end of the seventh century to restore the Sasanian
dynasty, a matter on which Chinese documents have thrown some
light.[1]

As for the Negus, we lack precise information. If van Berchem's view
is accepted and the picture symbolizes the victories of Walīd I, then
there can be no doubt that he is the originator of the building, which
in that case must be placed between 711 (battle of the Guadalete), or
712 (victory at Samarqand), and 715, the year of his death.

The Raison d'être of Qusayr 'Amra

Hatred of the narrow enclosures of cities and of a settled life char-
acterized the Arab conquerors on every front, hence the adoption of
Jabīya, the old camp-city of the Ghassānid Phylarchs, about 15 miles
south-east of Kuneitra, as the centre of the Arab Government after the
conquest of Syria.

Half-Bedawīn Life of the later Umayyad Khalifs

As for the Umayyad Khalifs, their instincts were likewise nomadic;
although Mu'āwiya, the founder of the dynasty, made Damascus his
capital and resided there, his successors only visited it when state ceremonial required their presence. At other times, 'by a kind of atavism
of the Bedawīn hīra', as van Berchem has expressed it,[2] they

---

1. *Journal des Savants*, 1909, pp. 367–70.
2. *Ibid.*, p. 307.

preferred the *bādiya*, or spring pasturage, when the desert is covered with green after the winter rains.

The oasis of Dūmat al-Jandal and the splendid city of Damascus merely reminded them, in the words of the poet Akhtal, of the pallor and rigors of the fevers caught by them in the gardens of the Ghūta.[1] Jāhiz (*d.* 869) expresses the same feeling when he says: 'Beware of the *rīf* (cultivated land); it is death and a quick death to approach it.' Likewise the Bedawī poet Ibn Mayāda when he said to Walīd II, 'The proximity of springs does not suit us; mosquitoes and fevers devour us.'[2]

And so each Umayyad Khalif, the members of his family, and the principal men of state, each possessed their camping ground. These encampments, at first no doubt of tents, gradually increasing in luxury, developed into a standing camp, and later on buildings of a permanent nature came to be erected. In some cases they even occupied Roman–Byzantine frontier forts, such as Azraq, forming part of the great block-house line which ran from the Gulf of 'Aqaba to Damascus, and from Damascus to Palmyra. Thus from *bādiya* developed *hīra*, an agglomeration of buildings half mobile, half permanent.

Mu'āwiya's successor, Yazīd (680–83), was the son of a Bedawī woman; he loved wine and dancing and died at Hauwārīn. Marwān I lived among the Bedawīn, Walīd I moved about a great deal, but his various places of residence always seem to have been on the edge of the desert, e.g. Khunāsira al-Ahāss (55 km. south-east of Aleppo), Qaryatain and Usays (= Tell Seis, 105 km. south-east of Damascus), where there are still remains of a *qasr* about 70 m. square, a camp mosque, and a *hammām*. 'Umar also chose Khunāsira as his favourite place of residence. Yazīd II (720–24) was the great-grandson of a Bedawī woman, and liked to spend his time at Muwaqqar (between Mshattā and Qasr Kharāna, amusing himself with poets, singers, dancers, and musicians).

Hishām (724–43) lived at Qasr al-Hair (below, p. 111 ff.), in the desert, 50 miles beyond Palmyra. His dissolute successor, Walīd II (743–4), had lived in the desert for twenty years before he became

1. Lammens, 'La Bâdia', in *Mélanges de la Faculté orientale, Beyrouth*, IV, p. 94. The Ghūta is the great belt of orchards, 7–8 miles broad, which borders the south side of Damascus.

2. Lammens, *ibid.*, pp. 100–102.

Khalif, and it is expressly stated that even when he was Khalif he never set foot in a town.[1] Tabarī speaks of his going to Azraq (12 miles east of Qusayr 'Amra), and of his staying near 'the water of al-Aghdaf', sometimes called al-Ghadaf in the *Kitāb al-Aghānī*, for which reason Musil[2] identified it with the Wādī Ghadaf on which Qasr at-Tūba stands (below, p. 134 ff.). At the time he was murdered he was staying at the Qasr al-Bakhrā', a Roman fort on the edge of the desert, about 15 miles south-west of Palmyra. After his murder the Khalifate passed to his cousin, Yazīd III, who had to promise that he would live in Damascus and 'lay neither stone on stone nor brick on brick',[3] so strained had the finances been by the extravagant building activities of his predecessors.

Six years later the Umayyad Khalifate came to an end, and with it the period of Arab ascendancy.

The Inspiration of the Fresco Paintings

The paintings of Qusayr 'Amra clearly belong, not to the hieratic art of Byzantium, but to the late Hellenistic art of Syria, and they bear eloquent witness to its vitality. Not only have we the four personifications of Poesy, History, Philosophy, and Victory (labelled in Greek), but a winged cupid also. The lozenge diaper on the vault of room *D* recalls a favourite treatment of mosaic pavements, e.g. at Mādaba, less than 50 miles away, the mosaic pavement discovered at Jerusalem in 1892,[4] another on the Mount of Olives,[5] and a fourth recently excavated at Antioch.[6] I would now call attention to the resemblance between the costume of the dancing-girl on the vault of the *Apodyterium* (Plate 22) and the costume of the winged Victories in a tomb at Palmyra. The costume is identical in both cases: a long underskirt, very full and reaching almost to the feet, an over-garment reaching to the knee only, fastened close to the waist, full above, sleeveless, and gathered together on either side of the neck (a Greek *chiton* in fact), so that the point of the shoulder is exposed.

1. Ibn 'Abd Rabbihī, *al-'Iqd*, II, p. 351, quoted by Nöldeke, *loc. cit.*, LXI, p. 226.
2. *Palmyrena*, pp. 155–6.　　3. Ibn al-Athīr, v, p. 220, l. 12.
4. *Revue Biblique*, 1892, fig. on p. 118.
5. *Ibid.*, 1895, p. 86.　　6. *Ars Islamica*, IX, 'Notes', Fig. 2.

That the paintings are derived from the Hellenistic art of Syria has been recognized by practically everyone who has discussed them: Brünnow, Strzygowski, van Berchem, Diehl, Herzfeld, and Dalton. The latter says:

They show us how absolutely the art of the early Mohammedan period depended upon the Hellenistic art of Syria and Mesopotamia. In the second place they show us how tenacious of life and of its old traditions the Hellenistic art of Hither Asia really was. ... Here, as in Constantinople, the old genre scenes retained their popularity, and at once found favour with luxurious princes of the conquering faith.[1]

Diez says:

The painted decoration of 'Amra shows us how long the Hellenistic tradition remained in activity, and of what charmingly gifted creations it was still capable at the beginning of the eighth century. The 'Amra series of paintings is the last great creation of a secular character that Hellenistic art has left us. The happy sensuality of the antique here flares up once more for the last time.[2]

There is, however, one trace of Persian influence, and that is the inspiration behind the painting depicting the Enemies of Islam. This, as Herzfeld has shown, must have been derived from a Persian prototype in which the Kings of the Earth do homage to Chosroes on his throne.[3] Such a composition existed, and is referred to by Yāqūt as follows:

At Qarmīsīn (i.e. Kirmānshāh) is the *dukkan* where the Kings of the Earth, amongst them Faghfūr – the King of China, Khāqān – the King of the Turks, Dāhir – the King of Sind, and Kaisar – the King of Rūm, are convoked by Kisrā Aparwīz.

Thus we can readily admit that the inspiration of this painting is Persian. But of the total surface it occupies only about a twentieth part, moreover it is Persian in inspiration only, not in execution, so the Persian element in the whole decoration is less than a fortieth part.

1. *Byzantine Art*, p. 279.
2. *Die Kunst der islamischen Völker*, p. 24.
3. *Die Malerei von Samarra*, pp. 5–6.

Nationality of the Artists

Brünnow [1] and Becker [2] have pointed out that the Arabic inscriptions have obviously been executed by one accustomed to write Arabic, whereas the letters of the Greek inscriptions have first been outlined in a darker colour and filled in afterwards. They therefore conclude that the artists knew Arabic better than Greek, but not perfectly, for they have written Kisrā as they heard it pronounced and not as it should be written. Becker also points out that the use of the title Kaisar for the Byzantine Emperor is not taken from Byzantine practice and would not have been employed by a Greek. One can even go further, and say that a Greek would not have understood the term, for Procopius, writing in the second half of the sixth century, says: 'Chosroes was indignant that the envoys had not been sent him by Kaisar', and then feels bound to add by way of explanation, 'For thus the Persians call the King (βασιλευς) of the Romans.' [3] Brünnow and Becker come to the conclusion that the artists were either Syrians or Aramaeans.

The Question of the Lawfulness of Painting in Islam

The paintings of Qusayr 'Amra raise, in an imperative fashion, the question of the lawfulness or otherwise of painting in Islam.

Even at the present day the belief is very widely held that all forms of painting are forbidden by explicit passages in the Qurān, but this is a popular error for no such passages exist, as Orientalists have frequently pointed out.

We have seen above (p. 2) that paintings existed in the Ka'ba as rebuilt in A.D. 608, and Azraqī says that when Muhammad entered it after he had taken Makka in 630, he ordered the picture of Mary with Jesus on her lap to be preserved, and that this picture remained until the Ka'ba was destroyed in 683. We are also told that on the capture of al-Madā'in, or Ctesiphon, in 637, the great Īwān was used for the Friday prayer in spite of the paintings which decorated it,[4] paintings which still existed in 897.

1. *Wiener Zeitschr. für die Kunde des Morgenlandes*, XXI, p. 282.
2. *Zeitschr. für Assyriologie*, XX, p. 382–4.   3. *Wars*, II, xxi, 9.
4. Tabarī, I, p. 2441, l. 13, and p. 2444, l. 7. The paintings represented the siege of Antioch by Khusrau Anūshirwān; al-Buhturī, *Diwān*, pp. 108–9.

Yet in spite of the silence of the Qurān, the *Hadīth* (Traditions) are uniformly hostile to all representations of living forms. When did the change take place? A valuable clue is provided, curiously enough, by the Patrology. Our first witness is John, Patriarch of Damascus and a great opponent of the Iconoclasts, who occupied a prominent place in the Court life of the later Umayyads. His active life was roughly between 700 and 750. He was well acquainted with the doctrines of Islam, and his quotations from the Qurān in Greek are sometimes almost literal translations from the original. But although he was a violent opponent of the Iconoclastic movement and wrote treatises against the Edict of 726, and although he also wrote against Islam, he never accuses the Muslims of being hostile to pictures,[1] although it would have been the first thing he would have seized upon to reproach them with, had they held such opinions. But about the end of the eighth century we find Theodore Abū Qurra, Bishop of Harrān, differing from John, for he includes the Muslims among the people opposed to painting, saying: 'Those who assert that he who paints anything living will be compelled on the Day of Resurrection to breathe into it a soul.'[2] Although the Muslims are not actually named, the almost literal citation of the Muslim *hadīth*[3] proves that they are meant and, in addition, that the *hādith* in question was already in circulation among the Muslims in the time of Abū Qurra. Thus the movement must have grown up in Islam towards the end of the eighth century.

How did the feeling arise? I believe it was partly due to the inherent temperamental dislike of Semitic races for human representations in sculpture and painting, and partly due to the internal effect of Jews who had been converted to Islam, like (1) the famous Yemenite Jew Ka'b al-Ahbar, who was converted in 638, and who is frequently cited as an authority for *Hadīth*, and (2) 'Abd Allāh ibn 'Abbās, one of the earliest expositors of the Qurān, also (3) Abū Huraira and (4) Wahb ibn Munabbih.

1. Becker, 'Christliche Polemik und islamische Dogmenbildung', in the *Zeitschrift für Assyriologie*, xxvi, pp. 177–80.

2. G. Graf, *Die arabischen Schriften des Theodor Abū Qurra*, pp. 297–8.

3. First found in Bukhārī (*c.* 870): 'On the Day of Judgment the punishment of hell will be meted out to the painter, and he will be called upon to breathe life into the forms he has fashioned; but he cannot breathe life into anything'; Juynboll's ed., ii, p. 41, and iv, p. 106.

Finally, as a predisposing psychological basis, there was the feeling, so common among primitive peoples, that the maker of an image or painting in some way transfers part of the personality of the subject to the image or painting, and in so doing acquires magical powers over the person reproduced. This feeling was once very widely spread.

My conclusion therefore is that the prohibition against painting *did not exist in early Islam*, but that it grew up gradually, for the reasons given above, towards the end of the eighth century.

HAMMĀM AS-SARAKH

Hammām as-Sarakh was discovered by H. C. Butler of the Princeton Expedition in 1905. It is strikingly like Qusayr ʿAmra in plan and arrangement, but it makes a very much better impression, thanks to its well-finished masonry, which has taken a beautiful amber tint (Plate 23*b* and Figure 18). Like Qusayr ʿAmra, it is composed of two principal elements: (1) a rectangular audience hall measuring 8·95 by 7·90 m. (29½ by 26 ft) (against 8·75 by 7·58; 28¾ by 24$\frac{9}{10}$ ft), with an alcove, corresponding to the throne-recess at Qusayr ʿAmra, opening on the south-east side, flanked by two rooms A and A_1, each lit by three windows like arrow-slits opening on the south side, and (2) a bath with three rooms, the first tunnel-vaulted, the second cross-vaulted, and the third covered by a dome – the same sequence of vaulting systems as at Qusayr ʿAmra, the only difference being that to pass out of B we must turn to the right instead of to the left.

One would have expected to find the entrance to the audience hall in the centre of the side opposite the alcove, but this is not the case; although two-thirds of the wall on this side had been preserved when I first saw it in 1926, there was no door to be seen, so it was probably in the centre of the south-western side. This wall, however, has fallen and any trace of a door-sill which may exist is buried under the débris. As in ʿAmra, the audience-hall was roofed by three parallel tunnel-vaults resting on two transverse arches springing from very low wall-piers. A quarter-round moulding runs all round at a height of about 5½ m. (18 ft). A small doorway on either side of the alcove opens into the flanking rooms, which are roofed with stone tunnel-vaults.

A door in the north corner of the main hall leads into the tunnel-vaulted *apodyterium* (B), measuring 2·50 by 3·45 m. (8¼ by 10 ft) from

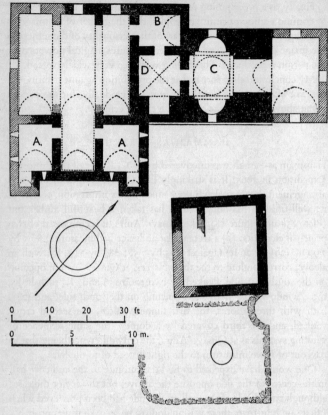

Figure 18. Hammām as-Sarakh: plan

which another door leads into the cross-vaulted *tepidarium* (*D*) measuring 3·40 by 2·20 m. (10 by 7¼ ft), on the far side of which, exactly
as at Qusayr ʿAmra, is a tunnel-vaulted recess, 1·70 m. (5½ ft) wide
and 1·20 m.(4 ft) deep. A door in the centre of the north-east wall leads
into the *calidarium* (*C*), covered by a dome on spherical-triangle
pendentives. There is a semi-circular recess to right and left covered by
semi-domes, beautifully constructed with voussoirs which radiate
from a saddle-block placed above the small window at the back.

The dome, which has an outer covering of pinkish waterproof cement, is built with nineteen projecting ribs, composed of long, thin, wedge-shaped pieces of shale, entirely unhewn, and the filling between the ribs is of shale also. It apparently had eight circular windows which have now become large holes.

The Decoration

This is no carved ornament but Butler, on the springing of the vault of the little recess in *D*, saw the remains of a painted medallion which had contained a life-sized bust. Only the shoulder, part of the neck, an ear with an ear-ring, and part of a head-dress could be seen; these were executed in good colours and were still bright. The background was yellow, the drapery of the shoulder dark red, and the head-dress was painted to represent a filmy white material, the transparency of which was well indicated.[1] But according to Musil there was more than this, for he says: 'On all the unimpaired walls are remains of paintings and it is evident that all the rooms were once painted.'[2] Unfortunately every trace of painting has since disappeared.

The Date

Hammām as-Sarakh, bath and audience hall like Qusayr ʿAmra, must have been built for an Umayyad prince for his own personal use. But it is better built and its arches are perceptibly more pointed (separation of centres one seventh to one-sixth of the span), though not yet so pointed as those of Mshattā (one-fifth), so I place it midway between them, say A.D. 725–30.

ARCHITECTURAL ORIGINS OF QUSAYR ʿAMRA

Similar Baths at ʿAbda and Ruhayba

Excluding the audience hall, the bath-houses at Qusayr ʿAmra and Hammām as-Sarakh closely follow a local type of which two pre-

1. *Ancient Architecture in Syria, A: Southern Syria*, Appendix, p. xxiii.
2. *Arabia Deserta*, p. 351.

Muslim examples have been preserved. At Ruhayba we have exactly the same sequence of vaulting systems: a tunnel-vault, a cross-vault, and a dome; in the walls are the same vertical grooves for pipes as at Qusayr 'Amra and Hammām as-Sarakh, and on the far side of the domed chamber is the same tunnel-vaulted passage. 'Abda is similar.[1]

These two baths, according to Jaussen and Savignac,[2] date from the Christian period, before the Arab conquest which sowed destruction in all the towns of the Negeb, and as the greater part of the tombstones that have been dug up in the cemeteries of Khalāsa, Ruhayba, and Sebaita date from the second part of the sixth century, they place these baths in the same period also.

The novelty, the addition of an audience hall, at Qusayr 'Amra and Hammām as-Sarakh, enabled the Khalif to hold his desert court there.

The Plan

Strzygowski, basing himself on Musil's plan, compares the audience-hall to a three-aisled church with apse and flanking rooms.[3] This impression, which the plan certainly gives, is erroneous, for one does not get any impression whatever of three aisles when standing in the hall. The effect produced is that of a clear interior, nearly square, without aisles, the triple division being confined to the vaulting above one's head.

The Pointed Arch

Pointed arches are arches in which the two halves are struck from a different centre. The less the separation of these two centres, the less the acuteness of the arch. The occurrence of the pointed arch at Qusayr 'Amra and Hammām as-Sarakh is proof of the priority of the East, for no European examples are known until the end of the eleventh or the beginning of the twelfth century. But H. C. Butler has called attention to a pre-Islamic Eastern example at Qasr Ibn Wardān

1. For these two buildings see Musil, *Kusejr 'Amra*, p. 67 and figs. 49–56 and 66–8.
2. *Les Châteaux arabes*, p. 112.
3. '*Amra als Bauwerk*', in the *Zeitschr. fuer Geschichte der Architektur*, I, p. 59.

(about 50 miles north-east of Homs), built between 561 and 564.[1] He maintains that the arch of the apse and the four arches that carried the dome are all struck from two points, 30 cm. (1 ft) on either side of the centre, i.e. they are 60 cm. (2 ft) apart.[2] Herzfeld has disputed this, yet a photograph taken by Thévenet, and published by Herzfeld himself,[3] clearly shows one of the dome-bearing arches to be pointed. In addition to this, the separation of the two centres, which Butler gives as 60 cm. (2 ft), is almost exactly the same as that found at Qusayr 'Amra, where the arches are on much the same scale (6·18 against 6·66 m.; 20¼ against 21¾ ft). Against this we have the fact, admitted by Herzfeld, that the pointed arch is absolutely unknown in Sasanian architecture.[4]

Even if we omit Qasr Ibn Wardān, the pointed arches of Qusayr 'Amra and Hammām as-Sarakh justify us in saying that this feature is of Syrian origin. And this view is confirmed by the fact that the very evolution of the pointed arch – i.e. the gradual separation of the two centres – can be observed there. At Hammām as-Sarakh, for example, the separation of the centres increases to one-seventh or one-sixth of the span, and at Mshattā to one-fifth, a ratio which becomes fairly constant henceforth, e.g. the Cistern at Ramla (below, pp. 228–30).

Thus we have:

		Date	Separation of centres
Qasr Ibn Wardān	Church, arches under dome	561–4	$\frac{1}{11}$th of span
Damascus	Great Mosque, arched frame at N. end of transept	705–15	$\frac{1}{10}$th of span
Qusayr 'Amra	Audience hall, transverse arches	712–15	$\frac{1}{10}$th of span
Hammām as-Sarakh	Calidarium of bath	725–30(?)	$\frac{1}{7}$th–$\frac{1}{8}$th
Qasr al-Hair	Mosque	728–9	Very slightly pointed
Mshattā	Section of vaults	744	$\frac{1}{5}$th of span
Qasr at-Tūba	Section of vaults	744	$\frac{1}{5}$th of span
Raqqa	Baghdād Gate	772	Four-centred arch

1. *Ancient Architecture in Syria, Sect. B: Northern Syria*, pp. 26–45 and pl. I–VII.

2. *Ibid.*, p. 32.

3. In his *Mshattā*, *Jahrb. der Preusz. Kunstsammlungen*, Taf. 2 *a*.

4. *Archäologische Reise*, II, pp. 91–2.

		Date	Separation of centres
Ukhaidir	Vault of great hall	last quarter 8th cent.	Slightly pointed
Ramla	Arches of cistern	789	⅛th of span
Fustāt	Mosque of 'Amr, windows	827	Slightly pointed
Sāmarrā	Bāb al-'Āmma	836	Four-centred arch
Fustāt	Nilometer, recesses	861–2	⅓rd of span
Qairawān	Great Mosque, arches lining transept and under dome	862	Pointed with slight return
Cairo	Mosque of Ibn Tūlūn	876–9	Irregular, about ¼th of span and stilted

Thus the first seven examples of this feature all occur in Syria.

The Low Springing of the Transverse Arches

This is a thoroughly local feature, good examples of which may be seen in a church at Tafhā, the fort of Qusayr al-Hallābāt, in the east church at Umm al-Jimāl, in the Bishop's palace at Bosrā, in a church and house at Lubbēn in the Lejā, etc.[1]

The Vaulting System of the Audience Hall

Architecturally the most remarkable feature of Qusayr 'Amra is its vaulting system, in which, the roof being carried on fixed points well apart, the wall between them becomes merely a curtain wall, which may be pierced at will and lateral lighting obtained. With a simple tunnel-vault running from one end of a hall to the other, adequate lighting becomes difficult, owing to the necessity of meeting the continuous thrust of the vault. I shall therefore attempt to trace this somewhat unusual solution to its earliest type, a type in which this potentiality for lateral lighting is not realized, and in which the arches, placed seldom more than 2 m. (6½ ft) apart, are roofed with stone slabs and never vaulted. This primitive type is found at the beginning of the Christian era in Nabataean tombs still existing in the Jabal Haurān, south-east of Damascus.

1. See Butler (H. C.), *Ancient Architecture in Syria, Sect. A: Southern Syria*, p. 63 ff.

This region does not produce any timber, so material necessity became the mother of invention and led to the discovery of new constructive methods. Thus the arch became the principal element of construction, and a series of parallel arches supporting ceiling slabs served to cover most of the halls. It may be asked, why did they not make the arch continuous and thus form a tunnel-vault? I think the answer must be that as they were not acquainted with the Mesopotamian method of building a vault without centering, a considerable amount of timber would be required for the centering, a very serious matter. But by building a series of arches the same piece of centering could be used over and over again directly one arch had set.

This system must have been known in Mesopotamia at a fairly early date, for it is found in the palace at Hatra built by the Parthians, whose dynasty came to an end in A.D. 226.

It was left to the keen architectural insight of the Persians to realize its potentialities, and to carry it to its full development. They were responsible for two innovations: (1) they were the first to use tunnel vaults to connect the transverse arches, thus making it possible to place them farther apart; and (2) they pierced windows in each of the curtain walls between these arches and thus obtained lateral lighting. The earliest existing building of this type is known as Tāq-Īwān at Khark, near Dizfūl in Khuzistān.[1] The surviving part consists of a gallery about 50 m. long by 9 m. broad (165 by 30 ft), the centre of which was occupied by a dome. Each half was spanned by transverse arches, brought up level and joined by tunnel-vaults, and in the side walls between each transverse arch was a window. Herzfeld has recently suggested that it may be of about A.D. 490.[2]

We now come to Qasr Kharāna, about 10 miles west of Qusayr 'Amra, where the same vaulting system occurs on the upper floor. I have given reasons elsewhere for believing that Qasr Kharāna is pre-Muslim, although it is generally regarded as Umayyad. In any case it is earlier than Qusayr 'Amra, and it is therefore the earliest building on the Syrian side of the desert in which the transverse arches are covered by tunnel-vaults.

1. See Dieulafoy, L'Art antique de la Perse, v, pp. 79–87, pl. VII–IX and figs. 55, 56, and 58–62; and Phené Spiers, Architecture: East and West, pp. 82–3 and fig. 37.

2. In Ars Islamica, x, p. 52.

Conclusion

The vaulting system of the audience hall at Qusayr 'Amra and Hammām as-Sarakh (and of the Mosque at Qusayr al-Hallābāt which we are going to describe) are of a perfectly normal local type with one modification – the slabs of basalt usually placed across the transverse arches are replaced by tunnel-vaults. This innovation was probably inspired by Qasr al-Kharāna, only 10 miles away. The low springing of the transverse arches is also Syrian and so are the famous fresco paintings. As regards the hammāms, they also follow a local type already developed in the sixth century, the very sequence of the roofing systems – tunnel-vault, cross-vault, and dome – being that adopted at Ruhayba.

THE MOSQUE AT QUSAYR AL-HALLĀBĀT

About 3 miles south of the Roman fort known to the Arabs as Qusayr al-Hallābāt is a little mosque measuring internally 10·70 by 11·80 m. (35¼ by 38¾ ft). Two wall-piers with the springing of arches above them suffice to indicate that the interior was divided into three aisles by two arcades, and Butler's measurement of the curve of one showed that the radius was such that there must have been five arches in each. There were three axial entrances, and the exterior was surrounded by a portico 3·30 m. (10¾ ft) deep, excluding the piers, which was covered by a sloping roof of timber, and ten of the holes which received the beams can be seen near the top of the west façade.

The walls are 82 cm. (32½ in.) thick, built of limestone in courses 40 cm. (15¾ in.) high, laid dry. The mihrāb was 1·20 m. (4 ft) in width, and above it was a bull's-eye window. A quarter-round moulding runs all round the interior at a level of 2·10 m. (7 ft) above the springing of the arches, and the remains above this moulding at the summit of the south wall show that the mosque must have been roofed by three parallel tunnel-vaults, exactly as in the two buildings we have just studied. At the end of each bay was a round-arched window, with a bull's-eye window above, close to the vault.

Date

The masonry of this mosque differs completely from that of the mosques of the twelfth and thirteenth centuries in the Haurān, all of which are of very poor workmanship and built of re-used material, set in mortar. The close resemblance of its vaulting system and its masonry to that of Quṣayr 'Amra and Hammām as-Sarakh justify us in grouping all three together. As there is a concave mihrāb it must have been built after 707–9 and, in view of the known historical circumstances, it can scarcely have been built after the fall of the Umayyad dynasty in 750.

CHAPTER 5

THE WORKS OF THE KHALIFS SULAYMĀN AND HISHĀM

The Later Umayyad Period

When al-Walīd died in February 715 the Umayyad dynasty had reached its zenith. Its decline was as rapid as its rise, and it only lasted for another thirty-five years. al-Walīd was succeeded by his brother, Sulaymān, who was followed by his cousin, 'Umar II. After a short reign he was succeeded by Yazīd II, who died in January 724 and was succeeded by his brother, Hishām, who had a comparatively long reign of nineteen years.

The Khalif Sulaymān

Sulaymān founded Ramla and built its congregational mosque, which, according to Muqaddasī, who saw it before it was destroyed by the earthquake of 1033, was a very fine building with marble columns and a marble pavement.[1] He also built the first Congregational Mosque at Aleppo. Ibn ash-Shihna, quoting Ibn al-'Adīm, says:

The Great Mosque of Aleppo rivalled that of Damascus in its decoration, marble panelling and mosaic (*fusaifisā*). I have heard that Sulaymān ibn 'Abd al-Malik built it, wishing to make it equal to the work of his brother al-Walīd in the Great Mosque at Damascus.[2]

He goes on to say that it was burnt down by the Byzantine Emperor (Nicephorus Phocas) when he entered Aleppo in 351 H. (962).

1. p. 165.
2. Beyrut ed., pp. 61–2; Sauvaget's transl., *Les Perles choisis*, pp. 56–7.

HISHĀM BUILDS THE MINARET OF THE
GREAT MOSQUE OF QAIRAWĀN

The existing structure (Plate 25) is a tower of three storeys, all square in plan, the lowest of which measures 10·67 m. (35 ft) a side at the base and 18·87 m. (61¾ ft) in height without its crenellations, the second 5 m. (16½ ft), and the third about 7·5 m. (24½ ft), the total height without the finial being 31·5 m. (103 ft). The first storey tapers slightly, but the second and third do not. The entrance, which is a metre wide and 1·85 m. (3¼ by 6 ft) high, is formed of two jambs and a lintel, all carved Roman fragments; above the lintel is a horse-shoe relieving arch. The first seven courses are formed of large blocks of stone, but the rest is built of small stone blocks only 13 cm. (5 in.) high – so small in fact that they look like bricks at a distance.

The staircase is not quite in the centre of the tower, its walls are of enormous thickness (3·30–3·50 m.; 10¾–11½ ft), and it is lit by three windows on the south-east side. There are also three more, like arrow-slits, on the north-western and two on the south-western side. Each flight of the staircase is covered by a short, nearly horizontal tunnel-vault. The leading end of each rests on a little arch, placed just before the turn, after which another tunnel-vault takes off at right angles *at a higher level*. The vaults thus rise in steps corresponding to the flights of the staircase and the problem of intersection is avoided, as is generally the case in really early Muslim architecture. The staircase continues through the second storey and comes out under the little domed pavilion, which opens on to the terrace on all four sides by horse-shoe arches.

Rivoira has suggested that the second storey is later than the first, saying: 'The materials, as far as can be judged from the very little which is visible inside, are different from those of the lower stage of the tower.' [1] This is not the case to-day, for the masonry of the sides and newel of the staircase are visible all the way up, and there can be no shadow of doubt that they are all one piece of work. But there is every reason for believing that the top storey is later. As Marçais has pointed out,[2] the measurements given by al-Bakrī (A.D. 1068) of 25 cubits at the base and 60 cubits high agree with the first two storeys,

1. *Moslim Architecture*, p. 37.   2. *Manuel d'art musulman*, I, p. 27.

for if 25 cubits = 10·63 m. (average of measurement of the sides of the base) then 60 cubits gives 25·51 for the first two storeys against my measurement of 25·03 m. (82 ft) – a very close agreement. Secondly, the domed pavilion is built of brick, and the squinches which carry the dome across the corners are like those of the Bāb Lalla Rejāna on the east side of the mosque, dated 693 H. (1294). So the domed pavilion probably forms part of the great Hafsid restoration of that year.

The Date of the Minaret

al-Bakrī says:

… Hishām, the son of 'Abd al-Malik, having ascended the throne of the Khalifate (Jan. 724) received a despatch from the Governor of Qairawān [at that time Bishr ibn Safwān] in which he stated that the mosque was not large enough, and that immediately to the north was a large garden. … The Khalif ordered the purchase of this land and its inclusion in the area of the mosque. The Governor obeyed … he built a minaret. … Today the minaret is just as Hassān [sic] constructed it; it is 60 cubits high and 25 wide.[1]

Hassān is obviously a slip for Bishr, who was Governor from 721 to 727, but the fact that he received his orders from Hishām narrows down the date of our minaret to 724–7.

Nevertheless, although I am convinced that the present minaret is that described by al-Bakrī, I wish to make a reservation here. Its masonry is so exactly like the exposed masonry of the buttresses on the south-east side of the mosque (Plate 47a), which cannot be earlier than 221 H. (836), that I cannot help feeling that this minaret, which I have placed here in homage to the text of al-Bakrī, may really form part of the new mosque built by Ziyādat Allāh in that year. But even if we put it forward to 836, it still remains the oldest existing in Islam, with the possible exception of that of Qasr al-Hair ash-Sharqī (below, p. 118 and Plate 27b, to left).

The Architectural Evolution of the Minaret

The typical Syrian church tower in pre-Muslim times, especially in the Haurān, the region first conquered by the Arabs, was a square

1. pp. 22–3; de Slane's transl., pp. 57–9.

stone shaft, sometimes slightly tapering as at Sama. A number have been preserved to the present day, as under:

(1) *Qasr al-Banāt* (in Northern Syria). Convent with square tower 23 m. (75 ft) high, probably built between 390 and 418.

(2) *Umm as-Surāb* (in the Southern Haurān). Church of SS. Sergius and Bacchus, with tall square tower, well preserved except the roof. Built 489.

(3) *Sama* (in the Southern Haurān). Monastery of St George, with square tower about 12 m. (40 ft) high. Built 624–5.

(4) *Umm ar-Rasās*. Square tower with Greek cross on east and west faces. About 12 m. high and 2·50 square (40 by 8¼ ft), alongside church. Undated.

(5) *Jerāda*. Tower of five storeys alongside narthex of church. Undated.

We can now say with confidence that the idea of the minaret arose in Syria under the Umayyad dynasty, the first minarets being the four ancient corner towers of the *temenos* at Damascus, and that the first minarets built by the Muslims were derived architecturally from Syrian church towers.

QASR AL-HAIR ASH-SHARQĪ

Qasr al-Hair lies in the desert nearly 60 miles north-east of Palmyra and about 40 miles south of Rusāfa.

The ruins consist of two fortified enclosures, roughly square, both flanked with half-round towers; one averages nearly 66 m. (215 ft) and the other about 160 m. (525 ft) a side internally (Plate 26a).

The Lesser Enclosure

This is formed by a curtain wall 2·03 m. (6¾ ft) thick, flanked by half-round towers, one at each corner and two intermediate ones on each side, making twelve in all, placed from 18·51 to 20·05 m. (61–66 ft) apart, except the two towers flanking the only entrance (on the west side), which are only 6·67 m. (22 ft) apart. The height of the wall, including the parapet, most of which has disappeared, must have been about 14·25 m. (46¾ ft). The stone, which has taken a beautiful amber tint, is a fine-grained limestone in courses about 35 cm. (14 in.) high.

The entrance is a well-designed piece of work. The opening is 2·98 m. (9¾ ft) in width; its height must have been about 4·20 m. (13¾ ft). The door-jambs have crumbled away, but the horizontal arch in the form of a lintel still remains in position (Plate 27a). Above it is a semicircular relieving arch, the tympanum of which is filled in with plain masonry; the spandrels are occupied by little niches with fluted heads.

The towers at their summits exhibit a most original and charming decorative scheme, carried out in brick and stucco. It begins below with a cyma recta moulding; then there are two courses of brickwork, then a row of small bricks about 10 cm. (4 in.) square set lozenge-wise, and then another course of brickwork. Immediately above this is the last course of stonework, and on this rests the attractive blind arcading, consisting of a series of rectangular panels divided by pairs of little columns, with shafts composed of a series of chevrons. The face of the arch above is decorated with acanthus foliage, but the design in the panels is badly damaged. This decoration is not carved but moulded, and four moulds appear to have been used. The whole is surmounted by a course of bricks placed so as to produce a dog-tooth motive, then by several courses of vertical brickwork, above which, set back from the face of the wall, is the brick dome which crowns the tower.

The arcaded frieze runs across between the towers, and in the centre, above the entrance, is a mâchicoulis of two openings resting on three moulded brackets.

The remaining towers are treated as follows: the first band of brickwork, of five courses, which runs along the curtain walls, is carried round each tower, then come three courses of masonry, then a band of small square bricks set lozenge wise, then three more courses of stone, and then a final band of four or five courses of brickwork, surmounted by a brick dome (Plate 26b). Each tower, when preserved above the rampart-walk, has a small domed chamber, except that flanking the entrance on the north, which appears to have contained a spiral staircase, but all the steps have disappeared and nothing but a hollow shaft is to be seen.

The Interior

This is in an advanced state of ruin (Figure 19), nevertheless it is still possible to see that the lower storey consisted of a number of vaulted chambers about 12 m. (40 ft) deep, but of varying width, arranged round a central court, now full of débris which must be more than 2 m. (6½ ft) deep. It is most probable that a portico ran all round this court, as at Minya (above, p. 82). The vaults are constructed as follows: the vault begins with from ten to thirteen courses of brick, laid horizontally in slightly over-sailing courses adjusted to the curve of the vault; above this are two rings of flat square bricks with their

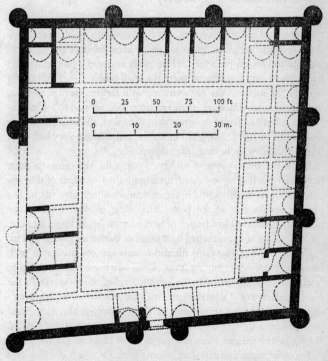

Figure 19. Qasr al-Hair: plan of Lesser Enclosure

faces at right angles to the axis of the vault; these rings are covered by an outer ring of bricks set edgewise. It is possible to see that the two best preserved chambers on the south side were divided into an inner and outer length by a partition wall, so I conclude that the rest were similarly treated.

Above these vaulted chambers was a second storey with rooms corresponding to those below. This upper storey, part of which still remains in the north-eastern and south-eastern corners, must have had a flat wooden roof, for a series of beam-holes are to be seen all along the enclosure walls, about a metre and a half below the ramparts.

The Greater Enclosure (Plate 26a)

The Greater Enclosure is formed by a curtain wall 2·12 m. (7 ft) in thickness flanked by towers 4 m. (13 ft) in diameter, with an entrance in the centre of each face. There is a tower at each corner and six intermediate towers on each face. Their pitch averages 25·25 m. (83 ft) from axis to axis. In addition, there is a small postern, 1·47 m. (48¼ ft) wide to the south of the east entrance. Still farther south is another, the function of which we shall see later (below, p. 116). This enclosure is built of larger masonry than the other, the courses varying from 50 to 70 cm. (20–27½ in.) in height, but it is in a very bad state, whole curtain walls having fallen down.

As all the towers appear to have been solid, the ramparts must have been reached by staircases running up the inner face of the curtain walls, presumably some of the curtain walls that have fallen. The parapet, unlike that of the Lesser Enclosure, is of stone; in many places it is preserved to a height of two courses. Its thickness is 41 cm. (16 in.), and it is strengthened by a series of buttresses placed 1·75 m. (5¾ ft) apart. The curtain walls and towers are not decorated with bands of brickwork, but the tops of the latter are built entirely of brick from a point one course below the level of the ramparts. At the top of each tower is a small room with three arrow-slits. Rousseau's sketch made in 1808 shows that all these towers at that time were crowned by a dome.[1] The height of the walls, if we allow 2·50 m. (8¼ ft) for the parapet, must have been about 12·25 m. (40 ft).

The four main entrances are almost identical; each consists of a

1. *Voyage de Bagdad à Alep, publié par L. Poinssot.*

rectangular doorway not quite 3 m. (10 ft) wide, with a joggled lintel surmounted by a stilted and slightly pointed relieving arch, the tympanum being filled up with masonry, the face of which is set back about 4 cm. (1½ in.) from the face of the arch. Above each entrance is a mâchicoulis of two openings resting on three brackets with three tiers of mouldings. The mâchicoulis over the northern entrance is wider and rests on five elaborate brackets, the central one being decorated with a sunflower. To return to the sunk tympanums, which are pitted with holes regularly spaced 25 cm. (10 in.) apart. Gabriel has suggested that these holes were intended to provide a grip for the cement with which a ceramic decoration was attached.[1] There is no known example of such ceramic decoration in Muslim architecture at this early date, and it seems much more probable that there was a panel of stucco ornament here, for we have seen that stucco ornament is used on the towers flanking the entrance of the Lesser Enclosure.

The Mosque (Plate 27b and Figure 20)

The interior is almost devoid of structures except for the remains of a building in the south-east corner, which must have been constructed after the enclosure was finished, for there is a complete vertical break between its masonry and the three piers which are in contact with it. There can be no doubt that it is a mosque, the arcade running parallel to the south wall being the façade on the sahn, and a moment's examination suffices to show that the two arcades of three arches each, which run from north to south, are nothing else but a transept, for the piers are T-shaped, and the two arcades which divided the sanctuary into three aisles must have stopped against their outer faces. The brick walls, over 4 m. (13 ft) high, which rise above these two arcades are, of course, the walls of the clerestory, as in the Great Mosque at Damascus. As for the isolated pier H which stands in a line with the northern arcade, it is, of course, a continuation of it; it corresponds in shape and dimensions with pier C, and it is separated from the transept pier by almost exactly the same distance (7·61 against 7·57 m.; 25 against 24¾ ft). Midway between C and the transept is a fallen column composed of four drums, and at D is another, half buried in the ground.

1. In *Syria*, VIII, p. 320.

Restoring our façade accordingly, we get a central arch 4·80 m. (15¾ ft) in span flanked by three averaging 3·25 m. (10¾ ft). But why are piers *C* and *H* L-shaped? Surely because they were the corner piers of the *sahn* from which the side *riwāqs* took off. If we repeat the arrangement – column, pier, column, pier, column, pier – along the sides we get a *sahn* 28 m. (9¼ ft) square. The purpose of the gate *A* now becomes clear: it must have been intended to give direct access to the mosque from the exterior, exactly as at Minya (above, p. 82).

The arches of the sanctuary must have rested on columns, for Sir Eyre Coote in 1771 'saw a number of arches supported by pillars of white marble finely polished ... several broken pillars of marble were scattered about the area.' [1]

It is not possible to say how high the transept originally was: it may have been a metre higher than the present height of the brick walls, nevertheless the actual remains of this, the second oldest congregational mosque in Syria, suffice to confirm the dominating influence of the Great Mosque of Damascus.

The Form of the Arches

The five existing arches of the transept are stilted and very slightly pointed, and the central arch of the façade is very slightly pointed but not stilted.

The Date

Rousseau found an inscription slab on pier *H*, and had it transported to Aleppo, where he made a careful sketch of it. It reads:

Bismillah. ... This city (*madīna*) has been built by 'Abd Allāh Hishām, Prince of Believers. This is one of the monuments which the inhabitants of Homs have erected by the hands of Sulaymān the son of 'Ubayd in the year [1]10 (= A.D. 728–9).[2]

1. 'Diary of a Journey with Sir Eyre Coote', *Journ. Roy. Geographical Socy*, XXX (1860), p. 207.

2. This sketch, although in his diary, was not published by Poinssot, but may be found reproduced with a commentary by Clermont-Ganneau in his *Receuil d'archéologie orientale*, III, pp. 285–90 and pl. VIII.

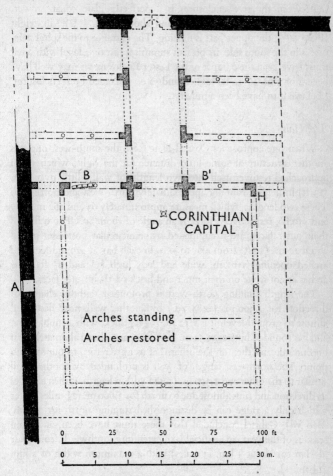

C B   B'

D ⊠ CORINTHIAN
         CAPITAL   H

A

Arches standing   — — — — —
Arches restored   — · — · — · —

| 0 | 25 | 50 | 75 | 100 ft |

| 0 | 5 | 10 | 15 | 20 | 25 | 30 m. |

Figure 20. Qasr al-Hair: Mosque in Greater Enclosure

The Minaret

Between the two enclosures is a perfectly plain square tower, averaging 2·94 m. (9¾ ft) a side and about 10 m. (33 ft) in height (Plate 26*b*); the upper part is missing. The entrance to the spiral staircase is in the south side. Its present summit is just on a level with what must have been the parapet of the Lesser Enclosure; it may well have been 2 or 3 m. (6–10 ft) higher, and so commanded both enclosures. I believe it to have been a minaret.

The Hair

When one approaches Qasr al-Hair from the south-west one sees another structure at some little distance on the right, which when approached resolves itself into two lengths of wall a little over 4 m. (13 ft) in height, running approximately north-west and north-east. These two lengths, which measure approximately 63 and 162 m. (207 and 530 ft), respectively, meet at an angle of about 80°. The walls, on their outer faces, are strengthened by semicircular buttresses placed about 12 m. (40 ft) from axis to axis. In each bay at ground level are arched openings 1·10 m. wide and 2·05 high (3½ and 6¾ ft). The arches are of stone on their inner and brick on their outer faces.

The length running north-west is prolonged without change of direction for 1,360 m. (1488 yd.) by another wall, now destroyed almost to ground level. It is 1·12 m. (3¾ ft) thick, with a rubble core, and has rounded buttresses 32 m. (105 ft) apart, placed alternately first on one side and then on the other. Let us now return to our starting point. The north-east length of wall is prolonged by another wall similar to the other and 1,300 m. (1,422 yd.) in length. It then changes its direction and runs almost due to north for 3,600 m. (2¼ miles), after which only a ridge can be distinguished running north for 750 m. (820 yd). Gabriel concluded that there must have been, at certain seasons of the year, an artificial lake extending southwards from Qasr al-Hair for about 5 km. (3 miles) with a maximum width of 2 km. (1¼ miles).

Seyrig, however, in 1931, suggested that these walls enclosed, not a lake but an artificial garden. Gabriel contested this, so Seyrig made further researches on the spot.[1] He found that the long walls of stone

1. *Syria*, XIII, pp. 317–18.

were still surmounted by the remains of a wall of mud bricks 42 cm. (16½ in.) square and 9 cm. (3½ in.) thick. It was 1·06 m. (3½ ft) thick, like the stone wall below it. In some places the wall had fallen *en bloc*, and some of the fallen pieces consisted of twenty courses, equal to fully 2 m. (6½ ft), which, added to 1·50 (5 ft) for the stone wall, gives 3·50 m. (11½ ft) for the minimum total height. The presence of this upper part of mud brick explains the need for buttresses. In addition, he actually discovered the bases of two monumental entrances, of stone below and mud bricks above, like the walls. He concludes that we have to do with a great enclosed garden or *paradeisos*, 850 hectares (3¼ square miles) in area, protected by a wall strong enough to keep out Bedawīn pillaging parties.[1]

Whence came the water supply? Early travellers such as Sir Eyre Coote, Irwin, and Rousseau all speak of *qanāts*, i.e. underground aqueducts, coming from 'Ain al-Kōm. Seyrig, guided by a villager, was able to follow one for 30 km. (18½ miles).

Meaning of the Word al-Hair

I submit quotations from two early Arabic historians, which throw light on this question.

(1) Ya'qūbī, describing the foundation of Sāmarrā by the Khalif al-Mu'tasim in 836, says:

And wherever these streets of al-Hair touched land granted to other people, he would order the wall [of al-Hair] to be built farther back. Behind the wall were wild animals, gazelles, wild asses, deer, hares and ostriches, kept in by an enclosing wall in a fine broad open tract.[2]

(2) Miskawaihī, under the year 315 H. (925–6) says:

This year there was a rising of the disbanded cavalry, who went out to the Oratory, plundered the Palace called ath-Thurayyā (the Palace of the Pleiades at Baghdād), and *slaughtered the game in the Hair*.[3]

I maintain therefore that the enclosure 5 km. long and 2 km. wide (3 by 1¼ miles) at Qasr al-Hair was neither an artificial lake nor a garden, but a game-preserve for the Khalif Hishām, and that the

1. *Syria*, xv, pp. 24–32.   2. *Buldān*, p. 263.
3. Margoliouth's text, I, p. 159; transl., I, p. 179.

walls were meant, not to keep the Bedawīn out, but to keep the animals in.

In other words, it was a *Paradeisos*, the very word used by Theophanes when speaking of the works of Hishām (below).

The Date of the Whole Group of Buildings

We have a fixed point for the dating in the inscription of 110 H. (728–9) seen by Rousseau on a pier of the mosque. The inscription dates the Greater Enclosure, for it refers to the *madīna* built for the Khalif Hishām. The mosque cannot be earlier, for its east and south sides are formed by the city walls, and I believe it to be the city mosque, expressly built immediately after the enclosure was completed. In addition to this we have two documents which cast a decisive light upon the matter: (1) Tabarī, speaking of Hishām, says: 'And he went out to Rusāfa because it was in the desert, and for that reason he had two castles (*qasrayn*) built there',[1] and (2) Theophanes (d. 818) says: 'And he began to found palaces in open country and town, and to make sown fields and paradises (παραδείσους) and bring water [there].'[2]

Thus we have: (1) Hishām built two castles in the desert of Rusāfa; we have seen that the Greater Enclosure is one, it is difficult to avoid the conclusion that the Lesser Enclosure is the other; (2) he carried out irrigation works and created 'paradises' and fields in open country. The open country must be the desert of Rusāfa, which was his known place of residence, and there can be little doubt that the irrigation works were the *qanāts* mentioned above.

Finally we have: (1) the Greater Enclosure (*madīna*) linked with Hishām by the inscription of 110 H. (728–9); (2) the Lesser, or Royal Enclosure linked with it by Tabarī's reference to *qasrayn* (the dual of *qasr*); (3) the Lesser Enclosure linked with the sluice-gates by its masonry, decorated with string courses of brick; and (4) the *qanāts* linked with Hishām by the text of Theophanes.

These three structures being thus indissolubly interlocked, and one being dated to Hishām in 110 H., I attribute all three to him *c.* 110 H. (728–9).

---

1. II, p. 1738, ll. 4–5.
2. Bonn ed., p. 620; de Boor's ed., p. 403.

ARCHITECTURAL ORIGINS OF QASR AL-HAIR

Joggled Voussoirs

These, although rare before the rise of Islam, are found scattered over a very wide area extending from Spain to the Euphrates. They are employed in a Roman bridge over the Salado, near Villa del Rio, close to Km. 53 (33 miles) on the road from Cadiz to Madrid, and also in another Roman bridge, over the Pedroches, 3 km. (1¾ miles) from Cordova, of which the joggled springer blocks of the arches still remain. They also occur in the Roman theatre at Orange, shortly after 44 B.C., at Spalato in the Porta Aurea and the Porta Ferrea of Diocletian's palace, c. 303–5, and at Ravenna, in the lower storey of Theodoric's mausoleum, c. 519. This feature is found in the pre-Muslim architecture of Syria, e.g. at Bethlehem, in the central doorway of the façade of the narthex which dates from Justinian, and in the Basilica of Sergios at Rusāfa, c. 600. It was from Rusāfa, probably, that the joggled voussoirs of Qasr al-Hair were derived, as it is less than 40 miles away.

The Mâchicoulis

The earliest examples of stone mâchicoulis occur in the pre-Muslim architecture of northern Syria, and at least ten examples may be cited. Of these, however, only three can possibly have been for the purpose usually assigned to mâchicoulis, viz. to enable the besieged to drop molten lead, boiling oil, or projectiles on a storming party attacking a doorway below. All the others are latrines,[1] and cannot have served any other purpose, for they are not placed over an entrance. The earliest example intended for defensive purposes is found at Dār Qītā, in what appears to have been an isolated watch-tower, dated 551. It is about 5½ m. (18 ft) square, with an entrance on the west side, and three storeys of it are still preserved. In the third storey, and directly over the entrance, are two brackets carrying a slab with a

1. Similar structures of brick resting on a pair of stone corbels occur on the walls of Rome in the part due to Maxentius in A.D. 354. They were known in early medieval Latin as *necessaria*, and had a sanitary and not a defensive function; see I. A. Richmond, *The City Wall of Imperial Rome*, pp. 84–6.

hole in it, and round the edges are the remains of thin walls which once surrounded it. Butler is convinced that it was undoubtedly intended for the delivery of missiles upon an enemy attempting to force an entrance.[1] These remarks could of course apply to the little tower of the guard at Khirbet Hāss, published by de Vogüé.[2]

Now the architecture of northern Mesopotamia at this time formed one with that of northern Syria, hence it is not surprising to find that this device was apparently employed at Amida (Diyārbakr) in A.D. 504, for Joshua Stylites (A.D. 515) says: 'It was difficult [for the Byzantine army] to fight with them [the Persians] because, being on the crest of the wall, and having built themselves little houses all along the rampart in which they hid themselves, they could fight without being seen by those who were outside',[3] a good non-technical description of a mâchicoulis.

The Arabic word for this feature is shown by the following passage in Abū Darr,[4] who says that when the Mongols came to Aleppo, the people in the Zāhirīya Madrasa defended it by making a saqqāta above the entrance and throwing stones on them. This madrasa has a recessed entrance porch with the usual stalactite vault; there is a large, roughly made hole in this vault, by means of which people above could drop heavy stones on anyone attempting to force the door. It thus served the same purpose as the holes in the floor of a mâchicoulis, for which the word saqqāta (falling) is obviously the Arabic equivalent.

The Combination of Brick and Stone

The use of brick at Qasr al-Hair constitutes an anomaly for Syria, before Islam, was a country of stone architecture, with two notable exceptions: Qasr Ibn Wardān and the great castrum of Andarīn, in both of which courses of brick alternate with stone. But the bricks used are thin Byzantine bricks 30 by 34 by 3·5 cm. (12 by 13½ by 1½ in.) and 34 by 37 by 4 cm. (13 by 14½ by 1½ in.), whereas the bricks

1. *Ancient Architecture in Syria, Sect. B: Northern Syria*, pp. 789–90.
2. *Syrie Centrale*, p. 95 and pl. 58.
3. *Chronicle*, Martin's text, p. 62; transl., p. lxii; Wright's text, p. 69; transl., pp. 59–60.
4. Quoted by Tabbākh, *I'lām an-Nubalā' fi Ta'rīkh Halab*, IV, p. 356.

used at Qasr al-Hair are smaller and thicker, resembling those used for the Baghdād Gate at Raqqa in 772 (p. 184, and Plates 32, 33), and the layers of mortar are less in thickness than the bricks, as in 'Irāqī brickwork. Qasr al-Hair therefore shows a mixture of two influences: the decorative use of brickwork to give a striped effect to masonry is Byzantine, but the bricks themselves and the thin layers of mortar are Mesopotamian.

CHAPTER 6

MSHATTĀ, QASR AT-TŪBA, AND HARRĀN

MSHATTĀ

MSHATTĀ, the most famous of all the Umayyad palaces, was discovered by Layard in 1840 [1] and, independently, by Tristram in
1872.[2] It lies about 20 miles south of 'Ammān and about 3 miles
north-east of the station of Zīza on the Hijāz Railway.

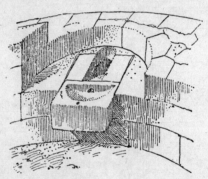

Figure 21. Mshattā: latrine

It consists of a great walled enclosure of stone, nearly 144 m. (473 ft)
square internally (Figure 22), flanked by half-round towers with an
entrance in the centre of the south side. The walls are preserved to a
height varying from about 3 to 5½ m. (10–18 ft), except where the
decorated part of the façade has been removed. All the towers are
solid except four, which were provided with latrines (Figure 21). The

---

1. His account, however, was not published until 1887, in his *Early Adven-
tures*, I, pp. 114–15.
2. *Land of Moab*, p. 195 ff.

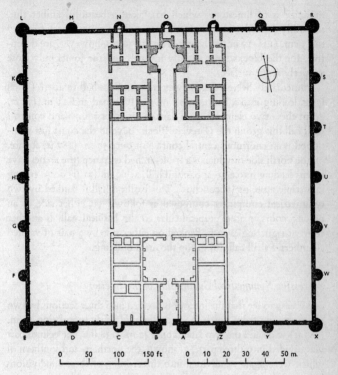

Figure 22. Mshattā: plan

buildings intended to occupy the lateral tracts have never been begun, and even those projected for the central tract have never been finished. Of the latter, however, the group at the north end must have been very nearly finished, and the plan of the group at the south end can be clearly seen, for a great stone grid is visible, formed by the foundation course of beautiful smooth stone blocks, which just projects above the ground.

The enclosure wall is 1·70 m. (5½ ft) in thickness, the corner towers measure about 7 m. (23 ft) in diameter, and the intermediate towers about 5·25 m. (17¼ ft), except the two towers flanking the entrance, which are half octagonal and measure 6·30 m. (20¾ ft) in width. The masonry is of limestone, which has taken a beautiful amber tint, smoothly dressed with very fine joints, and the courses vary from 37 to 43 cm. (14½–17 in.) in height. The fine joints, however, are deceptive, for the blocks taper slightly inwards and the joints only close properly at the surface.

Immediately behind the gateway is an entrance hall 17·40 m. (57 ft) long, leading into a court, 27·14 m. (89 ft) broad and 23 m. (75 ft) deep; these two elements were flanked by other rooms and courts. I shall call this group the Gateway Block. Beyond the court just mentioned is an enormous central court, just over 57 m. (187 ft) square, on the north side of which is a triple-arched entrance (the arches have fallen) leading into a great basilical hall, 21·60 m. (71 ft) deep, ending in a triple apse, or 'triconchos'. This basilical hall is flanked by two symmetrical complexes composed as follows: on either side of an oblong court, placed perpendicular to the basilical hall, is another court at right angles to it, flanked on either side by a pair of vaulted chambers. I shall call this group the main building.

Successive Symmetrical Subdivision of the Interior

It is easy to see that the interior is divided into three sections by two walls running from north to south, the middle division being 57 m. (187 ft) wide and the two lateral ones 42 m. (138 ft). The central part was divided into three parts, as shown, the northern and southern of which were again subdivided into three, some of these subdivisions being subdivided once more into three (Figure 23). Thus the system which we have observed at Minya (above, p. 84) is here carried much farther.

The Gateway Block

The gateway (now in Berlin) has been preserved to a height of about 3·80 (12½ ft). The width of the opening is 3·46 m. (11½ ft), and immediately behind it is the entrance hall, 9·23 m. wide and 17·40 deep (30½ by 57 ft). A row of rectangular plinths on either side were probably intended to support columns carrying transverse arches; if so, I suggest that these may have been brought up level to carry transverse vaults, as at Qusayr 'Amra. Beyond, to the east, is a rectangle

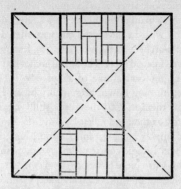

Figure 23. Mshattā: diagram showing
successive symmetrical subdivision
of the interior into three

13·40 m. broad and 28 m. deep (44 by 92 ft), with a semicircular
niche 1·62 m. (5¼ ft) wide, flanked by recesses to take columns. This
niche was undoubtedly intended as the mihrāb of the palace mosque.
To the west the subdivisions are more numerous. Passing forward
from the entrance hall we enter a court 27·40 m. wide and 21·70 deep
(90 by 71 ft). On all four sides are placed plinths 1·25 m. (4 ft) square
and 3·30–3·40 m. (10¾–11¼ ft) apart; they were presumably intended
to take columns which may have carried arches, thus forming a series
of arched recesses all round, exactly as in the Court of Honour at
Ukhaidir (Plate 37).

From this court one passes out into the great central court, 57 m.
(182 ft) square, on the north side of which is the Main Building. Two
doors, 1·92 m. (6¼ ft) wide, on each side of this court opened into the
side tracts.

The Main Building (Plate 30)

This is the only completely built structure in the enclosure; it
forms the central point of the whole and must be considered as the
royal part of the palace. The foundations of the burnt brick walls consist of four courses of limestone blocks, of which three and a half rise

1·50 m. above the floor level. This rectangle, like the gateway block, is divided into three main divisions, the two lateral ones being closed towards the south whereas the central one was entered from the great court by a triple-arched entrance (Plate 30) resting on two free-standing and two engaged piers. The lateral arches had a span of about 3·25 m. (10¾ ft), the central one of about 6·80 (22¼ ft). All three arches have been thrown down, presumably by an earthquake, and when Schulz saw them in 1903 they were still lying in contact with each other exactly as they had fallen.[1] Above the capitals was a perfectly preserved impost block 31 cm. (12¼ in.) high, and between it and the capital was a single course of brickwork 9 cm. (3½ in.) high. Embedded in this was a piece of wood 9 by 9 cm., in cross section, the remains of a tie-beam, of which each arch had a pair.

He found that the arches must have been stilted semicircles, their intrados being formed of four torus mouldings, and there was a torus moulding on each face, which ran round each arch, then horizontally above the impost block, then round the next arch, and so on, finally running up vertically at each side and then horizontally along the top so as to form a rectangular frame. Above the top of the moulded frame was one more course of masonry. There were also six rosettes, like those of the outer façade (below, p. 132, and Plates 28, 29). The background of the rosettes bore traces of red paint. Figure 24 shows his reconstruction.

On the inner face of the two free-standing piers are pilasters, 76 cm. wide and 65 deep (30 by 25½ in), to which piers with similar stone pilasters correspond at the northern end of the hall. Between them is a foundation wall of well-cut blocks. The eastern was smooth, but on the western Schulz found the grey marble base of the first column from the north, still in position, and a place cut for the second. The spacing showed that there must have been five columns, i.e. six arches. The two northern piers also served as supports for a transverse arch 6·99 m. (23 ft) in span, which opened into the triple-apsed hall. This arch (part is now in Berlin) is decorated with a pair of undulating vine-stalks which repeatedly cross each other, forming loops with little rosettes at their crossings. Each loop is occupied by a vine-leaf or a bunch of grapes.

1. Schulz and Strzygowski, 'Mschatta', in the *Jahrbuch der Kgl. Preusz. Kunstsammlungen*, xxv, pp. 216–17.

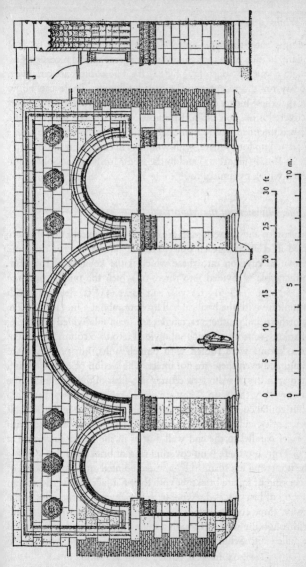

Figure 24. Mshattā: triple entrance to basilical hall (throne room)

The Triple-Apsed Hall (Plate 30b)

We now enter the triple-apsed Hall, which is exactly 9·85 m. (32½ ft) square. In each of its three side walls is a great apsidal recess 5·25 m. wide and about 3·80 deep (17¼ by 12½ ft). The corners are cut away, obviously for the reception of engaged columns. There can be no doubt that these niches ended in semidomes, but how the central part was covered is not so certain. Brünnow [1] and Schulz [2] believe that a dome was intended, but I cannot help feeling that the walls may have been carried up four square, with windows in each, as in the Bishop's Palace at Bosrā (Figure 27) and in the Red Monastery at Sohāg, and crowned with a pyramidal roof.

The Side Divisions of the Main Building

The eastern and western parts are exactly alike, except that they are reversed in relation to each other. Here again we observe the same successive subdivision into three which is the keynote of the plan. Each rectangle is divided into three, of which the middle ones are 18·55–18·70 m. (60¾–61½ ft) wide and 10·25 (33½ ft) deep, and both communicate with the basilical hall by doors about 3 m. (10 ft) wide. The northern and southern rectangles are again subdivided into three. The flanking sections are each subdivided into two rooms, as shown.

These rooms were roofed with tunnel-vaults, but only two are standing, and even these are not intact. The section of each vault is a pointed arch struck from two centres one-fifth of the span apart, the first example of this ratio. They are constructed as follows: there are two horizontal courses above the offset, above which begins the vault proper, a brick and a half thick, composed of flat square bricks set with their faces parallel to the end wall, just as in the Lesser Enclosure at Qasr al-Ḥair, but there is no covering ring of bricks laid flat.

The doorways are spanned by a stilted pointed arch, constructed of an inner ring of square bricks set with their flat faces outwards, and an outer ring of bricks set edgewise. In the brickwork at the sides of the doorway, three courses below the springing, is a gap which extends right through the wall, as though a stone lintel or wooden beam had been pulled out. Schulz, however, over fifty years ago, was able to

1. *Die Provincia Arabia*, II, p. 126.   2. *Loc. cit.*, p. 218.

find traces which convinced him that there was first a solid wooden ceiling, $12\frac{1}{2}$ cm. (5 in.) thick, the whole depth of the doorway, and on top of it a layer of bricks set vertically.[1] The object was to give a rectangular top to the doorway, and in the wooden ceiling it was easy to make a socket for the door-spindle; the tympanum would serve to admit light when the door was shut.

The decoration of the Main Building was apparently never begun, but it was evidently intended to have had a dado, for Schulz found several great blocks of a magnificent green stone lying in the east side tract. They had already been partly sawn into slabs, 2–3 cm. ($\frac{7}{8}$–$1\frac{1}{4}$ in.) thick, for use as a panelling.

The Side Tracts

No foundation walls are to be seen in the side tracts, nor did Schulz find any by excavation, but the bonding stones left for the attachment of transverse walls, which are to be seen on the inner walls of the enclosure, show that such were meant to be constructed. These bonding stones are arranged in pairs, jutting out from the wall in vertical rows in every alternate course. Their outer breadth varies from 97 to 1·14 cm. ($38\frac{1}{2}$–$\frac{1}{2}$ in.), thus indicating varying thicknesses of wall, and the distance apart of the pairs indicates the width of the rooms to be built against the wall. Now if we take one of the groups of five rooms in the side divisions of the Main Building and turn it round, there are no less than four places where such a group can be placed against the west wall – A_1, A_2, A_3, and A_4 (Figure 25). The attachments in the north-western corner obviously give four little rooms and a court (B_1); two similar groups (B_2 and B_3) will fit the attachments on the wall between A_2 and A_3 and a similar group can be placed in the south-west corner. As for the attachments for walls 2·50 and 2·90 m. ($8\frac{1}{4}$ and $9\frac{1}{2}$ ft) thick, I follow Schulz's suggestion that they were intended for staircases, running up perpendicular to the outer wall.[2]

The Decoration of the South Façade

The sumptuously decorated façade between towers C and Z consists of a plain socle 47 cm. ($18\frac{1}{2}$ in.) high, a richly decorated base

1. *Loc. cit.*, p. 215.   2. *Loc. cit.*, Taf. VII.

1·28 m. (4¼ ft) in height, a decorated wall face 2·95 m. (9¾ ft) in height, and an entablature of 90½ cm. (35¾ in.). The latter runs down vertically at the west end, turns again at right angles somewhat above the base, and stops suddenly against the flank of tower C (Plate 28). It apparently did the same at the east end also.

The torus moulding of the base is decorated with a network of interlacing vine-stalks which form loops; in each loop a vine-leaf rising upwards is generally paired with a bunch of grapes hanging downwards, just as of some of the tie-beams of the Dome of the Rock (Plate 9b). The entablature is equally elaborate, vine-ornament playing a prominent part; the cornice springs boldly forward and its crowning member is decorated with a row of great outward curving acanthus leaves.

The wall surface between the socle and the entablature is divided into twenty upright and twenty inverted triangles by a cornice-like moulding, which runs up and down zigzag fashion from the socle to the architrave. The triangles are c. 2·85 m. (9½ ft) in height and 2·50 m. (8¼ ft) in width at the base. Exactly in the centre of each is a great rosette; those in the upright triangles are lobed hexagons, those in the inverted triangles are straight-sided octagons. The rosettes divide the triangles into three parts of roughly equal height, viz. a broad lower strip, two small surfaces flanking the rosette, and the little triangle above it (Plates 28, 29).

The decoration of the triangles to the west of the entrance is so different from that of those to the east that it seems probable that they were executed by two entirely different schools of craftsmen. The triangles of the western half are generally filled with vine-stems, in which birds appear plucking at the grapes. In triangles IV to IX a pair of animals affronted appear in the centre, sometimes on either side of a vase. Some of these are the most successful of the whole series, being unsurpassed for richness and decorative value (Plate 29).

Schulz [1] points out that the distance (1·58 and 1·54 m.; 5½ and 5²/₂₀ ft) between the side of each tower and the outer edge of the door-post has evidently been calculated so as to allow room for the whole entablature of the façade to turn up vertically at right angles, before forming a relieving arch or lunette over the lintel, Syrian fashion (e.g. Qal'at Sim'ān), as was almost certainly intended.

1. *Loc. cit.*, p. 211.

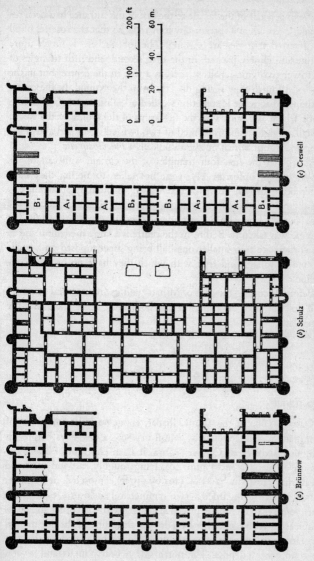

B₄ A₄ A₃ B₃ B₂ A₂ A₁ B₁

200 ft
60 m.

0   100   200 ft
0   20   40   60 m.

(a) Brünnow   (b) Schulz   (c) Creswell

Figure 25. Mshattā: Western side court, proposed reconstructions

133

The upper half of the façade to the east of the entrance had been removed, even when Tristram saw it in 1872, so that the rosettes of all the inverted triangles are missing. The foliage here is much more minute and closely packed. In the first, second, and fifth triangles of the tower two vine-scrolls start from a vase in the centre, but in the third and fourth they spring directly from the ground. In the centre of the third is what is sometimes called a 'palmette tree', a curious motif which also occurs on the tie-beams of the Dome of the Rock; the tall, straight trunk is formed of two twisted stems and above is a wing-like motif which Strzygowski calls a *Flügelpalmette*.

As regards the first four triangles of the curtain wall east of the tower, which, unfortunately, were not taken to Berlin, they have either been thrown down or taken away as building material, e.g. like the rosette of the third triangle, which has been built in over the doorway of a house on the east side of Zīza village. Nearly all the last triangle was taken to Berlin. In the centre is a large medallion and in the corners are two smaller ones, all being superimposed on a background of foliage and fruit with which they have no organic connexion.

Before discussing the date of Mshattā and its architectural origins, I will describe Qasr at-Tūba, because both must be of practically the same date.

QASR AT-TŪBA

Description

Qasr at-Tūba in the Wādī Ghadaf, about 60 miles south-east of 'Ammān, was discovered by Musil in 1898, a few days before his famous discovery of Qusayr 'Amra. It is an enormous oblong enclosure (Plate 31*b* and Figure 26), lying roughly east and west and measuring 140·50 by 72·85 m. (461 by 239 ft), almost a double square. It may in fact be regarded as two symmetrical enclosures, each a little over 70 m. (230 ft) square, placed in contact with each other and communicating with each other by a door in the centre of the side in contact, access to which is expressly provided for by a corridor that can have no other purpose. The north side is nearly intact and several

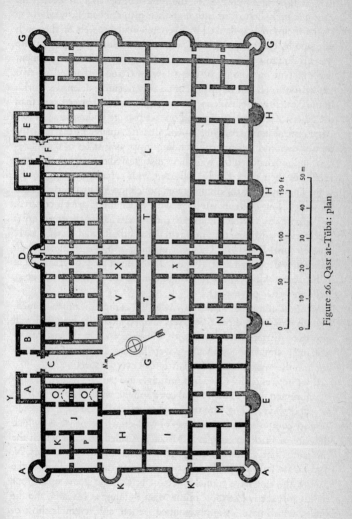

Figure 26. Qasr at-Tūba: plan

lengths of curtain wall exist on the west side; the two other sides are almost entirely destroyed, although their plan can be followed.

The enclosure was flanked by five semicircular towers on the south side, and by two on the east and west sides, in addition to which there was a round tower at each corner. On the north side the arrangement was different on account of the gateways C and F, flanked by two square rooms (B and B¹) which in no way resemble defensive works. In the curtain wall between is a ruined semicircular tower larger than the others. Each gateway opened on to a passage leading straight to a large central court, roughly 30 m. (100 ft) square. In the plan the parts shown in black are still standing in varying states of completeness; in those hatched the walls have disappeared down to the ground level, but their trace can be followed with certainty, owing to the white lines made by the disintegrated stone showing up clearly against the dark colour of the basalt chips with which this district is covered.

The gateway C which leads into the western half of the enclosure is preceded by a passage 6·42 m. (21 ft) in width, flanked by the nearly square rooms B and B¹. The door opening into B is spanned by an elaborately decorated lintel (Plate 31a), the finest piece of ornament at Tūba, above which was a relieving arch. Room B¹ is similar, but its walls are better preserved.

Mention must be made of tower D; although much ruined, enough remains to show that it was divided internally by a thin wall into two quarter circles, each with a little recess. On the analogy of Mshattā I would suggest that they were latrines. The gateway F, leading into the eastern half, is similar to C in every respect.

If we now enter by C we find ourselves in a passage which runs between ruined walls to the central court, on the west side of which are two doorways leading into two smaller courts, M and M¹. The walls here are composed of three courses of well-dressed stone, above which they are of brick, exactly as at Mshattā. A small door, of which the east jamb, partly preserved, is of great richness, leads into a court, N, 7·92 m. (26 ft) wide, flanked by two rooms on each side, of which the pair to the east have tunnel-vaults of brick. The doors of all four rooms are exactly like those of the Main Building at Mshattā, and the vaults, which have a slightly pointed section, also resemble those of Mshattā in every respcet. The two rooms, P and P¹, on the other side of the court correspond in every way except that they are not vaulted, although a few bricks have been placed so as to project at the summit of the side walls, ready for the springing of a vault.

The rooms on the other side of the entrance passage, between it and tower D, correspond exactly to those just described and their measurements are almost identical, but the work here is far less advanced, for only the first three courses of stone have been built, and the walls never reached the bonding stones left for the purpose in the outer wall.

The arrangement on the south side was the same, except that, as there is no gateway and long entrance passage here, the two *bayts* have been made wider – so wide, in fact, that none of them can have been vaulted, for the walls are too thin. It is therefore probable that all these rectangles except the pair at either end were merely enclosures (*ḥōsh*) open to the sky, with walls some 4 metres in height, in which the prince's Bedawīn followers encamped. I must now mention the two niches which form part of two shapeless masses of masonry, all that remains of towers I and I^1. As they come on the axis of court R and R^1 respectively, they may well have been intended for miḥrābs.

The decoration of the whole building is confined to the doorposts and lintels, e.g. the lintel over the door into B (Plate 31a), and the jambs of the doors leading from M to N, L into M^1, and M^1 into R.

The eastern half of the enclosure appears to have been an exact replica of the western.

THE DATE OF MSHATTĀ AND QASR AT-TŪBA

This question may be treated as one problem, for these two buildings resemble each other in so many respects that they must be of practically the same date; whatever conclusions are arrived at as to the date of one must be equally valid for the date of the other.

The points of resemblance are as follows:

(1) Stone employed for the exterior walls and brick for the interior walls, on a finely dressed foundation grid three or four courses high.

(2) Bonding stones in enclosure wall for attachment of the brick walls of the interior.

(3) Size and texture of bricks.

(4) Interior arranged in *bayts*.

(5) Brick vaults, with offset, and rings of bricks set Mesopotamian fashion.

(6) Pointed section of vault.

(7) Bull's-eye windows in vaulted rooms.

(8) Construction of doorways.

(9) Latrines in towers.

(10) Winged motif and tulip-like motif in decoration of each.

(11) Unfinished state of both.

As van Berchem has pointed out, Mshattā is a monument that 'has made more ink flow than any other in Syria'.[1] But there is no space here to repeat the synopsis of the discussion lasting for two generations which I gave in 1932.[2] I must confine myself to saying that the three principal attributions proposed are (1) Lakhmid, (2) Ghassānid, and (3) Umayyad. I will now give my objections against a Lakhmid or Ghassānid attribution, and my reasons for supporting an Umayyad attribution.

Objections Against the Lakhmid Theory

Of all the theories put forward in this connexion, the Lakhmid appears to me to be the most fantastic. On the strength of the Nabataean-Arabic inscription of Nemāra, on the outer edge of the Safā,[3] recording the burial of a man calling himself Mār al-Qais bar Ĭmru, King of all the Arabs, on the 7th day of Keslūl, 223 (= 7 December 328), it was suggested that this man was the Imru' al-Qais ibn 'Amr whose name appears in the list of Lakhmid kings. But there is nothing to show that the Lakhmids had already established themselves at Hīra at this early date, nor is there any proof that this Imru' al-Qais was a vassal of the Persian king. Had he been, it is scarcely probable that the era employed to express the date of his death would have been the Era of Bosrā which began in A.D. 106, when the Romans created the Provincia Arabia.

Nöldeke[4] believes that the simplest explanation is that he was a Lakhmid vassal of the Romans, as is evident from the words of the in-

1. *Journal des Savants*, 1909, p. 402.
2. *Early Muslim Architecture*, I, pp. 390–400.
3. The Safā is the region of lava, to the south-east of Damascus.
4. In *Florilegium Melchior de Vogüé*, pp. 464–5.

scription, that his tribe lived on the Roman border like the Ghassānid Phylarchs later on, and that his descendants, for some reason still obscure, crossed over to the Persian side of the desert, settled at Hīra, and became Persian vassals, not later than 420, for Nu'mān was then King of Hīra and a vassal of the Persian king, as we know from Simeon Stylites. But once established there, there is not a particle of evidence to show that the power of the kings of Hīra ever extended to Transjordan, where Dussaud suggests that one of them may have built Mshattā. And even if it did, is it conceivable that one of them would build a magnificent residence 500 miles from his capital, and only a few miles from the line of Roman frontier forts? No! When Roman rule was strong such a thing would have been impossible, and when the Roman hold on this region was weaker and its resources strained, it was the Ghassānids (the deadliest enemies of the Lakhmids) who took their place and, as allies, protected the frontier here.

Objections against the Ghassānid Theory

From the historical point of view the Ghassānid theory is a much sounder one than the Lakhmid, for the Ghassānids did actually occupy the eastern frontier of Syria, from the Euphrates to Transjordan, from at least as early as A.D. 500.[1] But there are three main objections: (1) the total lack of Christian symbols, as Littmann points out,[2] shows that Mshattā cannot have been constructed by these fanatical Jacobite Christians; (2) it is very doubtful if any of them, even the most famous, had the enormous resources required, and (3) how could Arabs of Syria, expressly under the protection of Byzantium, have erected buildings with a strong imprint of Persia and Mesopotamia? Those who have been led to adopt the Lakhmid theory have done so to escape this very difficulty.

This last objection has now been strengthened; Ghassānid architecture is no longer an unknown quantity, as it once was, for four definitely Ghassānid buildings have been identified and there is a possible fifth and sixth. The first of these is the building, either church or praetorium, outside the north gate of Ruṣāfa, built by al-Mundhir

1. A Ghassānid is mentioned in A.D. 498 under Anastasius; see Theophanes, Bonn ed., p. 218.
2. *Göttingischer gelehrter Anzeiger*, 170. Jahrgang, p. 150.

himself (569–82), with a Greek inscription in his name over the windows of the apse.[1] Its plan is a cross-in-square, and it is built of stone, including the vaults, without any admixture of brickwork; its pier capitals resemble those of Qal'at Sim'ān. It is a completely Syrian building. The second is the stone tower near Dumayr, the corner tower of an enclosure that has disappeared; [2] the third is the house at al-Hayāt on the northernmost slopes of the Haurān, built, according to an inscription, by Flavios Seos (a Roman–Nabataean name) as Procurator under Alamoundaros (= al-Mundhir) in A.D. 578.[3] All the rooms have transverse arches carrying corbel and slab ceilings, in the style typical of the Haurān. The fourth is the Monastery with tower at Qasr al-Hair al-Gharbī, built by Hārith ibn Jabala in A.D. 559.[4] A possible fifth is the building in the Citadel at 'Ammān, which closely resembles the first mentioned, and a possible sixth is Qastal.

Answers to Objections against the Umayyad Theory

Van Berchem writes:

Here is an objection taken from epigraphy: all Muslim monuments bear inscriptions, and these form one with the architecture or the decoration. ... The beautiful band of inscription of 'Abd al-Malik in the Dome of the Rock is well-known; those of Walīd in the mosques of Damascus and Mekka have doubtless disappeared, but authors have preserved the memory of them. ... Nothing like that at Mshattā or in palaces of the same type.[5]

Now if we take the monuments one by one in chronological order we shall see that this objection is scarcely justified. It is true that there is a fine Kufic frieze in the Dome of the Rock, but we have seen that at Damascus the dating inscription was merely 'on a marble slab in the sanctuary, near the roof and next to the minaret' (above, p. 66). In the Mosque of 'Amr at Fustāt the date (Ramadān 92 =June–July

1. See Guyer, in Sarre and Herzfeld, *Archäologische Reise*, II, pp. 39–43 and Abb. 151–6; Spanner and Guyer, *Rusafa*, pp. 42–4, 66–9, Abb. 11, 12, and 16, and Taf. 31–2; and Musil, *Palmyrena*, pp. 163–5, 323–6, figs. 80–82 and 113–15.

2. Brünnow and von Domaszewski, *Die Provincia Arabia*, III, p. 200.

3. H. C. Butler, *Ancient Architecture in Syria, Sect. A: Southern Syria*, pp. 362–3 and illus. 322.

4. Schlumberger, in *Syria*, XX, pp. 366–72.

5. *Journal des savants*, 1909, p. 406.

711) of Qurra ibn Sharīk's rebuilding was apparently recorded on the enigmatic 'green board'. At Qusayr 'Amra and Hammām as-Sarakh the exterior is without any inscription whatever. At Qasr al-Hair ash-Sharqī there are no inscriptions on either enclosure; as for the mosque, the dating inscription was on a slab on one of the piers. The well-preserved east façade of the Great Mosque at Harrān (preserved right up to the very eaves) is absolutely plain. At Raqqa there is no inscription on the well-preserved Baghdād Gate, nor at Ukhaidir. At Cordova the two oldest periods of the Great Mosque are perfectly plain, likewise at Qairawān. The first example of a dating inscription forming one with the architecture and the decoration is provided by the Bū Fatātā Mosque at Sūsa, built between 223 and 226 H. (838–41).

In other words, we may say that in *really early* Muslim architecture, the exteriors seem to have been almost invariably without inscriptions, except perhaps over the entrance. The absence of an inscription on the exterior of Mshattā need not surprise us; had there been one it would almost certainly have been over the entrance (as in the Dome of the Rock), but the entrance, unfortunately, was only completed to about two-thirds of its height. As for the interior, the same remark applies; had there been inscriptions they would have been executed in mosaic or painted on stucco, but the interior decoration was never even begun, except for the sawing up of some green stone for the dadoes. Mshattā never reached the stage where its embellishment with inscriptions became possible.

Van Berchem raises a second objection, viz. that Mshattā cannot be Umayyad because it is fortified and the Umayyad frontier was in Transoxiana and beyond the Indus, whereas the Belqā (Transjordan) was the home of the Umayyads; there they were among their own people and had no need of fortifications.[1]

We have seen that Umayyad princes sometimes lived in Roman frontier fortresses such as Azrak, Qusayr al-Hallabat, and the Qasr al-Bakhrā, and that when they built palaces for themselves at Minya and Qasr al-Hair they apparently felt bound to imitate these fortresses and give them a fortified appearance.

And Qasr al-Hair answers another objection of van Berchem's. How can Mshattā be Umayyad in view of the fact that the Umayyad Khalifs built Syrian monuments? Qasr al-Hair proves that they built

1. *Journal des savants*, 1909, pp. 405–8.

monuments in mixed style, and this mixing had already begun as early as A.D. 691, in the mosaics of the Dome of the Rock.

Historical Reasons for an Umayyad Attribution

In the first place, it is obvious that only a powerful ruler in possession of great resources can have contemplated the creation of a structure like Mshattā. This at once suggests an Umayyad Khalif, whereas, as Nöldeke and Littmann have pointed out, it is doubtful whether any Ghassānid ever had the necessary means. In further favour of an Umayyad date is the known fact that the Belqā was their favourite resort (see above, pp. 93-5), and the *Kitāb al-Aghānī* expressly says that Walīd II built in this region. Another historical fact of great importance is the known practice of the Umayyads of conscripting labour from all parts of the empire, e.g. for the Great Mosques at Madīna, Damascus, and Jerusalem. The Ghassānids were not in a position to conscript labour from 'Irāq and Egypt, yet Mshattā shows signs as we shall see (below, p. 150) of craftsmen from both these regions having worked on it.

Finally we have the passage in Severus ibn al-Muqaffa' to which Lammens has called attention:

Since, however, his people hated him, he [al-Walīd II] began to build a city named after himself in the desert, for he gave his name to it, but the water was fifteen miles distant from it. He collected workmen from all quarters, and built that city by means of forced labour; and on account of the multitude many died every day from the scarcity of water, for though the water was carried thither by twelve hundred camels daily, yet this was not enough for them, the camels being divided into two convoys, six hundred carrying water one day and six hundred the next. Then al-Walīd was attacked by a man named Ibrāhīm, who killed him, and seized the government instead of him. Ibrāhīm released the enslaved workmen, who departed each one to his own place. [1]

Lammens says that the geographical part suits Mshattā, and that fifteen miles is just about the distance to the Arnon (Mujīb). He also points out that this story explains why Yazīd III, on his accession, had to promise not to spend money on building.[2]

1. The above is Evetts' transl. in the *Patrologia Orientalis*, v, pp. 114-15.
2. *Études sur le siècle des Ommayades*, pp. 348-50.

Architectural Reasons for an Umayyad Attribution

Let us now tabulate the principal reasons.

(1) Brick, or a mixture of brick and stone, is foreign to the Classical architecture of Syria, and is absolutely unknown before the second half of the sixth century, the first example being the *castrum* at Andarīn, A.D. 558, followed by Qasr Ibn Wardān (palace, church, and barracks), A.D. 561–4. But Mshattā cannot be affiliated to these for technical reasons. In Byzantine brickwork the layers of mortar between the bricks are always equal to the very thin bricks employed, not only at Constantinople, but also in Syria, whereas in early Muslim works the joints are thinner and the bricks thicker. In this respect the brickwork of Mshattā and Qasr at-Tūba is exactly like that of Qasr al-Hair, and the Baghdād Gate at Raqqa (below, pp. 184–7).

(2) There is no example of an arch braced with a tie-beam in the pre-Muslim architecture of Syria.

(3) The arches of the doorways are not constructed like those of Qasr Ibn Wardān.

(4) Vaults of pointed-arched section, such as those of Mshattā, where the separation of the two centres is one fifth of the span, cannot be earlier than the eighth century, as may be seen from the list given above (pp. 103–4).

(5) To the above may now be added the new evidence provided by the ornament on the tie-beams and mosaics of the Dome of the Rock. For example, the decoration of the great torus moulding below the triangles at Mshattā, in which a vine-stalk forms circular loops, each filled as a rule by one bunch of grapes and one five-pointed vine-leaf, cannot be matched by any pre-Muslim work, but is closely matched by the decoration of one of the tie-beams in the Dome of the Rock (Plate 9*b*).

(6) In the early 'Abbāsid palace of Ukhaidir we have four *bayts* arranged to right and left of the Court of Honour and Audience Hall, which must have been intended for the self-contained households of the four lawful wives of the Muslim prince who built it. Surely the four *bayts* which flank the Audience Hall at Mshattā and the four *bayts* in each of the two enclosures at Qasr at-Tūba can only mean that these palaces were built for Muslim princes also.

(7) And at Ukhaidir there is an entrance hall, and on the right side

of it (the side of honour) is a mosque courtyard with a miḥrāb. At Mshattā also, to the right of the entrance, is a courtyard, and in the centre of its south wall is a niche, with flanking recesses to take columns, which can only be a miḥrāb.

I therefore maintain that Mshattā and Qaṣr aṭ-Ṭūba on historical and architectural grounds are Umayyad palaces built, in all probability, by Walīd II in 743–4, and left unfinished at his death.

ARCHITECTURAL ORIGINS OF MSHATTĀ

The Triple-Apsed Hall

Let us endeavour to arrange the earliest examples in some sort of chronological order. Leaving aside Classical examples of open courts with exedrae on three of their sides, for they really have nothing to do with the present problem, I once thought it possible that the earliest examples were to be found in Roman baths. But the more I think about it, the more doubtful it appears to be. For example, I cited the Palace of Diocletian at Spalato, A.D. 303–5, under reserve, for no trace of the part containing the trefoil shown in Adam's plan [1] exists to-day. Even the basement beneath the main floor has disappeared at this point. I believe that Adam may have restored it from insufficient indications, and I am supported in this by the fact that Clérisseau, who accompanied Adam and also made a plan, *only shows the central apse*.[2] Another example, Thelepta, which I cited in 1932, is equally suspect. I visited Thelepta about twenty years ago and was able to recognize most of the elements shown on Saladin's plan, including the two oblong rooms on the west side, each with an apse at each end, but not the third apse shown projecting beyond the alignment of the west wall. The west wall had disappeared at the two places in question and there was nothing but bare ground. As Saladin does not speak of making excavations, I conclude that the third apse is pure speculation.[3]

1. *Ruins of the Palace of the Emperor Diocletian*, pl. v.

2. His plan was published by Joseph Lavallée, *Voyage pittoresque de l'Istrie et de la Dalmatie*, pl. 54 bis.

3. 'Rapport', in the *Archives des Missions Scientifiques*, 3e sér., t. XIII, pp. 116–19 and figs. 206–10.

Next in chronological order are three little ruined structures in the cemetery of Callixtus on the Via Appia Antica near Rome:

(1) SS. Xystus and Cecilia.
(2) St Soteris.
(3) A structure connected with S. Sinforosa, at the ninth milestone on the Via Tiburtina.

These little edifices, until recently, have been regarded as of the third century, but it now appears that in the first two side apses may have been inserted at a later date.[1]

We are on firmer ground when we come to the Church of St John the Baptist at Jerusalem, which was built by the Empress Eudocia between 450 and 460. Here we have three apses of large size preceded by a narthex, but there is no nave.[2] This is certainly the oldest example in Syria.

A number of examples are to be found in North Africa, but it is very doubtful if any go back to before the middle of the fifth century.

But when and where was the trefoil plan first employed for a Throne Room? Apparently at Bosrā in the Haurān, where a perfect example occurs in the Episcopal Palace (Figure 27), which Butler believes to be contemporary with the Cathedral (512–13). I give Butler's section here because of its close analogy with the triple-apsed hall at Mshattā, and because the central part has a clerestory, with three windows in each face, which was probably covered by a pyramidal roof, as in the White Monastery at Sohāg.[3]

Examples of the use of a triple apse for a hall of audience do not appear to exist outside Syria until much later, the earliest examples known to me being:

(1) Ravenna: Palace of the Exarchate, seventh to eighth century.[4]
(2) Aachen: Aula Regis of Charlemagne.[5]
(3) Rome: Triclinium of Pope Leo III, 795–816.[6]

1. Marucchi, *Nuovo bullettino di archeologia christiana*, XVI (1910), pp. 220–21.
2. Vincent and Abdel, *Jérusalem*, II, pp. 642–68, figs. 263–9, and pl. LIII–LV.
3. Butler, *op. cit.*, pp. 286–8 and illus. 248 and 250–3.
4. For the excavations, see *Kunstchronik*, XXI, col. 476.
5. Thordeman, 'Der Karolingerpalast in Aachen als Trikonchos', in *Studien zur Kunst des Ostens*, 1923, pp. 241–2.
6. Lauer, *Le Palais de Latran*, pp. 105 and 121, and figs. 40–42 from manuscript drawings by Ugonio.

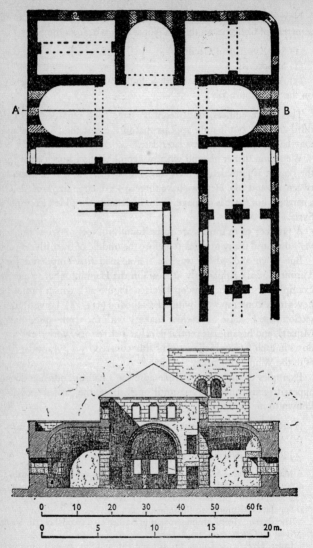

Figure 27. Bosrā: Bishop's Palace, plan and section

(4) Constantinople: Triconchos, built in the palace by the Emperor Theophilus in 839. It had three apses – north, east, and south – and on the west side were three doors.[1]

Thus it would appear that the custom of using a triple-apsed plan for a throne-room arose in Syria.

Finally which are the earliest examples of the *combination* of a trifoil apse and a basilical hall? The answer, fortunately, is easy to give.

(1) Nola: Basilica of Paulinus *c.* 401–3.[2]
(2) Sohāg: White Monastery, *c.* 440.[3]
(3) Sohāg: Red Monastery, *c.* 440.[3]
(4) Dendera: Basilica, end of fifth century.[4]
(5) Bethlehem: Church of the Nativity, alteration of Justinian, i.e. before 565.

Thus out of the five earliest examples of this feature, no less than three occur in Egypt. I therefore conclude (1) that the adoption of this feature for a throne-room or audience-hall first took place in Syria, and that the further development, in which the triple-apsed hall is preceded by a basilical hall, was due to Egyptian influence.

The Bayts

In early Oriental palaces the rooms are generally arranged in threes or fives round a court, so that each group forms a self-contained unit, a habitation in itself (*bayt*). This is exactly what we find at Mshattā; but the *bayts* are different from those found in Sasanian palaces, a point ignored hitherto. At Qasr-i-Shīrīn, in the Palace of Khusrau Parvēz (590–628), we have a deep līwān, with flanking chambers all opening into a triple-arched portico. A passage at the side leads to a court at the back (Figure 28). At Ukhaidir (Figure 40) the arrangement is almost identical – that is to say the 'Abbāsids followed the Sasanian tradition. But in Syria the *bayts* are quite different. Two examples have survived, and in both of them the arrangement resembles that at Mshattā and Qasr at-Tūba. The first of these is Qastal, about 4

1. See the continuation of Theophanes, Bonn ed., III, p. 139 ff.
2. As reconstructed from the description of Paulinus by Holtzinger, in the *Zeitschr. für bildende Kunst*, XX, pp. 135–8 and fig. 1.
3. For the date see Monneret, *Les Couvents près de Sohâg*, pp. 15–33.
4. *Ibid.*, pp. 47–8.

miles west of Mshattā. Here there are six *bayts* arranged round the interior so that a central court is left over. Externally, it resembles the fortresses of the Roman frontier line, but the internal arrangement does not. In the sixth century the care of the frontier was handed over to the Ghassānid Phylarchs, and this leads me to believe that it was built for one of them. This is confirmed by Hamza al-Isfahānī (tenth century), who says that it was built by Jabala ibn al-Hīrith.[1] We find a similar grouping of rooms on the upper floor of Qasr Kharāna, which I believe to be pre-Muslim. The *bayts* here are identical to those of Mshattā; those of Qastal, in which two small rooms giving access to the corner tower (? a latrine) are added on one side, bear the closest possible resemblance to these of Mshattā. In this respect, therefore, Mshattā and Qasr at-Tūba are Syrian and not Persian.

The Decoration of the Façade

The decoration of the triangles of Mshattā can readily be divided into four groups, as follows:

A–C (= three triangles). This group is distinguished by the following features: (1) the division of the field into two parts by a horizontal band touching the lower edge of the rosette; (2) the living forms are limited to birds only, except for the human-headed feline in the apex of *A*; (3) in *A* and *C* the lower field is filled by four tangential and nine intersecting circles respectively, which are knotted together at their points of contact.

D–L (= seven triangles). In these triangles two animals (some mythical) are affronted, and in every case (except in *J* and *K*) they are placed on either side of a central chalice.

M–T (= eight triangles). These are dominated by vine scrolls and there are neither birds nor animals, moreover the scrolls are quite different from the naturalistic ones of *A–L*.

U–V (= two triangles). An extraordinary mixture of motifs: pine-cones, winged palmettes, etc.

We can therefore readily admit that several groups of craftsmen worked at this wonderful façade. From what countries did they

1. Gottwaldt's ed., p. 117; quoted by Brünnow and von Domaszewski, *op. cit.*, II, p. 100.

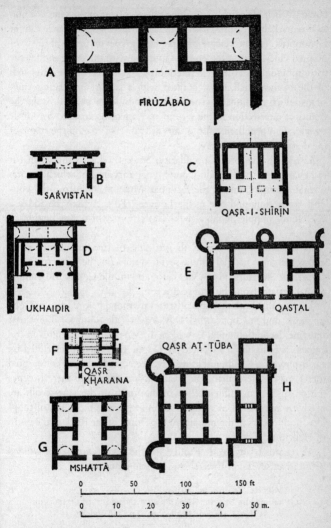

A — FÎRÛZÂBÂD

B — SARVISTÂN

C — QAŞR-I-SHÎRÎN

D — UKHAIDIR

E — QASTAL

F — QAŞR KHARANA

G — MSHATTÂ

H — QAŞR AȚ-ȚÛBA

| 0 | 50 | 100 | 150 ft |

| 0 | 10 | 20 | 30 | 40 | 50 m. |

Figure 28. Bayts: Persian and 'Irāqi types compared with those of Syria

come? When we come to examine the treatment of the vine, we find two remarkable features, so rare in fact that their significance cannot be doubted: (1) the placing of three little grapes on many of the five-pointed vine-leaves at the point of junction with the stalk; and (2) the torus mouldings of the socle and doorposts, and also on the inner arch of the basilican hall, are decorated with a pair of undulating vine-stems which continually cross each other to form pointed ovals, the points of intersection in the second and last being marked by a little rosette. This peculiarity also occurs at Qasr at-Tūba, on the frame of the door between M and N.

As regards the former peculiarity, Strzygowski has shown that it is a characteristic of certain Coptic ivory carvings, of which he cites several examples, one in the Egyptian Museum, one from the Fouquet Collection, and one in the Louvre.[1] To these may be added a very fine example in the Benaki Collection, which was bought in Egypt.[2]

As regards the rosettes at the crossing of two undulating vine-stalks, the only parallel found so far occurs on the door from the Church of Sitt Burbāra at Old Cairo, now in the Coptic Museum. It probably dates from the fifth century.[3]

The fact that both these peculiarities are found before Islam in Coptic work, and in Coptic work *only*, leaves little room for doubt that the vine decoration cited, as well as the vine foliage and birds in triangles *A–L*, has been executed by Coptic craftsmen, conscripted by an all-powerful Khalif, just as we have seen that they were conscripted for Damascus, Jerusalem, and Madīna. Yet even here there is penetration of Persian influence, for in the midst of the vine-scrolls are mythical animals taken from Sasanian art, just as the Sasanian tulip-like motif occurs in the mosaics of the Dome of the Rock in the midst of Hellenistic motifs.

As regards triangles *M–T* and *U–V* the occurrence of the winged palmette in several of them shows Persian influence.

1. 'Mshatta', *loc. cit.*, pp. 303–5.
2. Published by Migeon, *Manuel d'art musulman*, 2e ed., I, fig. 146.
3. See my *Early Muslim Architecture*, I, p. 388 and fig. 483.

THE GREAT MOSQUE OF HARRĀN

Description

The Great Mosque of Harrān is a rectangle roughly 100 m. square, built of ashlar in courses averaging 37 cm. in height. The best-preserved part is the east wall, of which the eastern half is nearly intact except for a gap of about 6 m. (20 ft) in the middle. The last 9·42 m. (31 ft) are deflected 60 cm. (2 ft) to the west. There is an imposing entrance immediately north of the façade of the sanctuary as at

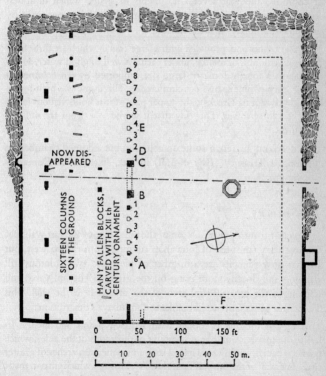

NOW DIS-APPEARED

9
8
7
6
5
4 E
3
2 D
1 C

SIXTEEN COLUMNS ON THE GROUND

MANY FALLEN BLOCKS, CARVED WITH XII th CENTURY ORNAMENT

B
1
2
3
4
5
6 A

F

0   50   100   150 ft

0   10   20   30   40   50 m.

Figure 29. Harrān: Great Mosque, plan

Damascus. The west wall has almost disappeared, but there was apparently an entrance on this side, corresponding to the one just mentioned, for a pair of parallel walls, about 2·75 m. (9 ft) apart, can still be traced leading up to this point. Several courses of the east half of the north wall remain, likewise the opening of the northern entrance, which is approximately in the centre (Figure 29).

About half-way between it and the north-east corner rises the tall square shaft of the minaret, which averages 5·30 m. (17½ ft) a side externally and 3·83 (12½ ft) internally.

In the *sahn* is an octagonal basin measuring 6·10 m. (20 ft) over all. Preusser says that the octagonal border bears clear marks of the bases of columns, and that several fragments of shafts, which doubtless served to support a dome, are lying near. This is fully confirmed by Ibn Jubayr, who says that the mosque

is of great beauty and provided with a large *sahn* in which are three lofty domes on columns of marble, under each is a well of good water, and in the *sahn* is a fourth dome of large size supported by ten columns of marble, each of nine spans in circumference. This dome was built by the Rūm (=Byzantine Greeks); the upper part of it is hollowed out in the form of a lofty tower. They say that it served as a depot for military equipment.[1]

Thus it was not merely a dome on columns, but a domed chamber on columns, a Treasury (*Bayt al-Māl*) in fact, like that at Damascus (above, pp. 58–9).

The Sanctuary

It is clear from an examination of the inner face of the east wall that the sanctuary consisted of four aisles running from east to west, but all that now remains are a number of piers and two columns still standing and dozens more lying on the ground. The only arch still standing is the great central arch of the arcade next the *sahn*. This arcade can be reconstructed thanks to Ibn Jubayr's description:

This blessed mosque is roofed with wooden beams and arches. Its beams are massive and long on account of the width of the aisles, which is fifteen paces. ... Nowhere have I seen a mosque with arches of greater span. The wall of the mosque next the *sahn*, through which entry is made

1. De Goeje's ed., p. 246, ll. 9–14.

into the mosque itself, is pierced with doorways. Their number is nineteen, nine right and nine left, and the nineteenth is a lofty door in the middle of these of which the arch occupies the whole height of the façade, of very beautiful aspect and well executed, like the gate of some large city. All these openings are closed with wooden doors of fine workmanship, covered with carved ornament which makes them resemble the doors of the audience hall of a palace. We have been astonished at the quality of the workmanship of this mosque.[1]

Let us now try to reconstruct the façade. The great central arch is of pointed form with stepped extrados. It rests on two great piers 8·32 m. (27¼ ft) apart, and to the west is a smaller pier (D); attached to it is a capital, but the column belonging to it is lying on the ground. The rear face of this pier is in exact alignment with the rear face of the great arch. To the west of D is a column (E) of pink limestone. From the west side of D to the centre of the column measures 7·32 m. (24 ft), which give 8·02 m. (26¼ ft) as the distance from centre to centre. The rear face of this column is in a line with the front face of D, so it doubtless belonged to a similar pier that has disappeared. It is obvious, however, that there must have been another such support between it and D, and if we insert another pier of 1·40 m. (4½ ft) we get two intervals of 2·61 m. (8½ ft), which is just what we require. If we mark off the piers accordingly, we find that there is just room for nine arches between the great arch and the junction with the west *riwāq*. The same process can be repeated on the other side, thus giving us the nineteen arches of Ibn Jubayr.

These eighteen flanking openings were each spanned by two arches, one resting on the piers and a larger one resting on the engaged columns; the latter were of slightly horse-shoe form [2] and formed a frame for the former.

As for the interior of the sanctuary, I am unable to suggest a reconstruction as the irregularities are so curious and so inexplicable; the supports of the various arcades do not appear to have corresponded with each other, nor do there appear to have been the same number of columns between the various piers. Again, whereas the central arch of the façade has a span of 8·32 m. (27¼ ft), the one behind it about 6 m. (19¾ ft), and central arch of the back row 3·30 m. (10¼ ft) only. In

1. p. 246, ll. 14–21.
2. The return of the first to the west of the great arch still exists.

addition to this the axis of the mihrāb is some 5 m. (16½ ft) to the west of the centre. Only excavation can settle the true form of the sanctuary.

The Date

An examination of the west façade makes one thing perfectly clear: we have to do with at least two periods, for there is a complete break in bond between the second and third bays, and the height of the base of the stone gables to the right of it is 1·70 m. (5½ ft) more than it is to the left. Secondly, the arches which once formed the façade of the sanctuary are lying in two cases exactly as they fell, face forward on the ground. But in some cases the stones are on their sides and the ornament is such that it cannot be earlier than the twelfth century, for there are many blocks with parts of an inscription in large Naskhī characters, surmounted by a guilloche border, which can scarcely be earlier than the twelfth century, for only one Naskhī inscription is known before A.D. 1100. Finally, Sachau in 1879 saw an inscription to the right of the east entrance in the name of Salāh ad-Dīn.[1] Salāh ad-Dīn was in Harrān in 1183, 1185, and 1186, but as the finished work was seen by Ibn Jubayr in 1184, one must conclude that it was probably ordered in 1183.

Harrān was famous as the city of the Sabians, and its inhabitants were regarded as pagans by the early Muslims. I very much doubt if Walīd I, or any other Khalif before Marwān II, ever thought of building a mosque there. But the latter, who was the last Umayyad Khalif (744–50) made Harrān his capital, and the need for a congregational mosque must then have made itself felt. I therefore attribute the oldest part to him.

Architectural Origins

Like all Umayyad monuments, the Great Mosque of Harrān exhibits a mixture of influences; its masonry is North Mesopotamian, which forms one with that of Northern Syria, its arches with a stepped extrados continue Classical tradition, but its square plan follows that of the earliest mosques of ʿIrāq. As for the façade on the *sahn*, with

1. *Reise in Syrien und Mesopotamien*, p. 221.

columns attached to the front faces of the piers, it at once recalls the work of the Inālides in the Great Mosque of Diyārbakr between 510 and 559 H. (1116 and 1164).[1]

1. See van Berchem and Strzygowski, *Amida*, pp. 52–3 and plates IX–XI and XII–XV.

CHAPTER 7

CONCLUSION TO PART ONE

We have seen that the Arab conquerors, for at least a generation, re-mained so untouched by any architectural ambitions that they showed not the slightest desire to make use of the developed architectural talents of the conquered peoples. In Syria, at first, they used divided or converted churches as mosques, and in 'Irāq, where they founded new cities on bare ground, the first mosques were primitive in the ex-treme. When at last they did begin to feel such ambitions, it was chiefly for political reasons. At first they turned to the conquered people for craftsmen, e.g. Ziyād ibn Abīhī, when about to rebuild the Great Mosque at Kūfa, employed a man who had been an architect of the Persian kings (above, p. 13), Ibn az-Zubayr employed Persian masons when rebuilding the Ka'ba in 684, and al-Walīd employed Copts from Egypt and Greeks from Syria when rebuilding the Mosque of Madīna in 707–9.

Nearly all the surviving monuments of this period are in Syria, which is not surprising, for Syria was the seat of the dynasty. Most of them are really splendid structures of cut stone, some of ashlar in courses 80–90 cm. ($31\frac{1}{2}$–$35\frac{1}{2}$ in.) high, with arcades resting on marble columns. The mosques were nearly always covered with a gable roof of timber, for the enormous timber resources of the Lebanon (the great timber reserve of the ancient world) had not been exhausted. The minarets were tall square towers, derived from the church towers of pre-Muslim Syria, and the triple-aisled sanctuaries were due to the same influence.

But although the influence of the Christian architecture of Syria dominated, another influence is apparent even in the earliest monu-ment – the Dome of the Rock – where late Sasanian motifs appear in the mosaic decoration alongside well-known Classical forms. This was due to a remarkable factor, the conscription of labour on a large scale, by the all-powerful Khalifs, from all parts of the Muslim Em-pire. For this reason all existing Muslim monuments exhibit a mixture of influences, Syria occupying the first place and Persia the second, and Coptic evidence is definitely demonstrable at the end of this period (Mshattā).

And there was another new factor also – the half-Bedawīn instincts of all the Umayyad Khalifs (except Muʿāwiya) and their love of the desert life –, which led to the erection of a number of desert residences, such as Quṣayr ʿAmra, Minya, Qaṣr al-Hair, Mshattā, Qaṣr aṭ-Ṭūba, etc. In constructing these residences, which were generally about 70 m. (230 ft) square, or multiples of that dimension, the fortresses of the Roman frontier line running from the Gulf of ʿAqaba to Damascus and from Damascus to Palmyra were taken for models, as far as their outer fortified enclosure was concerned, but the interiors were divided up differently into *bayts*. These *bayts*, each of which consisted of living-rooms and a court, were arranged round the interior of the enclosure so that a court was left over in the centre.

It was during the later Umayyad period that brick walls and brick vaults, hitherto almost unknown in Syria, again made their appearance, but it must be especially noted that the technique (joints thinner than the bricks) show that this innovation did not come, as previously, from Byzantium, but from ʿIrāq.

Umayyad architecture employed the following constructive devices: the semicircular arch, the round horse-shoe arch, the pointed arch, flat arches or lintels with a semicircular relieving arch above, arches braced with tie-beams, joggled voussoirs, tunnel-vaults in stone and brick, the latter constructed without centering, the system of roofing in which transverse arches support parallel tunnel-vaults, wooden domes, and also domes of stone on true spherical–triangle pendentives. The squinch does not appear to have been employed and the intersection of tunnel-vaults was avoided. In fortification, half-round flanking towers were employed, likewise the mâchicoulis, but the bent entrance does not appear to have been known.

In planning, a geometrical network, derived from earlier Syrian practice, was employed for laying out the Dome of the Rock, and a curious system of successive, symmetrical subdivision into three, not yet noted elsewhere, is found at Minya and Mshattā.

The decoration was of the most splendid kind, marble was used for panelling, the slabs being cut in half and opened like a book, so that the wavy grain ran from opposite sides towards the joint. The upper part of the exterior and interior walls was sometimes decorated with glass mosaic (*fusaifisā*), vaster surfaces being covered than had ever been known before. But the most surprising fact is that human figures were painted in fresco, for the hostility against painting had not yet taken decisive theological form.

And just as the Muslims in Syria were influenced by the Hellenistic traditions and Christian art of their environment, so those who found themselves in 'Irāq or Persia as a result of the fanwise invasion of the Arabs, were influenced by the Sasanian traditions of their environment. Although no monuments of the Umayyad period (except at Wāsit) have survived in 'Irāq or Persia, we know from the descriptions of early authors that a type of mosque prevailed there quite different from the stone-walled, gable-roofed mosques of Syria. This Persian type of mosque, which was constructed at Basra and Kūfa, and later on at Wāsit, Baghdād, and Sāmarrā, was square in plan (the result of the first mosques in this region having been marked out by arrow-casts), had walls of brick (sometimes of mud-brick), and its flat timber roof rested directly on the columns *without the intermediary of arches*. The columns were sometimes of stone, but frequently (as we shall see) of wood. In this type of mosque we have a direct link with the ancient Persian *apadāna*, or hypostyle audience-hall of the Achaemenian kings, and the *tālār* or flat-roofed portico of more recent Persian palaces.

In Persia, materials such as Persepolitan columns with bull-headed capitals were taken from older buildings, just as Corinthian columns from older buildings were used in Syria.

PART TWO

The 'Abbāsid Dynasty

*

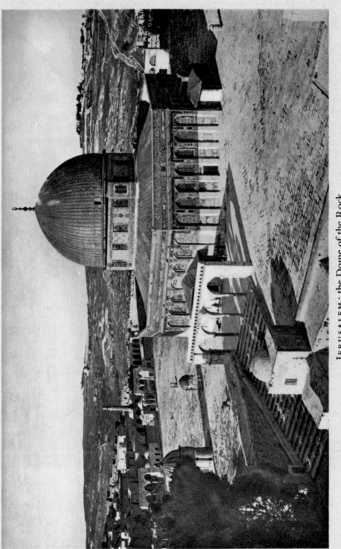

JERUSALEM : the Dome of the Rock

JERUSALEM: the Dome of the Rock, inner ambulatory

JERUSALEM: the Dome of the Rock, central part under dome

JERUSALEM: the Dome of the Rock, bronze-plated soffit of south doorway

4

JERUSALEM: the Dome of the Rock, octagonal arcade, west side, inner face

5

JERUSALEM: the Dome of the Rock, inner face of north-west pier of octagonal arcade

JERUSALEM : the Dome of the Rock, inner face of north-east pier of octagonal arcade

7

(a) JERUSALEM: the Dome of the Rock, soffit of an arch of octagonal arcade

(b) JERUSALEM: the Dome of the Rock, tie-beam of an arch of octagonal arcade

JERUSALEM: the Dome of the Rock, tie-beams of arches of octagonal arcade

JERUSALEM: the Dome of the Rock, flanks of piers of octagonal arcade

DAMASCUS: the Great Mosque, west side of ancient *temenos* and corner tower

DAMASCUS: the Great Mosque, south side

12

DAMASCUS: the Great Mosque, interior looking west

13

DAMASCUS: the Great Mosque, façade of sanctuary

14

DAMASCUS: the Great Mosque, western *riwāq*

DAMASCUS: the Great Mosque, marble
window grilles in western vestibule

16

DAMASCUS: the Great Mosque, remains of original quartered marble panelling, in east vestibule

DAMASCUS: the Great Mosque, left extremity of mosaic decoration
under western *riwāq*

18

DAMASCUS: the Great Mosque, mosaics under western *riwāq*

(a) Arch in vestibule

(b) Arch in *riwāq*

DAMASCUS: the Great Mosque, mosaic decoration on
soffits of arches of western vestibule and *riwāq*

(c) RAVENNA: mosaic in Sant'Apollinare Nuovo, showing the
Palace of Theodoric

20

(a) QUSAYR 'AMRA: from the north-west

(b) QUSAYR 'AMRA: interior of audience hall

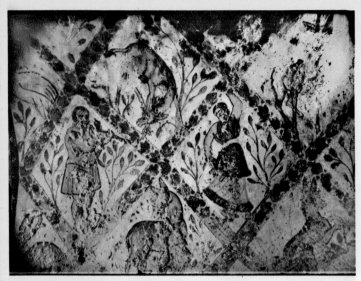

QUSAYR 'AMRA: painting

(a) QUSAYR 'AMRA: the painting of the Enemies of Islam

(b) HAMMĀM AS-SARAKH

JERUSALEM: the Aqsā Mosque. The arcade in the foreground is probably part of the Umayyad structure

QAIRAWĀN: minaret of Great Mosque

(a) QASR AL-HAIR ASH-SHARQI: the two enclosures from the south

(b) QASR AL-HAIR ASH-SHARQI: the Lesser Enclosure

(a) QASR AL-HAIR ASH-SHARQĪ: entrance to the Lesser Enclosure

(b) QASR AL-HAIR ASH-SHARQĪ: Mosque in Greater Enclosure

MSHATTĀ : façade to west of entrance, first triangle

MSHATTĀ: flanking tower on west side of entrance, third triangle

(a) MSHATTĀ: Throne-Room block

(b) MSHATTĀ: triple-apsed Throne-Room

(a) QASR AT-TŪBA: lintel of doorway

(b) QASR AT-TŪBA: north façade, right half

RAQQA : Baghdād Gate, outer face

RAQQA: Baghdād Gate, rear face and corner tower of main wall

(b) UKHAIDIR : decoration at top of first bay to east of north gateway

(a) UKHAIDIR : east gateway

34

(a) UKHAIDIR : entrance hall, with slots in vault, most of which has fallen, revealing vault of room above

(b) UKHAIDIR : transverse corridor

UKHAIDIR: Great Hall, looking north

(a) UKHAIDIR: Court of Honour, north side

(b) UKHAIDIR: Court of Honour, south side

(a) UKHAIDIR : east façade

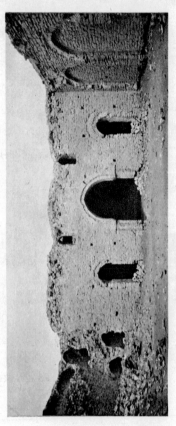

(b) UKHAIDIR : *bayt* D

(a) UKHAIDIR : panel of geometrical ornament in brick, on south side of Court of Honour

(b) UKHAIDIR : room 32, blind windows in wall between springing of transverse arches

(a) CORDOVA: the Great Mosque, west façade

(b) CORDOVA: the Great Mosque, Puerta di San Estéban

(a) CORDOVA: the Great Mosque, façade of sanctuary

(b) CORDOVA: the Great Mosque, arcades of sanctuary

JERUSALEM: the Aqṣā Mosque, wall-plates

RAMLA : the Cistern known as Bir al-Anezīya, with pointed arches of A.D. 789

The Mosque of 'Amr : north end of west side

(a) THE MOSQUE OF 'AMR: decorated wooden architrave with stump of broken-off tie beam (see below)

(b) THE MOSQUE OF 'AMR: the Sanctuary, west end

(a) THE MOSQUE OF 'AMR: carved woodwork of first window on south-west side

(b) THE MOSQUE OF 'AMR: carved woodwork of westernmost window on north-west side

(a) QAIRAWĀN: the Great Mosque, south side

(b) QAIRAWĀN: the Great Mosque, east side, showing an original door (left) and a late door

47

QAIRAWĀN: the Great Mosque, from the north-east

QAIRAWĀN: the Great Mosque, from the minaret

(a) QAIRAWĀN: the Great Mosque, the *sahn*, looking north

(b) QAIRAWĀN: the Great Mosque, the sanctuary, looking east

SĀMARRĀ : the Jausaq al-Khaqānī, the Bāb al-ʿĀmma

(a) SĀMARRĀ : the Jausaq al-Khaqānī, stucco dado in room to east of Throne-Room

(b) SĀMARRĀ : the Jausaq al-Khaqānī, wooden panel from Throne-Room (compare Plate 68)

52

(a) SŪSA: the Great Mosque, bay under first dome

(b) SŪSA: the Great Mosque, decorated tympanum of arch on west side
under first dome

SŪSA : the Great Mosque

SĀMARRĀ: the Great Mosque

(b) SĀMARRĀ: the Great Mosque, the *Malwīya*

(a) SĀMARRĀ: the Great Mosque, one of the windows, from within

SĀMARRĀ : al-Jaʿfariya, with Mosque of Abū Dulaf

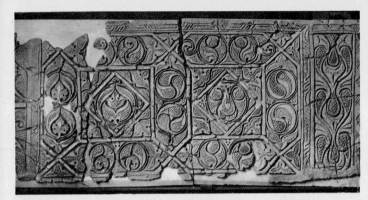

(a) SĀMARRĀ : ornament, style B. From house near Jubayrīya

(b) SĀMARRĀ : ornament, style A. From House II, room 41

(a) QAIRAWĀN : the Aghlabid Cisterns, junction of smaller cistern (of decantation) with greater cistern

(b) QAIRAWĀN : greater cistern

CAIRO : the Nilometer, with measuring shaft temporarily removed

QAIRAWĀN: the Great Mosque, mihrāb

(a) QAIRAWĀN: the Great Mosque, lustred tiles
decorating mihrāb

(b) QAIRAWĀN: the Great Mosque, marble panels
lining mihrāb

QAIRAWĀN : the Great Mosque, setting of dome in front of miḥrāb

QAIRAWĀN: the Great Mosque, sanctuary

(a) QAIRAWĀN: the Mosque of the Three Doors,
façade on street

(b) QAIRAWĀN: the Mosque of the Three Doors,
detail of ornament of spandrels

The Mosque of Ibn Ṭūlūn

THE MOSQUE OF IBN TŪLŪN: north-eastern *ziyāda* partly cleared

The Mosque of Ibn Ṭūlūn: door soffit (compare Plate 52b)

The Mosque of Ibn Ṭūlūn: façade of north-eastern *riwāq*

The Mosque of Ibn Tūlūn : arcades of sanctuary

The Mosque of Ibn Ṭūlūn: soffits of arches

(a) THE MOSQUE OF IBN TŪLŪN: detail of decoration of arcades

(b) THE MOSQUE OF IBN TŪLŪN: sixth window from left on south-east side

CHAPTER 8

THE FOUNDATION OF BAGHDĀD

The Fall of the Umayyads and the Rise of the 'Abbāsids

The last Umayyad Khalif was Marwān II, who became Khalif at the end of 744 and made Harrān his residence, greatly offending the Syrians thereby. His reign was a continuous struggle against Khārijite and 'Abbāsid conspiracies, and the latter eventually brought about the fall of the dynasty. The Persians were ready to revolt, for great numbers had gone over to Islam without receiving the promised advantages, viz. exemption from the poll-tax paid by all non-Muslims.

In 747 the Umayyad garrisons were expelled from Merv and Herāt and the whole of Persia was lost the following year. Marwān was defeated in 'Irāq in January 750 and put to death in Egypt in July. Meanwhile Abu'l-'Abbās, the first 'Abbāsid Khalif, had been proclaimed at Damascus in April. He was constantly occupied in exterminating the male descendants of the Umayyads, of whom hardly any escaped except 'Abd ar-Rahmān, destined to be the founder of the Umayyad Emīrate of Cordova.

The Dār al-Imāra of Abū Muslim at Merv

Abū Muslim, who had been chief agent of the 'Abbāsid family, built a Dār al-Imāra at Merv, and we fortunately possess sufficient information to form a general idea of its form. Istakhrī says:

Among the buildings of Abū Muslim is the Dār al-Imāra, and it is at the back (zahr) of the mosque. And in this dār is a domed chamber ... in which he used to sit. It is a domed chamber made of burnt brick and its measurement (sa'a) is 55 cubits. There is access to the flat part of the roof from the interior. And the domed chamber has four doors, each leading to an īwān, and the height of each īwān is ... (blank). And in front of each īwān is a square sahn.[1]

1. p. 259, ll. 4–9.

Figure 30. Merv: Dār al-Imāra, plan

The missing dimensions of these *īwāns* is given by Mustawfī as 30 by 60 cubits.[1] As for the date it must have been built between December 747 or January 748, when Abū Muslim had driven the Umayyad Governor out of Merv, and January 755, when Abū Muslim was executed by his savage and ungrateful master, al-Mansūr, the second 'Abbāsid Khalif. Figure 30 is an attempt to give form to this description. It almost follows from the plan that the diameter of the dome was equal to the width of the *īwāns*.

One cannot help being struck by the close resemblance of Abū

1. *Nuzhat al-Qulūb*, Le Strange's ed., p. 156.

Muslim's palace to the Palace of al-Mansūr at Baghdād and, later on, to the throne-room group in two of the palaces at Sāmarrā, viz. the Jausaq al-Khāqānī and Balkuwārā.

The Foundation of Baghdād

The Khalif as-Saffāh died in June 754 and al-Mansūr was proclaimed his successor. The outlook of the 'Abbāsids being towards the East, it was evident that a site on the Tigris or Euphrates was required, and al-Mansūr made many journeys in search of a site for his new capital, until he finally fixed on the site of Baghdād.[1]

Having decided on the site on 1 August 762, al-Mansūr wrote to every city to send engineers and people acquainted with building, surveying, and mensuration. Engineers, architects, and land-surveyors from Syria, Mosul, Western Persia, Kūfa, Wāsit, and Basra were gathered together, and not until thousands of men had been assembled did the work begin.[2]

Tabarī says that the plan of the city was first traced on the ground with lines of ashes, for al-Mansūr wished to see its actual form.[3] The plan was circular, with four equidistant gateways named after the city or province towards which they opened (Figure 31): the Kūfa Gate (SW.), the Basra Gate (SE.), the Khurāsān Gate (NE.) and the Damascus Gate (NW.). The foundations were laid at a moment chosen by the astrologer Naubakht, and the Arabic authors are almost unanimous as to the date, nearly all giving 145 H. (762-3), and most say the date of completion of the whole work was 149 H. (766-7). As for the size, the dimensions given by Ya'qūbī do not agree with the various traditions recorded by al-Khatīb: I am inclined, like Herzfeld, to adopt the figure which has come down from Rabāh, who was the actual architect of the walls, viz. circumference 16,000 cubits, which gives a diameter of 5,093 cubits.[4]

1. Compare this search for the site of a capital with that made by Idrīs in 805-6 before choosing the site of Fez (Rawd al-Qirtās, Beaumier's transl., pp. 31-5), al-Mutasim's search for the site of Sāmarrā in 836, and the first Fātimid Khalif's search for the site of Mahdīya in 912-13.

2. Ya'qūbī, Geography, p. 238.

3. III, p. 277.

4. Taking a cubit at 51.8 cm., we get 2,638 m. for the diameter.

The Bricks

The walls were made of mud bricks a cubit square (the thickness is not stated) and reeds were set in as a bond between each course. Burnt bricks were employed for the tunnel-vaults and domes.

al-Khaṭīb, on the authority of Rabāḥ, the architect of the walls, says: 'In each of the courses of mud bricks, there were 162,000. When we had built a third of the wall, we made it thinner and only laid 150,000 to a course; when we had built two thirds we reduced it again and only laid 140,000 bricks to the course up to the summit.' [1] Herzfeld remarks that as the distance from gate to gate was 4,000 cubits, total 16,000 cubits, i.e. bricks, the wall must have been 10 cubits or bricks thick, which would require 160,000, leaving 2,000 over for the towers. The number 150,000 for the courses of the middle third would provide for a wall $9\frac{1}{4}$ bricks thick (= 148,000) plus 2,000 over for the towers; 140,000 for the courses of the upper third provide for a wall $8\frac{1}{2}$ bricks thick (= 136,000), plus 4,000 over, which would enable the towers to be carried up above the crest of the wall.[2]

Reconstruction of the Fortifications

I shall begin with al-Khaṭīb's description, supplementing it by Ya'qūbī, whose description fills some of the gaps:

The height of the inner wall, which was that of the city, was 35 cubits. On it were towers which rose 5 cubits above it ... Then came the fasīl between the two walls (fasīl, therefore = intervallum), 60 cubits wide, finally the first (i.e. outer) wall, which was the wall of the fasīl, and beyond was the ditch. The city had four gates ... each was composed of two gateways, one in front of the other, separated by a passage (dihlīz) and a door opening on to the fasīl between the two walls; the first gateway was that of the fasīl, the second that of the city. When one entered by the Khurāsān Gate, one first turned to the left in an oblong passage with a vault of brick, 20 cubits wide by 30 long, the entrance of which was in the width and the exit in the length, and passed out into a courtyard, 60 cubits long and 40 wide, leading to the second gateway. At the far end of this court was the second gateway which was that of the city. To right and left of this court were two doorways opening on to the two fasīls; that to the right opened on to the fasīl of the Damascus Gate,

1. al-Khaṭīb, pp. 8-9.   2. Archäologische Reise, II, pp. 108-9.

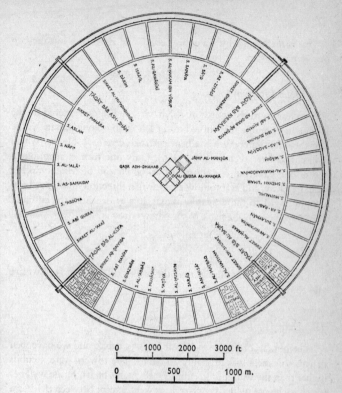

Figure 31. Baghdād: The Round City of al-Manṣūr, plan

that to the left opened on to the *fasīl* of the Basra Gate, which continued round to the Kūfa Gate. The four gates were constructed on the same model. ... The second gate, which was that of the city ... gave access to an oblong passage vaulted with bricks, 20 cubits long and 12 wide; it was the same with the other gates. Above the vaulted chamber of each gate was an audience-hall, with a staircase against the wall, by means of which one ascended to it. These halls of audience were each covered by a great dome 50 cubits high and gilt. Each dome was surmounted by a figure which turned in the wind.[1]

1. pp. 11–13.

The Moat

This is mentioned by Ya'qūbī, Tabarī, and al-Khatīb, but they do not give its width.

The Outer Gateways

It is clear from the words of al-Khatīb – 'when one entered by the Khurāsān Gate one first turned to the left in an oblong passage', etc., that the outer gateway was a bent entrance, a remarkable fact which is discussed later (below, pp. 174–9). Only one turn is mentioned, and as one passed into a courtyard at the far end of which was the main gateway, and as it follows that the first direction must have been at right angles to the direction of exit, it is evident that the entrance must have been in the flank of the gateway tower.

The Outer Wall

This was naturally thinner than the main wall, but that is all we are told about it.

The Main Wall

Its height, according to al-Khatīb, was 35 cubits, and we have seen that its thickness was probably 10 cubits. The towers were 5 cubits higher than the wall, i.e. 40 cubits (= 20·70 m.; 68 ft). In the wall between each gate were twenty-eight towers, except between the Basra Gate and the Kūfa Gate, where there was a tower extra.

The Main Gateway

We have seen that the passage through the main gateway was 20 cubits long by 12 wide; to this must be added 5 cubits for each end wall, for they were meant to withstand assault and to carry a domed upper storey; this gives a total depth of 30 cubits for the gateway tower. Herzfeld [1] assumes its width to have been the same as the court in front of it, i.e. 40 cubits. From the ground to the top of the

1. *Op. cit.*, II, 125.

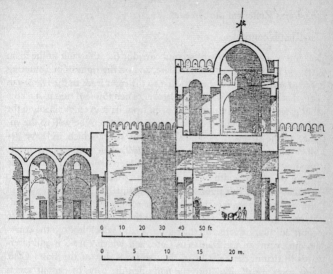

Figure 32. Baghdād: section of one of the four main gateways

dome measured 50 cubits. On the analogy of the central portion of the Palace of al-Manṣūr, which consisted of two superimposed domed chambers, each 20 cubits square and of equal height, totalling 80 cubits, let us assume that the vaulted hall and the domed chamber were each of equal height, also that the apex of the dome was 1 cubit thick and the vault 2 cubits. Then we have: apex of vault 23 cubits, floor level above 25 cubits, interior of dome 49 cubits, exterior 50. The domed chambers referred to in the Palace had a side measurement equal to half their height; taking this proportion we get 12 cubits for a side of our domed chamber, exactly the width of the passage below, a remarkable confirmation. In the Palace the vertical walls were half the total height, therefore the dome itself and the zone of transition must have made up the rest, that is to say, the walls of the domed chamber were 12 cubits in height and the zone of transition and the dome together 12 cubits, as shown (Figure 32).

The Inner Zone and the Arcades

al-Khaṭīb continues:

One enters afterwards by the second corridor (i.e. the vault of the main gateway) into a court 20 cubits square, and on the right of one entering is a road and another on the left; that to the right leads to the Damascus Gate, that to the left to the Basra Gate. ... Then this *fasīl* runs past all the other gates; the gates of the streets open from it; it extends all round the enclosure wall. The width of each of the *fasīls* from the wall to the entrance of the streets is 25 cubits. From the court which we have described one enters towards the arcades (*ṭāqāt*) which are 53 in number, excluding that of the entrance of this court. Here is placed a great double door of teak. The width of the arcades is 15 cubits and the length 200 [we shall see that this figure is much too small]. ... On both sides of these arcades, between each of them, are rooms reserved for the guard; it is the same for the other gates. ... After these vaults one passes out into a court 20 cubits square. On the right is a road which leads to the corresponding court of the Damascus Gate, and which curves round afterwards to that of the Kūfa Gate, then towards that of the Basra Gate. These gates are all alike. Into the *fasīl* open the gates of certain streets and in front of one is the Little Arcade ... by which one passes into the circular area in which are the palace and the mosque.[1]

The Residential Area

There was therefore a residential zone between the main wall and the central palace area. This zone was divided into four equal quadrants by the vaulted arcades which ran from the main gates to the gates of the palace area; it was bounded externally and internally by the ring streets, 25 cubits wide, from which opened the gates of the streets of the quarters. The latter, which ran like the spokes of a wheel, had a strong gate at each end. Yaʿqūbī actually gives the names of all these streets (see Figure 31), of which there were from eight to twelve in each quadrant.[2] He expressly says that none of these streets was connected with the central area, 'for the road runs all round the wall of the *Rahaba*', by which he means the Palace Enclosure.

1. pp. 14–15.
2. *Geography*, pp. 240–41.

The Great Arcades

Now let us attempt a reconstruction. In the first place we must imagine a long gallery, 15 cubits wide, spanned by fifty-three transverse arches. We have seen that to right and left were side rooms for the guard. There were therefore fifty-four rooms a side, for the fifty-three arches must have been independent of the end walls. Now, al-Khatīb says that there was a guard of 1,000 men at each gate.[1] For these and their officers we therefore have 108 rooms, say 100 for the men at ten per room, and eight for their officers. If we assume a width of 10 cubits and a depth of 15 for each room, with partition walls of 2 cubits and end walls of 5, then 54 × 10 = 540, 53 × 2 = 106, 2 × 5 = 10, total 656 cubits, or 340 m. If we assume that the rooms were only 8 × 12, we get 54 × 8, plus 53 × 2, plus 5 × 2 = 548 cubits, or 284 m. Herzfeld adopts this figure, and I follow suit (Figure 33). If we add 25 × 2 cubits for the two ring streets we get 598 cubits as the depth of this zone.

It is obvious that the spacing of the arches must have corresponded with the partition walls, for the sake of abutment, i.e. 8 cubits apart. But Ya'qūbī speaks of Byzantine windows (kiwā' rūmīya) in the vault, which admitted light but not rain.[2] Where were these windows placed? They must have been in the side walls above the level of the crown of the vaults of the rooms. Ya'qūbī[3] and Ibn Rusta[4] expressly say that these arcades were vaulted with burnt brick. If we assume that a tunnel-vault rested on the side walls its springing must have been very high, in order to clear the windows, and that would at once involve abutment difficulties, to say nothing of the difficulty of finding an analogy for such construction in our present field of study. There can be no doubt that such a series of transverse arches can only have served to support a series of transverse vaults (Figures 32–3), exactly as in Tāq Īwān, Qasr Kharāna, Qusayr 'Amra, Hammām as-Sarakh, the Mosque at Qusayr al-Hallābāt, Ukhaidir, and, several centuries later, in the famous Khān Ortma of 760 H. (1359) at Baghdād.

The Little Arcades

Ya'qūbī says: 'When one comes out from the Arcades one comes into a court, then to a long passage consisting of a vault of brick,

1. p. 17. 2. p. 239, ll. 16–17. 3. p. 239, l. 16. 4. p. 108, l. 20.

which had iron doors, whence one went out into the Great Rahaba' [1] (i.e. the central area). He does not give any measurements, but Herzfeld [2] suggests 10 cubits wide and 15 long. This would make it project beyond the inner ring wall. To avoid this he restores the Little Arcades as a free-standing vaulted arcade, but his restoration does not provide abutment for the thrust of the transverse arches.

On the analogy of the Court of Honour at Ukhaidir (below, pp. 196–7) and the walls of the *Ziyādas* of the Great Mosque at Sāmarrā, I prefer to restore them as a blind arcade on half-round piers as shown, the four entrances being flanked by quarter-round piers of the same projection as the half-round ones. This involves a slight reduction of the dimensions of the passage to 8 cubits wide and 10 long, as shown (Figure 33).

The Central Area

In the Central Area was the Palace (below, p. 179) and the Mosque (below, pp. 179–82). In addition there were seven *Dīwāns* (Government Departments), residences for the younger sons of al-Mansūr, and a kitchen. [3]

ARCHITECTURAL ORIGINS

The Circular Plan

The 'Round City' of al-Mansūr may fairly be considered as one of the most remarkable examples of town-planning that have come down to us. The Muslim historians insist that the circular form of the city was a feature that had never been known before, but such is far from being the case.

It appears probable that the earliest circular enclosures were the Assyrian military camps. Some it is true, were oval, but one at least, shown on a slab found by Layard at Nineveh, is a true circle, with cross-roads from north to south and east to west. But at least twelve circular cities, dating from before Islam, are known:

1. *Geography*, pp. 239–40.
2. *Op. cit.*, II, p. 129.
3. Ya'qūbī, *Geography*, p. 240.

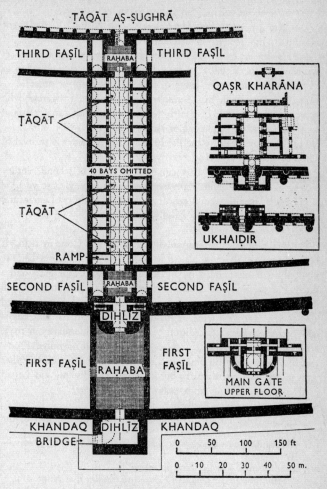

Figure 33. Baghdād: the *Tāqāt*

(1) *Sinjerli*, a Hittite city with a double wall forming an almost exact circle about 700 m. (770 yd.) in diameter.

(2) *Abra* (about 60 km. (37 miles) east of Nisibis). Circular enclosure 450 m. (490 yd.) in diameter.[1]

(3) *Hagmatana*, known to the Greeks as Agbatana, built by Deioces the Mede in the first half of the seventh century B.C. According to Herodotus[2] it had walls 'rising in circles one within the other'.

(4) *Mantineia*, built by Epaminondas in 371 B.C. Fougères,[3] who surveyed it, found it to be a fairly regular ellipse with a major axis of 1,340 m. (1,470 yd.) and a minor axis of 1,080 (1,180 yd.).

(5) *Ctesiphon*, built by the Parthians. Reuther makes it an oval of 3,300 by 2,800 m. (3,610 by 3,060 yd.).[4]

(6) *Takht-i-Sulaymān*, Parthian, probably end of second century B.C. Oval enclosure about 1,250 by 1,050 m. (1,370 by 1,150 yd.).[5]

(7) *Hatra*, first to second century A.D. A roughly oval enclosure, 1,700 by 2,000 m. (1,860 by 2,190 yd.).

(8) *Harrān*, likewise oval.

(9) *Dārābjerd* was first examined by Flandin and Coste in 1840.[6] It bears a remarkable resemblance to al-Mansūr's foundation because not only is it surrounded by a circular wall with four gates and a ditch, but there was an inner circular area with a concentric wall 675 m. (740 yd.) in diameter. Between the two was a ring-shaped area 262 m. (286 yd.) wide, exactly like the residential area at Baghdād. Sir Aurel Stein's expedition made a plane-table survey in 1933, according to which the area enclosed by the wall measured almost exactly 1 mile and 1 furlong, say 1,810 m.[7] The four gates, or rather gaps in the wall, were nearly but not quite equidistant, and a road could be traced leading from each towards the centre.

(10) *Hiraqla*, perhaps Parthian.

(11) *Gūr* (later Fīrūzābād) built by Ardashīr, the founder of the

1. Poidebard, *Mission archéologique en Haute Djézire*, in *Syria*, XI, p. 40.

2. Bk I, cap. 98.

3. *Bull. de corresp. héllenique*, XIV, pp. 65–79.

4. *Die Ausgrabungen der Deutschen Ktesiphon-Expedition 1928–29*, pp. 6–9.

5. Pope, in *Bull. of the Amer. Inst. for Persian Art*, V, p. 76; and E. F. Schmidt, *Flights over Ancient Cities of Iran*, Plates 87–9.

6. *Voyage en Perse: Perse ancienne, Texte*, pp. 31–3; *Planches*, I, pl. 31–2.

7. An 'Archaeological Tour in Ancient Persis', in *Iraq*, III, pp. 191–3 and plan 10.

Sasanian dynasty in A.D. 224, was circular 'even as though drawn with a compass', as Ibn al-Balkhī expresses it,[1] and, what is most interesting for our purpose is Ibn al-Faqīh's statement that it was built after the pattern of Dārābjerd;[2] like Dārābjerd it had four gates.[3] It was surveyed by Sir Aurel Stein's expedition, according to which it had an inner and outer wall, its overall diameter, scaled of his plan, being 2,240 m. (2,450 yd.).[4] Erich Schmidt's air photograph shows its form to be a remarkably accurate circle.[5]

(12) *Isfahān*. Ibn Rusta says that Isfahān was 'evenly round' and 6,000 cubits (say 3,000 m.; 3,270 yd.) in diameter.[6]

We are therefore justified in saying that circular cities had been known for fifteen centuries before the foundation of Baghdād, and concentric circular cities for several centuries before, in the region between Eastern Asia Minor and South-Western Persia, and that it was probably the remarkable plan of Dārābjerd that directly inspired the 'Round City' of al-Mansūr.

But apart from any military advantages, such as the avoidance of dead angles, there is another practical consideration which may have led to the adoption of the circular plan, viz. economy of walling, for if a given area has to be enclosed, the shape with the shortest boundary is the circle, the economy being roughly 11·38 per cent, which would represent a very considerable sum in the construction of the walls of a city.

Another Muslim example may be cited, for Muqaddasī says that Sabra (close to Qairawān), built by Ismā'īl, the third Fātimid Khalif, in 337 H. (948–9), was 'circular like a drinking glass' with 'the palace of the Sultan in the centre as at Madīnat as-Salām' (i.e. Baghdād).[7]

Reeds Used as a Bond

This is an ancient Babylonian practice. At Aqarqūf, attributed to the Kassite dynasty (thirteenth century, B.C.), Peters says that between every seven courses of bricks is a layer of palm matting.[8] Herodotus says that at Babylon they used hot bitumen for their cement, with a layer of plaited reeds at every thirteenth course.[9] Koldewey found

---

1. pp. 160–61.   2. p. 198.   3. Istakhrī, p. 124.
4. *Loc. cit.*, III, p. 117 and Plan I.
5. *Op cit.*, pp. 20–21 and pl. 18.
6. pp. 160–61.
7. p. 226, ll. 2–6.
8. *Nippur*, p. 188.
9. Bk. I, cap. 179.

that such layers occurred in the Qasr at a maximum distance of thirteen courses and a minimum of five.[1] The same practice was followed at Assur in all periods, the reeds being laid criss-cross.[2] In Sasanian times the same thing is found at Dawālīb, where a layer of reeds occurs between every course.[3]

The Bent Entrance

This presents a curious problem, for although it was known in Ancient Egypt, it apparently does not occur again anywhere until the eighth century A.D. The two Egyptian examples are at Kōm al-Ahmar and Shūnet az-Zebīb. The former is a mud-brick fortress on the Nile about 4 miles from al-Kāb. The walls are still about 9 m. (30 ft) high, and form a rectangular enclosure measuring about 75 by 66 m. (250 by 220 ft), surrounded by a thinner outer wall. The entrance consists of two gateways on opposite sides of a court about 5 by 4 m. (16¼ by 13 ft), but they are not quite on the same axis.[4] The outer wall is so ruined that it is not possible to say where the corresponding gateway was.

At Shūnet az-Zebīb, near Abydos, the arrangement is more advanced. Like Kōm al-Ahmar, it consists of a rectangular enclosure measuring 131 by 78 m. (430 by 255 ft), the walls being 11 m. (36 ft) high and 6 m. (19¾ ft) thick at the base. At a distance of about 3 m. (10 ft) all round is an outer and lower wall, at present about 6 m. (20 ft) high. There are four entrances, two straight through and two bent. The best designed is at the north corner. The gateway in the outer wall is placed opposite the gateway in the inner wall. The latter opens at the back of a recess 8 m. wide and 3.50 m. deep (26¼ by 11½ ft), and leads into a small court 3.40 m. (11¼ ft) wide, a veritable pit, in fact; the exit from it is at right angles to the entrance.[5] These two forts are generally regarded as dating from the sixth to twelfth Dynasties.

But now comes a gap of at least 2,500 years, which is remarkable, as there is no lack of gateways. We have the city gateway at Atchana,

1. *Das wieder erstehende Babylon*, p. 31.
2. Andrae, *Die Festungswerke von Assur*, p. 15.
3. Herzfeld, *op. cit.*, II, p. 90.
4. Quibell, *Hierakonpolis*, II, pp. 19–20 and pl. LXXIV.
5. Ayrton, *Abydos*, II, pp. 46–9 and pl. 69.

excavated by Woolley and placed by him in the thirteenth century B.C.; the Hittite city of Boghaz-Keui, where all four gateways provide a straight passage through the double walls. At Sinjerli we have an outer gateway flanked by square towers, a courtyard, and a second gateway on the same axis, a forerunner, therefore, of the Roman *propugnaculum*. The same with the three gates of Shalmaneser III (858–824 B.C.) at Assur, and in the seven gates of Khorsābād, built by Sargon (722–705 B.C.). At Babylon the famous Ishtar Gate of Nebuchadnezzar (604–561 B.C.) follows the same pattern.

Neither did the Romans know the bent entrance. All the forts of the Roman *limes* in Transjordan have simple straight-through entrances, likewise the north gate of Baalbek and the Roman gateway of Qasr ash-Sham' at Old Cairo. It was the same also in Roman Africa, where all the gateways of the Roman period are straight-through entrances. Even at Rome itself, all the gates of the city wall (Nomentana, Latina, Appia, Asinaria, Pinciana, Tiburtina, etc.) built by Aurelian, A.D. 271–5, are of this type. [1]

The first step forward was to arrange things so that the assailants, after passing through the outer wall, had to turn to the left and walk along the *intervallum* towards the main gate, which, instead of being on the same axis at the outer gate, was a little distance from it. This would compel them to present their right sides, i.e. the side not protected by a shield, to fire from the top of the wall. It recalls the passage in Vitruvius: 'The roads should be planned so as to approach the gates, not in a straight line, but from right to left, for as a result of this, the right-hand side of the assailants, unprotected by their shields, will be next the wall.' [2] This system may be called 'the oblique approach'; we will meet it at Raqqa (below, p. 186).

When did the bent entrance first appear? Diehl,[3] Monneret,[4] and Deschamps,[5] say that it occurs in certain fortresses of the period of Justinian in North Africa. It is not going too far to say that *no example* of such an entrance is to be found *in any work that is certainly of Justinian's reign, or before it, either in North Africa or anywhere else in the Byzantine Empire.*

1. Richmond (I. A.), *The City Wall of Imperial Rome*, Oxford, 1930.
2. Bk. I, cap. 5.   3. *L'Afrique byzantine*, p. 160.
4. *Il Monastero di S. Simeone presso Aswân*, I, p. 20.
5. 'Les Entrées des châteaux des croisés en Syrie', in *Syria*, XIII, pp. 372–3.

Let us begin on the eastern frontier. On the Euphrates, about 50 miles south-east of Raqqa, is Halabīya, the ancient Zenobia, whose walls were rebuilt by Justinian. There are two straight-through entrances flanked by square towers. On the opposite bank is Zalubīya, which has one straight-through entrance only.[1] About 30 miles south-west of Raqqa is Rusāfa, also built by Justinian. It has four gates, one of which is single, the other three consisting of two gates on the same axis, with a small court between.[2] At Palmyra all the gates of the enclosure of Justinian shown on Gabriel's plan [3] are simple, straight-through entrances. The same remark applies to Antioch. At Ancyra (Angora) all the gates except one, which is of the ninth century, are of the usual type; according to Jerphanion they date from about A.D. 630. To these may be added the Constantinople Gate and the Lefka Gate, at Nicaea. Even at Constantinople, the capital of the Empire, we have no example of a bent entrance, either in the work of Theodosius II (413 and 447), or Heraclius (627), or later.

We have seen that all the gateways of existing Roman enclosures in North Africa are the ordinary type; if we take those known to date from the time of Justinian, the same remark holds good, e.g. Madauri and Tebessa, both built by his general Solomon.[4]

In addition to this there are several enclosures which, although not exactly dated, are known to have been built by Justinian, viz. Ammaedara, Laribus, Milevum, Tigisis, Timgad, and Lemsa. To these may be added two of uncertain date: Tifech and Tobna. All these, without exception, have straight-through entrances.

The four alleged examples of a bent entrance are Gigthis, Thelepta, Thignica ('Ain Tunga), and Bellezma. Gigthis may be eliminated at once, for Constans says that the entrance is 'précédée d'un palier carré surélevé auquel on accédait non point de face, mais par le côté gauche'.[5] It therefore belongs to the 'oblique approach' class.

Diehl gives a plan of Thelepta showing a rectangular enclosure flanked by twelve towers with only one entrance, a bent one, in the central tower of the west side. He says:

1. For Halabīya and Zalubīya, see Herzfeld, *Archäologische Reise*, II, pp. 367–9 and 374–81.

2. Spanner and Guyer, *Rusafa*, pp. 18–22.

3. In *Syria*, VII, pl. XI–XII.

4. Gsell, *Monuments antiques de l'Algérie*, II, pp. 378–82 and 356–7.

5. In the *Nouvelles Archives des Missions Scientifiques*, n. s. Fasc. XIV, p. 98.

Unfortunately the fortress of Thelepta is one of the worst preserved of those that have come down to us from the Byzantine period. Its fallen walls can no longer be distinguished except as confused piles of stones; its towers can be recognized with difficulty by slightly higher mounds. However, important excavations, carried out in 1885 under the direction of Commandant Pédoya, have laid bare a part of the ramparts.[1]

Pédoya, therefore, is our basic authority. He says:

The walls are completely overthrown. ... Excavations, very difficult because of the enormous clearance which had to precede them, permitted us to reach the foundations and to trace the perimeter of the fortifications with sufficient exactitude, as well as a great part of the detail of the towers and bastions.[2]

And what did he find? *Six* gateways, two in the east, south, and west sides, as well as a small postern, all of the straight-through type. As for Diehl's alleged bent entrance, Pédoya shows it as a hollow square tower with a small door leading from the town into its interior! I therefore decline to accept the alleged bent entrance at Thelepta, for Diehl, who did not stop there long enough to make excavations, appears to have modified Pédoya's plan without secure grounds for doing so.

'Ain Tunga (Thignica), however, is certainly a good example of what we are seeking, the entrance being in the flank of a tower and wide enough to serve as the main entrance.[3] But Saladin calls attention to the setting of the masonry round the entrance and exit arch, and points out that both door-frames and arches have been taken, stone by stone, from some ruined Roman monument and re-erected here, and that there is no proper fitting of the masonry round the stepped extrados of the two arches. What are we to think? The masonry of the rest of the enclosure and towers does not show such gross incompetence. Is it not possible that these two archways are a subsequent insertion, and that the original entrance was somewhere else? So convinced was I that this must be the case that I decided to visit 'Ain Tunga when I was in Tunisia in 1934. I examined the bent entrance and noticed the bad jointing and packing round the extrados, and I observed at the same time that the masonry was perfectly fitted round

1. *Rapport*, in the *Nouvelles Archives des Missions Scientifiques*, IV, pp. 337–43.
2. 'Notice sur les ruines ... de Thélepte', *Bull. Archéologique*, 1885, pp. 133–6.
3. Saladin, 'Rapport', in the *Nouvelles Archives des M.S.*, II, pp. 542–7.

the stepped extrados of an arched doorway leading into the south-east corner tower. I then proceeded to walk round the enclosure. When I arrived on the west side I saw, in the centre of the curtain wall, the very thing the existence of which I had predicted, but scarcely expected to find visible above ground – viz. the top of an arch with enormous voussoirs about a metre (3¼ ft) deep, which can only be the top of the original straight-through entrance to the fortress, standing as it does on the road from Carthage to the interior.

This leaves Bellezma only, a rectangular fortress measuring 125 by 112 m. (410 by 370 ft), flanked by eight rectangular towers. According to Diehl, the only entrance is in the central tower on the west side; he shows it as a bent entrance, with entrance and exit only 1·25 m. (4 ft) wide.[1] Is it possible that the only entrance to an enclosure of this size was a little postern, too narrow even for a loaded donkey to pass? So convinced was I that this cannot have been the main gate that when I met Monsieur Leschi of the Service of Antiquités in 1937, I mentioned my doubts to him, saying that I was convinced that the original entrance, when found, would prove to be of the normal Roman *propugnaculum* type, and I expressed the hope that excavations might be conducted to settle the question. He replied that this had already been done by his predecessor, M. Albertini. The north gate, which formed a rectangular salient, had been laid bare, and was found to consist of two gateways on the same axis, with a court 6·35 by 6·10 m. (20¾ by 20 ft) between. Above the inner gateway was a lintel with a much-damaged inscription in the name of Solomon, Justinian's Prefect of Africa.[2] In other words, it was exactly the type of gateway I had predicted. As for Diehl's west gate, it was covered by earth and nothing was to be seen (if indeed it ever existed).

So we need have no hesitation in saying that *there is no known Roman or Byzantine bent entrance in North Africa or Syria*, and that the four entrances of al-Mansūr's city are the earliest examples of a bent entrance after Shūnet az-Zebīb.

The next example of a bent entrance would appear to be the south gate of the Citadel of Ancyra (Angora). On the south side is a gate in the flank of a great salient, leading into a court measuring about 17 by 11 m. (56 by 36 ft), from which a gate about 3 m. (10 ft) wide,

1. 'Rapport', *loc. cit.*, IV, pp. 303–6 and plans iv–v.
2. *Bull. de la Soc. Nat. des Antiquaires de France*, 1934, p. 136.

at right angles to the first, gives access to the Citadel.[1] There are two inscriptions in the name of the Emperor Michael; Grégoire has shown conclusively that the Emperor in question must be Michael III (847–67), and he has succeeded in deciphering the date at the end of the second as the Year of the World 636, 7th Indiction = 10 June 859.[2]

This is the first example known to me of a Byzantine bent entrance; so we most certainly *cannot* say, with Deschamps, that it was 'un procédé emprunté à la construction militaire byzantine qui en présente de nombreux exemples'.[3]

The Palace of al-Mansūr at Baghdād

al-Mansūr's palace was known as the Palace of the Golden Gate. It was a square of 400 cubits a side, and lay in the middle of the 'Round City'. There was an *īwān*, that is to say a tunnel-vaulted hall open at one end, measuring 30 cubits deep and 20 cubits wide, with a room at the back, 20 cubits square and 20 cubits high, covered by a dome. Above this was a second room, of the same area and height, also covered by a dome. This was the celebrated Green Dome, on account of which the palace was also known as al-Qubbat al-Khadrā. The total height was 80 cubits.[4]

THE GREAT MOSQUE OF AL-MANSŪR

The only description of this mosque that we possess is that given by al-Khatīb. It runs as follows:

> Abū Ja'far al-Mansūr had established the principal mosque ... in contact with his palace – it is [what is now known as] the Old Court – he built it with sun-dried bricks and clay: its dimensions were as follows: the dimensions of the palace of al-Mansūr were 400 by 400 cubits and those of the mosque 200 by 200; and the columns of wood of the mosque each consisted of two pieces. ... Ibn 'Arabī says: the qibla needed turning slightly towards the Basra Gate. The great mosque

---

1. Jerphanion, in *Mélanges de l'Université Saint Joseph*, XIII, pp. 175–9, 208–12, and 300–301.

2. 'Inscriptions historiques byzantines', in *Byzantion*, IV, p. 445.

3. 'Les Entrées des châteaux des croisés', in *Syria*, XIII, p. 372.

4. al-Khatīb, p. 10.

remained in the same state until the time of Hārūn ar-Rashīd. Hārūn ordered its demolition and reconstruction with kiln-baked bricks and gypsum. This was done and they inscribed the name of Hārūn ar-Rashīd on it, mentioning ... the name of the architect, of the carpenter, and the date; this inscription is to be seen to this day, on the outside wall of the mosque on the side next to the Khurāsān Gate. [Here follows another account.] The mosque of Abū Ja'far al-Mansūr was demolished, enlarged, and solidly rebuilt; the work, commenced in [1]92, was finished in [1]93 (= 808-9). The Friday prayer was celebrated in the Sahn al-'atīq (the old court), which had been the mosque before it had been enlarged by taking in the Dār al-Qattān which had been a Government Office of al-Mansūr. This became the praying place for the people and that in the year 260 (873-4) or 261 (874-5). al-Mutadid billāh afterwards added the first court, which was [part of] the Palace of al-Mansūr; he joined it to the mosque by opening 17 arches in the partition wall between the Palace and the Old Mosque, of which 13 opened into the *sahn* and 4 into the side arcades. He transported the pulpit, the mihrāb and the *maqsūra* into the new mosque. [Another account.] – al-Mutadid billāh was informed that there was not sufficient room ... and that this want of room compelled people to pray in places where prayer was not permissible (i.e. the Dār al-Qattān). He then ordered its enlargement at the expense of the Palace of the Commander of the Faithful. A mosque was built there after the pattern of the first one, of the same size or nearly so. Then the *sadr* [i.e. the qibla wall] of the old mosque was opened and joined to it, and the people found ample room there. The completion ... took place in 280 H. (893-4).[1]

Reconstruction

Herzfeld remarks [2] that the statement that seventeen arches were made in the partition wall, of which thirteen opened into the court and four into the side aisles, shows that the old mosque must have had seventeen aisles from left to right and that the side aisles must have been two deep. As for the aisles of the sanctuary, he suggests five on the analogy of the Mosque of Ibn Tūlūn. That is as far as I follow him. I must emphasize that al-Khatīb merely says the mosque was built in contact with the palace, without specifying on which side. We are therefore free to choose so let us place it, not as Herzfeld does on the south-west side of the Palace, but where one would expect it to be,

1. pp. 59-61.   2. *Archäologische Reise*, II, p. 137.

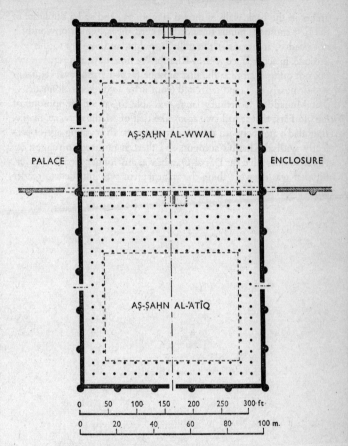

Figure 34. Baghdād: The Great Mosque, plan

viz. on the north-east side, with its *qibla* wall in contact with the Palace, so as to enable the Khalif to pass from the latter directly into the *maqsūra* through a door in the *qibla* wall, as was the practice in the first few centuries of Islam, and see how this fits the facts. Now for the part added, which was (1) built against the *sadr*, i.e. part farthest from the entrance, and (2) built on part of the ruined Palace area. Let us cut arches in the back wall, as shown (Figure 34) and add a duplicate of the first mosque, minus the north-eastern *riwāq*, which obviously is not needed, and transfer the mihrāb, pulpit, and *maqsūra* to the new mosque, in accordance with al-Khatīb. We now have a mosque nearly but not quite as large as the first mosque (as al-Khatīb says: 'equal in size or nearly so'), and separated from it by a covered colonnade, so that Muqaddasī, a century later, was able to say of the mosque of Fasā in Fārs, that it had two *sahns* like that of Madīnat as-Salām (i.e. Baghdād), and between them a covered part. Everything agrees perfectly with al-Khatīb's account, and there is no need to suggest (as Herzfeld does) that the Dār al-Qattān was any longer used for prayer, for that was the very thing the enlargement was intended to render unnecessary.

CHAPTER 9

RAQQA

The Walls

Tabarī says that Raqqa was built after the pattern of Baghdād in respect of its gates, *fasīl* (or *intervallum*), *rahabas*, and streets,[1] nevertheless the town is not really round, for the south side is straight and the rest of the wall forms a slightly pointed and distorted horse-shoe (Figure 35). At present it is about a kilometre from the Euphrates, which presumably once washed its south side. It measures about 1,500 m. (1,640 yd.) from east to west and the same from north to south.

The walls were double as at Baghdād; remains of the inner wall have been well preserved on the west and north, less well on the east, and for a few hundred metres only on the south side at the east end. This wall, which in some parts towards the north-west is still about 10 m. (33 ft) high, is flanked by small round towers at distances of about 35 m. (115 ft).

At the south-east corner is the remains of a great round tower with a radius of about 7·80 m. (25½ ft); it appears to have been solid. It was 7–8 m. (23–26 ft) high when I first saw it; it consists of a core of mud bricks with an outer coating of kiln-burnt bricks nearly 2·30 m. (7½ ft) thick below, tapering to about 1 m. (3¼ ft) above. The burnt bricks are 24–26 cm. (9½–10¼ in.) square and 7 cm. (2¾ in.) thick, the mud bricks 42 cm. (16½ in.) square and 11–12 cm. (4⅓–4¾ in.) thick.

Thanks to trenches, very kindly made by M. Schlumberger of the Department of Antiquities at my request in July 1933, it was found that the exact thickness of the main wall was 5·85 m. (19¼ ft), the *fasīl* was 20.80 m. (68 ft) and the thickness of the outer wall about 4·50 (14¾ ft). As for the ditch it was 15·90 m. (52 ft) wide at the top, diminishing to about 9·50 m. (31¼ ft) at the bottom. The walls rest directly on the rocky soil, and the two lowest courses of the main wall consist of a white chalky stone like gypsum,[2] each course being 65 cm.

1. III, p. 276, ll. 14–15, and p. 373, l. 14.
2. We are at once reminded of the instructions given by Philo of Byzance to build the walls of fortifications on foundations of gypsum.

(25½ in.) high. The wall, which is of mud brick, does not appear to have been faced with burnt brick, like the towers, which had a casing of burnt brick 55 cm. (21½ in.) thick = 2½ bricks.

The Baghdād Gate

Although nearly three-quarters of it have disappeared, enough still remains to enable us to form a pretty clear idea of its original form (Plates 32, 33). Assuming that the façade was symmetrical, it must have been an oblong rectangular tower of 18·07 by 14·50 m. (59½ by 47½ ft; = 35 by 28 black cubits of 51·8 cm.), with a fine arched entrance 3·19 m. (10½ ft) wide in the centre of the east façade; its present height is about 11·30 m. (37 ft). On either side of the entrance was a shallow niche. Within was an oblong arched chamber, about 12 m. (39½ ft) in length, of which the two ends were tunnel-vaulted and the central part cross-vaulted. Unlike the great tower behind it, it is built throughout of burnt brick, and horizontal grooves on the inner face show that timber was let in as a bond.

The splendid arch is built of two rings of square bricks, each ring being two bricks thick, so that the total depth is about a metre. It is our first example of a pointed arch outside Syria, but it is not the two-centred type to which we have been accustomed; it is a new type struck from four centres. In view of the many wild statements that have been made, such as: 'From Persia the pointed arch spread through Mesopotamia to the Mediterranean',[1] and 'by the ninth century it appears in practically every building (in Mesopotamia and Persia),[2] it should be especially noted (1) that Raqqa, where this new type of arch, so frequently regarded as Persian, first appears is separated from Syria only by the width of the Euphrates, and that it is only a little over 100 miles from Aleppo, whereas it is over 350 miles from the nearest point on the Persian border, and (2) that in the Tārīk Khāna at Dāmghān, the only contemporary, or nearly contemporary monument in Persia, the arches are closely related to the old elliptical Sasanian form, except that they exhibit a slight tendency to a point.

1. A. U. Pope, in *Country Life*, 3 January 1931.
2. Talbot Rice, in *The Architectural Review*, July 1935, p. 16. What does the expression 'practically every building' really amount to? There is *not a single building* standing on Persian soil which dates from the ninth century.

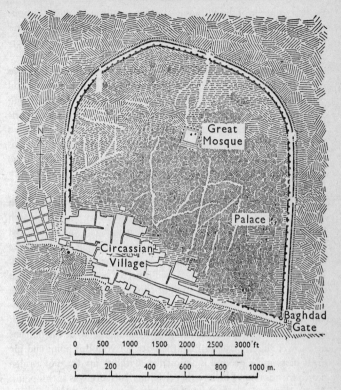

Figure 35. Raqqa: plan of the city of al-Manṣūr

In other words, the evolution that had already begun in Syria in the second half of the sixth century had scarcely begun in Persia at the end of the eighth.

The Ornamental Brickwork

The arched hood of the niche to the left of the archway is decorated with a geometrical design consisting of four swastikas and five squares. The design is executed entirely in the brickwork, the elements of the pattern and the background all being one brick broad. This is the first example of this technique, known locally as *hazārbāf* (=thousand twistings), which was destined to be elaborately developed later on in Persia. The pattern is raised slightly, and the hollows are decorated with rows of rhomboids in stucco.

The façade for the purpose of decoration has been divided into two parts, the lower containing the great archway and the two blind panels, the upper, which is about 4·40 m. (14½ ft) in height, being decorated with a series of three-lobed niches with very stilted keel-arched frames resting on engaged colonnettes. Eight of these niches have been preserved; as the axis of the sixth corresponds with the axis of the gateway, I conclude that there were eleven originally. In the treatment of the hoods the craftsman has given free play to his fancy (Plate 32).

It is clear from an examination of the site, and still clearer from air photographs very kindly made at my request by the French 39th Regiment of Aviation, 7th Squadron, that this gateway is only the gateway of the outer wall. As the long ridge marking the line of the eastern wall runs directly on to the side of the tower at the point where the exit would have been, had it been a bent entrance, it must therefore have been of the straight-through type. Where was the gateway of the inner wall? The south wall is still preserved for a considerable height to the west of the great round bastion (Plate 33), but before reaching it, it suddenly stops at what appears to be the remains of a tower slightly stouter than the rest; between this point and the great bastion the ground is almost flat, without any trace of a ridge worth mentioning. I believe that the inner entrance was at this point. An attacking party, which had forced the outer gate, would then have to pass close under the great bastion, with their right sides exposed to the fire from the parapet, before being able to reach the inner gate which is commanded by it. In other words, we have here the 'oblique approach' arrangement. The bent-entrance system had not yet taken root.

The Date

Herzfeld [1] attributes this gate to Hārūn ar-Rashīd, who is known to have taken up his residence at Raqqa in 180 H. (796). Both the inner

1. *Archäologische Reise*, II, p. 359.

and outer enclosures admittedly belong to al-Manṣūr, and there must always have been a gate at this point for the ancient road along the Euphrates. It seems unlikely that a gate built in A.D. 772 would need rebuilding twenty-four years later and, failing further evidence, I attribute it with the rest of the enclosure to al-Manṣūr.

THE GREAT MOSQUE

The Great Mosque, which stands in the northern half of the enclosure, consists of a rectangle measuring internally about 92·90 m. (305 ft) in width and 108·10 (350 ft) in depth – proportions therefore almost exactly 6 : 7 – surrounded by the remains of mud-brick walls strengthened by half-round towers. The bricks are 45 cm. (17¾ in.) square and 10 cm. (4 in.) thick. In spite of the gaps in the walls and their terribly ruined state, it is still easy to see that there was a tower at each corner, and four intermediate towers on each side, i.e. twenty in all. The thickness of the walls must have been about 1·70 m. (5½ ft) (Figure 36).

The only things standing within the enclosure are a minaret, probably twelfth century, a mean mausoleum, and a row of eleven arches which formed the façade of the sanctuary. This arcade, which gives us a fixed point for the reconstruction of the interior, is constructed of burnt bricks. Its total height is about 10·50 m. (34½ ft), but it must originally have been about 13 m. (42¾ ft). The rear façade is smooth and plain, but the front is quite otherwise; not only is each arch set in a shallow recessed bay, but the corners of the piers are decorated with slender engaged shafts of brick with capitals executed in stucco, and at the base of each pier is a small shallow mihrāb.

The stucco capitals of the engaged shafts are distinctly related to the 'lyre-capitals' of the Mosque of Nūr ad-Dīn at Mosul. This is not surprising, for above the central arch of the façade is an inscription saying that Nūr ad-Dīn restored this mosque; it continues: 'And by that is meant eleven arches and the piers belonging to them, and the gable roof, in the year 561 H. (1165-6).' [1] Nūr ad-Dīn's work, therefore, was merely the restoration of an earlier building, and was expressly confined to the eleven arches still standing and the gable roof.

1. Van Berchem, in Sarre and Herzfeld, *Archäologische Reise*, I, pp. 3–6.

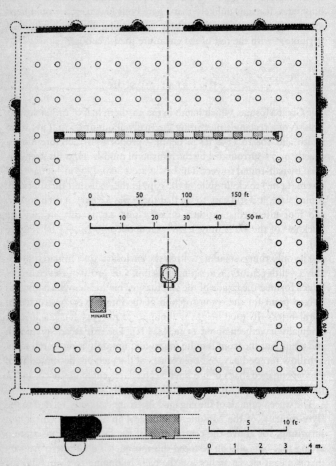

Figure 36. Raqqa: Great Mosque, plan

MINARET

The end piers, however, as Herzfeld has pointed out,[1] differ considerably from the rest, not merely because they are the corner piers of the *sahn*, but because they lack the slender corner shafts, and because the side from which the arch springs is treated as a massive half-round pier, 1·73 m. (5¾ ft) in diameter. In addition to this, the remains of an acanthus cornice in stucco has been preserved on the north side of the east pier; it is still quite Classical in style, so it cannot possibly have been executed under Nūr ad-Dīn. He therefore believes that the end piers belong to the older structure which Nūr ad-Dīn restored. To this argument one might add that Nūr ad-Dīn's inscription only implies the reconstruction of ten piers, for had he rebuilt the end piers, he would have been compelled to reconstruct the arch taking off from each of them towards the north, that is to say thirteen arches instead of eleven. We may therefore regard it as certain that the end piers belong to the earlier structure – in other words, to the original mosque dating from the foundation of the town by al-Mansūr in 155 H. (772). This would be in perfect keeping with the acanthus cornice, the bastioned walls of mud brick, and the corner piers, which are just like those in the palace mosque at Ukhaidir. It is on account of them that I have restored the other piers as round ones, as at Ukhaidir, instead of rectangular ones as Herzfeld has done.

Two deep trenches,[2] behind Nūr ad-Dīn's row of arches and parallel to it, mark the two lines of piers which divided the sanctuary into three parallel aisles. It averages 30·50 (100 ft) in depth, and must have been covered with three parallel gable roofs, the ends of which must have appeared above the east and west walls. There can be no question of a transept, for no pilasters are provided for the pair of parallel arcades which would have been required, running back at right angles to the façade, nor is there any trace higher up of the springing of a pair of arches, the brickwork of the back of the façade being quite smooth and unbroken.

It is clear that the side porticoes must have been 12·52–12·70 m. (41¼–41¾ ft) deep, with two rows of piers, and that the *sahn* must have been 67·67 m. (225 ft) wide and 75·30–12·52 = 62·78 m. (205 ft) deep, which gives room for ten lateral arches only instead of eleven.

---

1. *Op. cit.*, II, p. 360.

2. The trenches are the work of brick robbers, doubtless from the Circassian colony which settled here about 1879.

Architectural Origins

This mosque, which stands on the dividing line between Syria and Mesopotamia, provides an interesting example of the blending of two types. The nearly square plan of mosque and *sahn*, the bastioned walls, and the large number of entrances (instead of the three axial ones usual in Syria) is Mesopotamian, likewise the combination of material – mud brick for the walls and burnt brick for the arcades – a combination found in the Nestorian churches of Hīra,[1] but the triple-aisled sanctuary and the parallel gable roofs which covered it (in contrast to the flat roofs of 'Irāq) are Syrian features which we have already met with at Damascus and Qasr al-Hair. We have also met with a sanctuary roofed in exactly the same way at Harrān, a region which belongs architecturally to Syria.

GROWTH OF PERSIAN INFLUENCE

As Browne has pointed out,[2] the 'revolution which placed the 'Abbāsids on the throne entirely altered the status of the Persians, who at once rose from the position of a despised and slighted subject race to the highest and most influential offices and commands. It was their swords which won the victory for the House of 'Abbās, whom al-Bīrūnī, not without good reason, calls a Khurāsānī, an Eastern Dynasty. ... The fall of the Umayyads was the end of the purely Arabian period'.

During al-Mansūr's reign this Persian influence began to have a marked effect on the manners and habits of the Muslim world. Persian costumes, with the tall Persian hat (*qalansuwa*), became the fashionable dress at Court. Magians came over in large numbers to the new faith, and brought their learning with them, and the Persian New Year began to be observed. The Arabs lost their pre-eminence not only in the army and at Court, but also in society. Hitherto the dominant caste, looking down with contempt on nations every way their superior in science, art, and culture, they were now fast sinking

1. Talbot Rice, 'Hira', in the *Journal of the Roy. Central Asian Soc.*, XIX, p. 265; and in *Ars Islamica*, I, pp. 55–6.

2. *Literary History of Persia*, I, p. 247.

to a lower level. The power of the sovereign began to rest primarily on Persian troops, who were more amenable to discipline than Arabs, and the whole of the Byzantine frontier at this time was full of troops from Khurāsān.

The effect of this on Muslim art has been well expressed by Terrasse:

The Khalifate passed from Hellenistic soil to a country where the traditions of the ancient East remained full of life. In 'Abbāsid Mesopotamia an art was about to develop which in almost everything is opposed to the semi-Classic art which still prevailed on the shores of the Mediterranean.[1]

1. *L'Art hispano-mauresque*, p. 54.

CHAPTER 10

UKHAIDIR AND 'ATSHĀN

UKHAIDIR

THE fortified palace of Ukhaidir lies in the desert on the Wādī 'Ubayd about 120 miles south of Baghdād. Its present name is doubtless modern: the earliest mention of it that I have found occurs in 1625 in Pietro della Valle's Travels.

Ukhaidir in its loneliness is one of the most impressive buildings I have ever seen (Plate 38). It consists of a fortified rectangular enclosure measuring 175 by 169 m. (575 by 555 ft), with a gateway in the centre of each side. There are four round corner towers and ten intermediate half-round towers, not counting the peculiar gateway towers, on each side. Within this great enclosure, and in contact with its northern face, is the Palace proper, measuring 112 m. (370 ft) from north to south and 82 m. (270 ft) from east to west (Figure 40). It also is provided with half-round towers. Its main entrance forms one with the northern entrance of the main enclosure. The masonry is composed of thin, roughly shaped slabs of limestone, set in gypsum mortar.

The Outer Enclosure

The present height of the walls is about 17 m. (55 ft), but the parapet has gone, so it must have been at least 19 m. (62 ft) originally. The corner towers are 5·10 m. (16¾ ft), in diameter, the intermediate ones 3·30 m. (10¾ ft) only, with a pitch of 13 m. (42½ ft) and a projection of 2·60 (8½ ft) beyond the face of the wall arches. The wall is 2·60 m. (8½ ft) thick with pilasters carrying arches on both faces, as a result of which the thickness at the floor level of the gallery is about 4·60 (15 ft). On the outer side of the gallery, which was tunnel-vaulted, are recesses averaging 1·40 m. (4½ ft) in width and 50 cm. (19½ in.) in depth. Every fifth one opens into one of the small round chambers in the top of each tower; the remainder serve arrow-slits. Along the outer edges of each recess is a gap 17 cm. (6¾ in.) wide; its inner edge corresponds with the outer face of the wall at the back of the arched recesses, consequently it opens in the crown of the arch at its inner end. Missiles could be discharged through these slits at an enemy standing at the foot of the wall. This provision for a downward fire throughout the whole length of the gallery almost amounts to continuous mâchicolation, a feature unknown in Europe before the fourteenth century.

The point where the curtain wall has been preserved to the greatest height is on the north side. It is clear that it was terminated by a little blind arcade of horse-shoe arches (Plate 34b).

In each of the four corners of the enclosures is a staircase to the gallery which runs all round, but they are all badly ruined, except the south-eastern. It could also be reached by the double staircases which flank the eastern, southern, and western gateways.

The Gateways

The three gateways just mentioned are exactly alike. The arched entrance, 3 m. (10 ft) wide, is set between two quarter-round towers which project exactly the same distance as the others (Plate 34a). To right and left is a groove about 20 cm. wide and 30 cm. deep (7¾ by 11¾ in.), which shows that there must have been a portcullis here. At the back, at a distance of 1·95 m. (6½ ft), is another arch, 1·83 m. (6 ft) in span, and between the two is a vestibule measuring 3 by 1·95 m. (10 by 6½ ft), covered by a tunnel-vault in which are three slits, 17 cm. (6¾ in.) wide, running from wall to wall (Figure 37). Now, supposing Ukhaidir was likely to be attacked, the portcullis would be kept in a hauled-up position by means of a windlass in the top chamber, until a party of men entered the vestibule and tried to break down the door behind the inner archway. At a signal, given by men looking through the slits in the vault, the portcullis would be released and missiles, molten lead, or boiling oil dropped on the storming party trapped below.

The portcullis (cataracta) was known to the Romans. It is mentioned by Polybius (Bk. x, 33, 8) and Livy (Bk. xxvii, 28) in their account of the attempt on Salapia in 208 B.C. It is also described by Vegetius (Epitoma Rei Militaris, IV, 4): 'But more useful is the ancient

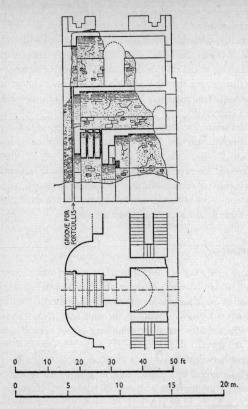

Figure 37. Ukhaidir: east gateway, plan and section

device of adding in front of the gate a projecting tower, in the entrance to which is placed a portcullis, suspended from iron rings in such fashion that if the enemy gets in, it could be dropped behind them and they, so imprisoned, be dispatched.' [1]

The Herculaneum Gate of Pompeii (before 78 B.C.) had a portcullis, and likewise the Roman gateway at Qasr ash-Sham' at Old Cairo.

1. I owe this reference to Mr Sidney Toy.

The Main Entrance

This is in the centre of the north side, where the series of half-round towers is broken by a great salient projecting 5·12 m. (16¾ ft) and measuring 15·90 m. (52¼ ft) in breadth. The entrance is in the outer face of this tower; it leads to a narrow vaulted room 3 m. wide and 5·80 long (10 by 19 ft). To right and left are small doorways opening into unlighted rooms, rectangular in shape except for a curved piece of wall in their inner corners.

The vault over the entrance hall consists of seven transverse arches, 65 cm. (25½ in.) wide, opening into the room above (Plate 35a). These slits, like those in the other gateways, would enable people in the room above to pour molten lead or boiling oil on a storming party that had forced an entrance. The centre parts of all these arches have fallen and the vault of the room above can be seen from the entrance passage. On either side of the hall at a distance of 1·70 m. (5½ ft) from its inner end is a groove, 18 cm. (7 in.) in width and depth, and 55 cm. (11½ in.) farther north is a complete break in the masonry clearly visible to a height of about 2·50 m. (8 ft). It can only mean, as Reuther has pointed out,[1] that the present entrance, with its two flanking rooms, did not form part of the original design, which provided only for the domed chamber, archway, and portcullis, the latter part being flanked by two quarter-round towers and the whole having been designed exactly like the other three entrances. The two curved pieces of masonry in the unlighted rooms are, of course, the outer faces of these towers. Then, after the building had risen about 3 m. (10 ft), the great outer enclosure was decided upon, likewise the great rectangular entrance tower with its slotted vault and flanking rooms. The north wall was then begun in contact with the 3 m. that had already been built of the north wall of the palace; above this point the work is all of one piece. At the far end is an arch opening into a chamber 4·15 m. long and 3 m. wide (13½ by 10 ft). It is reduced to a square by an oblong arch, and on this square has been set a fluted dome, which is carried across the corners on flat triangular brackets (Plate 35b).

Three pointed arches lead out of this domed chamber: two open into vaulted corridors nearly 35 m. long and 3·45 wide (115 by 11¼ ft), leading to the east and west parts of the Outer Enclosure (Plate 35b).

1. *Ocheïdir*, p. 17.

The doorways at each end are not placed in the axis of the corridor, but close against its south side. The explanation of this is that these two corridors were used as stables for horses, and remains of the feeding-troughs still exist along the north wall.

On the south side of the domed square is an arched doorway leading into a great vaulted hall about 7 m. (23 ft) wide and 15·50 (51 ft) deep, and 10·33 (34 ft) in height, with arched recesses to right and left (Plate 36).

Behind these recesses are unlit vaulted chambers, probably store-rooms. Beyond these again, to the west, is a mosque with a rectangular mihrāb recess; to the east is a court surrounded by vaulted rooms (Figure 40).

The Mosque

This is entered from the western arm of the transverse corridor by two doors, which open into a space 24·20 m. wide and 15·65 deep (79½ by 51½ ft). It was once full of débris, but the Directorate of Antiquities has since cleared it, and sufficient remains are now visible to render its reconstruction easy. It is obvious that there was once a single aisle of five arches on the *qibla* side resting on round rubble columns a metre (3¼ ft) in diameter. This arcade supported a tunnel vault, but as the wooden tie-beams which took the thrust have disappeared, the vault has pushed the arcade over and collapsed. The same remark applies to the eastern and western *riwāqs*, which were 3 m. deep and 10 m. long (10 by 33 ft). There was no *riwāq* on the north side, so the *sahn* must have measured 16·20 by 10·30 m. (53¼ by 33¾ ft). Approximately in the centre of the south wall is the mihrāb, a rectangular niche, 1·05 m. wide and 52 cm. deep (3½ by 1¾ ft), covered by a semi-dome carried across the corners on horizontal brackets. Mihrābs rectangular instead of semicircular in plan are a distinctive feature of the Persian–Mesopotamian area in early times, e.g. the Tārīk Khāna at Dāmghān, the Great Mosque at Sāmarrā, and Abū Dulaf, Nāyīn, etc.

The Court of Honour

Let us return to the great hall. At its outer end is a small domed square, from which a vaulted corridor 3·50–3·60 m. (11½–11¾ ft) wide leads off to right and left. If we continue forward we find ourselves in the great Court of Honour, 27 m. wide and 32·70 deep (89 by 108 ft), the sides of which are formed of blind arcades, six on the north and south sides (Plate 37), and nine on the east and west. On the south side is a vaulted līwān 6 m. wide and 10·74 m. deep (19¾ by 35¼ ft), with a square room at the back of it. The arch (now fallen) over this opening must inevitably have risen well above the façade on either side, and was doubtless set in a rectangular frame. We therefore have here the first example of that ubiquitous feature of later Persian architecture, the *pīshtāq* or frontispiece. The shallow, semi-domed hoods of the recesses on either side are constructed of bricks in whole, two-third, and one-third lengths, some being set horizontally and some vertically, so as to form geometrical patterns (Plate 39a), as on the Baghdād Gate of Raqqa (above, pp. 185–6). As we have seen, it is called *hazārbāf*, and is found everywhere in later Persian and ʿIrāqī architecture. On each side of the great līwān, and opening out of it, are a pair of vaulted rooms, those on the right having a decorated vault (Plate 39b). This group was evidently the Hall of Public Audience, the Hall of Private Audience, and the waiting-rooms attached.

The long vaulted corridor already mentioned runs completely round the central block of 70·82 by 31·20 m. (232 by 102 ft) and separates it from another group of vaulted chambers and two courts. On its east and west sides are four isolated and self-contained sets of vaulted chambers, each with its own courtyard, which I regard as four *bayts*, as at Mshattā in Trans-Jordan.

The Four Bayts

These four *bayts* have no communication with each other, and each is accessible by one door only from the Great Corridor, except the south-eastern, which has a door opening into the outer enclosure as well. B and C differ from each other, but each is almost identical with its fellow opposite, except that everything is there transposed from right to left (Figure 40). The court of B measures roughly 15 m. (50 ft) from north to south and 16½m. (54 ft) from east to west. The side next the Great Corridor is bounded by a blind arcade of five arches resting on half-round piers, the central arch being occupied by the door. The far side was bounded by a portico 2·80 m. (9¼ ft) deep, of five arches, resting on four round piers and covered by a tunnel-vault. The north and south sides are occupied by a triple-arched façade, the central arch being wider than the rest. These arches form a portico, behind which are three parallel tunnel-vaulted rooms. Each side room has two doors, one placed as usual near the outer end of the side wall and opening into the central room, and one into the portico.

Here we have an architectural group which is found in all four *bayts* and which I shall call a 'līwān group'. The central room with the wide archway was presumably the reception-room, and the side rooms ordinary living-rooms. The group facing south would form the winter quarters and the rooms facing north would be used in summer. On the outer side is the entrance of a staircase leading to the roof. Between this staircase and the outer wall is a narrow passage leading to a room 17·60 m. long and 3½ wide (58 by 11½ ft), which is placed transversely behind the three tunnel-vaulted rooms. A similar passage on the opposite side of the court leads to an identical room behind the other tunnel-vaulted rooms. Both these two transverse rooms are covered by two lengths of tunnel-vault with a space open to the sky between them. It must have been intended to contain a fire, for in each case the vault next the outer wall is pierced by a pair of terra-cotta pipes which must have served as chimneys. These places must have been intended for kitchens. *Bayts C* and *D* (Plate 38*b*) differ from *A* and *B* in having no porticoes in front, but the rooms are much deeper in consequence.

Let us leave the problem of the date of Ukhaidir until we have described 'Atshān.

'ATSHĀN

'Atshān is a khān-like building in the sandy plain to the east of the Hindīya Canal, roughly midway between Ukhaidir and Kūfa. It is a rectangular building measuring internally 25·57 m. (84 ft) from north to south and 24·90 m. (82 ft) from east to west. The walls, which are built of burnt bricks, 33 cm. square and 7 cm. thick (13 by 2¾ in.), are flanked by four corner towers and four intermediate towers, all projecting about 2 m. (6½ ft), except the gateway tower on the north

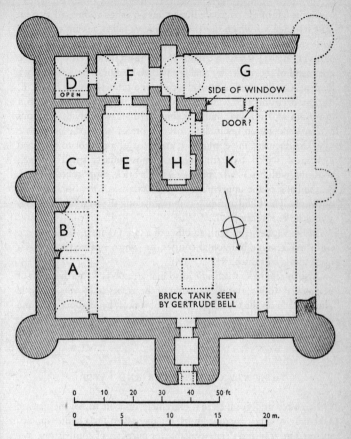

Figure 38. ʿAtshān: plan

side, which projects 4·40 m. (14½ ft). It bears a striking resemblance to those of Ukhaidir, for the corners are rounded off, and the massive arched entrance, which is only 1·33 m. (4½ ft) wide, is set back 1·10 (3½ ft) between the rounded salients. On either side, as at Ukhaidir, is a groove 15 cm. (6 in.) wide, close up to the arch, showing that there must have been a portcullis (Figure 38).

On the left of the court are three tunnel-vaulted rooms, all 3·39 m. (11¼ ft) wide, of which the west walls have fallen, taking the vaults with them. In the south-eastern corner is a vaulted room, 3·42 by 4·04 (11¼ by 13¼ ft), with a space 80 cm. (2½ ft) wide left open at the north end of the vault; by analogy with Ukhaidir, it was probably a kitchen. On the south side of the court is a tunnel-vaulted līwān, E, 7·46 m. deep and 4·79 wide (24½ by 15¾ ft), and on the west side of it is a room 2·98 m. wide and 6·65 long (9¾ by 21¾ ft), with a curious external decoration resembling that still preserved on the north side of Ukhaidir, next the entrance. It consisted of a row of four arched niches, of which two still remain almost intact; small engaged columns, with bases and capitals of a single brick, support little arches. At the back of the upper part of each niche was a flat brick set face outwards. This blind arcading continued along the west face also, and along the north face of G.

All the vaults begin with an offset of 4 cm. (1½ in.); above this are from five to nine horizontal courses, on which rest vertical rings a brick and a half thick.

'Atshān resembles Ukhaidir in so many respects – e.g. the form of he gateway tower, the construction of the arches and vaults, the little blind arcade on the top of H, etc. – that it must be of about the same date. We shall see that it was probably built in connexion with Ukhaidir.

THE DATE OF UKHAIDIR AND 'ATSHĀN

On architectural grounds it is extremely difficult to fix the date of Ukhaidir between narrow limits, for there is so little contemporary material in 'Irāq and Persia available for purposes of comparison. We have Qasr-i-Shīrīn on the Persian border, which was built between A.D. 590 and 628, after which there is a gap of 150 years until we come to the Baghdād Gate of Raqqa, A.D. 772, and the earliest monument at Sāmarrā – the Bāb al-'Āmma – begun A.D. 836.

Let us proceed on this basis and try to narrow down the limiting dates. The *bayts* at Ukhaidir, as we have seen, are of a type which first appears at Qasr-i-Shīrīn; nevertheless Ukhaidir must be later than this for it contains a mosque, and is therefore a Muslim building which cannot have been built earlier than A.D. 637, the year in which ʿIrāq was conquered. But this mosque contains a concave mihrāb, a feature which was first introduced in A.D. 709. Ukhaidir must therefore be placed after A.D. 709.

Two other architectural features present themselves as a basis for argument: (1) the groined vault, which occurs eight times at Ukhaidir in the Great Corridor, and (2) the geometrical patterns (hazārbāf) executed in the brickwork on the south side of the Court of Honour. These features are unknown in Sasanian architecture, but they both appear in the Baghdād Gate of Raqqa. However, we can scarcely place Ukhaidir at the end of the eighth century for this reason alone, because of the gap of 150 years before the latter monument, and the possibility that other monuments built during this period may have possessed both features. There is a third feature which is very frequently employed at Ukhaidir, viz. niches covered by shallow hoods which are carried across the corners on horizontal brackets. Exactly similar niches decorate the base of the Malwīya tower at Sāmarrā, 234–7 (848–9 to 851–2).

A terminus ante-quem is provided by the fact that the pointed arch is not fully established at Ukhaidir, as it is at Sāmarrā in A.D. 836, so Ukhaidir is evidently earlier.

On architectural grounds, therefore, it is difficult to fix the date of Ukhaidir closer than A.D. 720–800.

We must now proceed on historical lines. Ukhaidir was certainly not built by an Umayyad Khalif, for they all resided on the Syrian side of the desert, with the single exception of Marwān II (A.D. 744–50), who lived at Harrān. Nevertheless only a prince, or some all-powerful Governor of ʿIrāq such as Hajjāj (A.D. 694–713), can have built it. Hajjāj, however, lived at Wāsit, and subsequent Governors must have lived unavoidably at some important capital such as Kūfa and Basra. Thus a date prior to A.D. 750 seems to be excluded, and there is no architectural objection to putting Ukhaidir after this date.

As for the ʿAbbāsid Khalifs, they did not lead the semi-nomadic life of their Umayyad predecessors, but were town dwellers, and resided, at least after A.D. 764, at Baghdād. If the ʿAbbāsid Khalifs are excluded also, who then can have built it?

I suggest ʿĪsā ibn Mūsā, the powerful nephew of as-Saffāh and al-Manṣūr and head of the 'Abbāsid family, for his history seems to fit it.

We are told by Tabarī that as-Saffāh, the first 'Abbāsid Khalif, on getting his brother al-Manṣūr recognized as Khalif, had nominated 'Īsā ibn Mūsā as the latter's successor, and that the people had accepted him as such.

al-Manṣūr when he first became Khalif honoured 'Īsā, made him Governor of Kūfa, and, after the foundation of Baghdād, gave him a great palace in the city. At audiences he took precedence of everybody. But later on, in 147 H. (764–5), he did his best to get rid of him by the same methods that David adopted towards Uriah the Hittite, sending him to the most dangerous places during his campaigns, hoping that he would be killed and so leave the way clear for the recognition of his own son al-Mahdī as heir. This method failing, he evolved the following trick.

'Abd Allāh son of 'Alī, whose revolt against al-Manṣūr had failed, was in prison. al-Manṣūr, before leaving on the Pilgrimage, said to 'Īsā ibn Mūsā: 'Take this man and put him to death in prison the day I leave, without letting anyone know.' 'Īsā, knowing full well the infamous character of the man with whom he had to deal, took no action, but when al-Manṣūr wrote to him from Kūfa asking whether he had executed 'Abd Allāh, he replied in the affirmative. When al-Manṣūr returned to Baghdād, he arranged that 'Abd Allāh's relations should appeal for his release. al-Manṣūr then told 'Īsā to release him. 'Īsā replied: 'He is dead, you told me to kill him', but al-Manṣūr replied: 'God forbid that I should order the execution of my uncle,' and, turning to the petitioners, said: 'Here is 'Īsā; take him and do what you like with him. If you want to put him to death you are free to do so.' 'Īsā then said: 'The trick, if it had succeeded, was well thought out. But 'Abd Allāh is not dead, and I will send for him.'

After this al-Manṣūr tried poison; 'Īsā recovered, but lost his beard and the hair of his head, and remained a permanent invalid.

al-Manṣūr then consulted Khālid the Barmecide, who was evidently as evil as his master. He tried to persuade 'Īsā to surrender his rights, but failed. He then got three false witnesses, who agreed to swear that 'Īsā had consented to surrender his rights. al-Manṣūr then convoked a great assembly and publicly thanked 'Īsā, who naturally protested and denied that he had ever done anything of the sort. Khālid the Barmecide and the three false witnesses then rose and stated that 'Īsā, a few days previously, had done so in their presence. The assembly then covered 'Īsā with reproaches.

A little later al-Manṣūr came to the conclusion that 'Īsā's reluctance was due to his anxiety to preserve the right of succession for his son after him, so he summoned both to the palace and ordered his chamberlain to pretend to strangle the son in his father's presence. When the leather thong had been drawn tight and the victim was half strangled, his father agreed to renounce his rights in order to save his son's life.

It was then agreed that 'Īsā, on signing a renunciation of his rights in favour of al-Mahdī, should receive ten million dirhems (£500,000) and have the right to succeed al-Mahdī if he outlived him. al-Manṣūr died in 158 H. (775) and was succeeded by his son al-Mahdī, who, three years after his accession (i.e. in 778), wished to proclaim his son Hārūn ar-Rashīd as heir instead of 'Īsā. He could not obtain the latter's consent, so he deprived him of the Governorship of Kūfa, which he had held for thirteen years. 'Īsā, disgusted with life, then retired to his estates, where he lived in complete isolation, only going to Kūfa once a week to attend Friday prayers. He used to ride to the door of the mosque, dismount, accomplish his devotions, and ride away again.

Does not this suit Ukhaidir perfectly? It could only have been built by a man with the wealth of 'Īsā, and he alone of all the 'Abbāsid princes of this period is definitely known to have lived in such isolation. Moreover, its distance from Kūfa (about 50 miles) could have been covered in two easy stages if a relay was available, and this brings us to 'Atshān, which is obviously of about the same date and placed at just the distance required on the direct route from Ukhaidir to Kūfa.

Moreover, it is a khān of quite exceptional type, for it does not consist of a central courtyard surrounded by dozens of cells, all alike. On the contrary, there is a large līwān, a kitchen close to it and a large tunnel-vaulted hall nearly 12 m. (40 ft) long with a semi-domed alcove at one end (G), which I suggest must have been intended for a princely hall of reception, on account of the close resemblance which it bears to the vaulted reception hall at Jebel Seis.

If my conclusions are correct, Ukhaidir and 'Atshān must have been begun in 161 H. (778), the year of 'Īsā's retirement.

CHAPTER II

THE AQSĀ MOSQUE AND THE GREAT MOSQUE OF CORDOVA

THE AQSĀ MOSQUE

How long did al-Walīd's structure last? It appears to have been badly damaged in the great earthquake of 747 or 748, but the first mention of its rebuilding occurs in a late work, known as the *First Muthīr*, written in 1351. It attributes the work to al-Mansūr (754–75).[1] According to the same work another earthquake took place a few years later and the Khalif al-Mahdī rebuilt the part damaged. I cannot help feeling that these two earthquakes may be a duplication of the same event, of which the former is well documented but *not the second*. Even Muqaddasī, a native of Jerusalem, who wrote in 985, does not give its date, merely referring to it as 'an earthquake in the days of the Abbāsids', which he says 'threw down the sanctuary except the part round the mihrāb' and he goes on to say that it was rebuilt 'stronger and more massive in construction than it had been, and the more ancient portion remained, even like a beauty spot, in the midst [of the new]. This portion extends as far as the limit of the marble columns, for beyond, where the columns are built up (*mushaiyada*), the later part commences'.[2] He does not say which Khalif carried out the work, but according to the *First Muthīr* it was al-Mahdī. As for the year, Le Strange suggests 163 H. (780),[3] for in that year, according to Tabarī, he went to Jerusalem and prayed in the Aqsā Mosque.

Here is the only description which we possess of this mosque. Muqaddasī says:

The sanctuary has twenty-six doors. The door opposite the mihrāb is called the Great Brass Door ... To the right hand of it are seven large doors ... and on the left the same. And on the eastern side are eleven

1. Le Strange's text in the *Journ. Roy. Asiatic Socy*, n.s. xix, p. 303; transl. p. 286.

2. p. 168.   3. *Palestine under the Moslems*, p. 93.

doors, unornamented. ... Over the centre part of the sanctuary is a mighty gable roof, above which rises a beautiful dome. The roofs everywhere ... are sheathed with lead.

What was this mosque like? Let us leave this question for a moment and follow the history of the building.

A great earthquake in 1033 damaged the mosque and necessitated its rebuilding by the Fātimid Khalif az-Zāhir in 1035. The Aqsā Mosque in its present form has often been regarded as mainly due to the Crusaders and Saladin, but this is a mistake, for a great deal of az-Zāhir's mosque remains. The late Kemāl ad-Dīn, the very able Turkish architect who carried out repairs between 1924 and 1927, laid bare many details of the structure which prove this.

(1) He stripped the plaster from the north face of the northern dome-bearing arch, and exposed a splendid decoration in glass mosaic, consisting of great scrolls of acanthus surmounted by a long Kufic inscription, just below the roof-beams, in the name of az-Zāhir. This proves that the great dome bearing arch cannot be later than 1035.

(2) He partly stripped the lead covering from the lower rim of the wooden dome. This lower rim or 'lip' is turned out slightly, so as to throw off rain-water and snow. It is maintained in this position by a series of projecting beams, or wall-plates, exactly as in the Dome of the Rock (above, p. 29 and Figure 5), where they project about 85 cm. against 75 only in the Aqsā (33½ against 29½ in.). I was fortunate enough to see them exposed; most were very badly worm-eaten, but a few, which had escaped more or less, were carved with Fātimid ornament. This proves that the drum of the dome cannot be later than az-Zāhir, and therefore the four dome-bearing arches also, and not merely the one below the inscription.

(3) All the arches of the mosque are braced by double tie-beams, and nailed to the underside of each pair is a plank with painted decoration. This had been hidden by a deal casing, which was removed in ten or twelve cases. One tie to the west of the dome bore a band of eleventh-century Kufic. Some of the arches near the dome therefore cannot be later than az-Zahir. The same remark applies to the first tie-beam next the dome, on either side of the central aisle.

(4) The roof of the nave consisted (until recently) of roof principles, fairly closely set, resting on flat consoles of two sizes, some about 35 cm. broad and 90 long (13¾ by 35½ in.), others 60 cm. broad and

110 long (23½ by 43¼ in.). They are carved with ornament that can scarcely be later than the eighth century. They presumably have been taken from al-Mahdī's mosque and re-employed (Plate 42).

Now let us look at the plan (Figure 39). We observe that a row of great round columns still exists intact to the east of the nave arcade and at a distance of 7·10 m. (23¼ ft) from it. One more column has survived in the next aisle going east. As for the part on marble columns, two arcades have survived to east and west of the dome, and part of a third to the east. We also notice that the northern and southern dome-bearing arches are continued east and west, so as to carry the thrust through to the side walls, thus creating a sort of T-plan on paper, but not in reality, for all the aisle arcades are carried right through to the *qibla* wall.

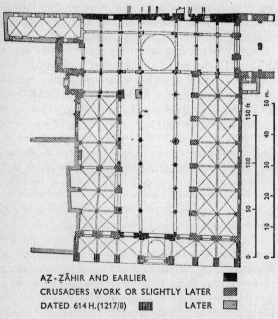

AZ-ẒĀHIR AND EARLIER

CRUSADERS WORK OR SLIGHTLY LATER

DATED 614 H. (1217/8)   LATER

Figure 39. Jerusalem: The Aqṣā Mosque, plan

Thus it is clear that a large part of the present mosque is the work of az-Zāhir, viz. the arcades of the central aisle, the four arches under the dome and the drum up to its top edge, an arcade to the east of the nave arcade, the arcades to the left of the eastern dome-bearing arch, and the two corresponding ones on the opposite side.

The Form of az-Zāhir's Mosque

The northern limit of az-Zāhir's mosque must have been the same as to-day for two of the three central doorways, on account of their mouldings, must date from the eighth century at the latest. Here are my general conclusions:

(1) Quite a large part of the present Aqsā mosque is the work of az-Zāhir.

(2) His mosque consisted of seven aisles, formed by arcades perpendicular to the *qibla* wall, of which all but the two central ones consisted of eleven arches.

(3) The central aisle was nearly double the width of the rest (11·80 against 6·50 m.; 38¾ against 21¼ ft); it had a clerestory and the first seven bays were covered by a gable roof, beyond which was a great wooden dome.

(4) The transverse dome-bearing arches were carried through to the side walls on account of their thrust.

(5) The side aisles were covered by gable roofs at a lower level than the great gable and parallel to it.

(6) I am inclined to believe that his mosque was no wider than the present building.

Reconstruction of al-Mahdī's Mosque

Let us turn back to Muqaddasī's description. No one can fail to be struck by the resemblance of the main features of the mosque he saw to the salient features of az-Zāhir's mosque, e.g. the great central doorway with seven smaller ones to right and left, the mighty gable roof over the central part with a beautiful dome rising above it, the roof covered with sheets of lead, etc.

But there is more than this. We have seen that the columns are of two sizes, those in the nave and to the east of it averaging about 90 cm.

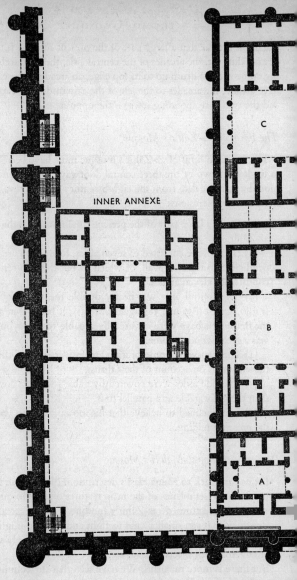

INNER ANNEXE

C

B

A

Figure 40. Ukhaidir: plan of Pal

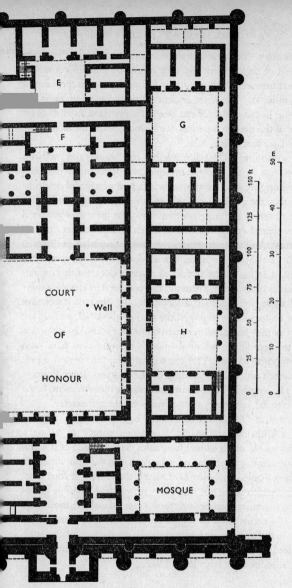

E

G

F

COURT

OF

HONOUR

Well

H

MOSQUE

150 ft

125

100

75

50

25

0

50 m

40

30

20

10

0

mplex and part of outer-enclosure

(3 ft) in diameter. Now, these are not columns at all, for they have been stripped of their plaster and turn out to be built in courses of stone. This at once recalls the words of Muqaddasī when speaking of al-Mahdī's mosque: 'The more ancient portions remained, even like a beauty spot, in the midst [of the new]. This portion extends as far as the limit of the marble columns, for beyond, *where the columns are built up*, the later part commences.'

Thus the mosque of al-Mahdī was partly on columns and partly on round piers, just as the present mosque, and the central part was covered by a mighty gable roof, over which rose a beautiful dome. In addition to this, the great central aisle and the aisle to right and left of it must have been of the same width as now, for their axes are fixed by the three central doorways, two of which cannot be later than the eighth century. And is it not remarkable that the number of doors in the east side of al-Mahdī mosque, viz. eleven, correspond exactly to the number of arches in the arcades of to-day; does not this suggest that the arcades of al-Mahdī's mosque also consisted of eleven arches? Taking all these points into consideration, the obvious conclusion seems to be that az-Zāhir respected the plan of al-Mahdī, leaving the round piers as they were and reconstructing everything more or less on the same lines. The width of al-Mahdī's mosque must have been 11·80 (from centre to centre) for the central aisle, plus 6·50 × 14 m. for the fourteen aisles corresponding to the fourteen lesser doors = 102·80 m. The length from north to south, inside measurement, being 69·20 m. (230 ft), we have a proportion of almost exactly 3 : 2 a favourite ratio in 'Abbāsid architecture, e.g. al-Mansūr's work at Baghdād, at Ukhaidir, and in the following century at Sāmarrā. Fifteen aisles would mean adding four aisles on either side of the present mosque. Is it not a curious coincidence that in the little annexe to the east, the so-called 'Mosque of 'Umar', there are just four bays, their average width being not quite 6·75 m. (22 ft)? The east side of this annexe, therefore, corresponds to the east side of the mosque of al-Mahdī, if reconstructed as suggested, and the wall piers on the south side of this annexe are approximately on the axis of the wall-piers required by my theory. Figure 41 is an attempt to show what al-Madhī's mosque must have looked like.

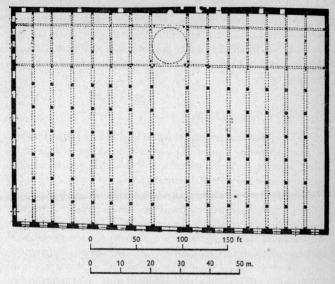

Figure 41. Jerusalem: The Aqsā Mosque of al-Mahdi, proposed
reconstruction

The Wooden Consoles

These, applied to the roof-beams at their two ends, are of two
sizes, as mentioned above (p. 205–6). Two of them are illustrated
here (Plate 42). They are obviously much earlier than az-Zāhir, and I
believe they come from the mosque of al-Mahdī. When I published
them in the *Illustrated London News* of 16 January 1937 (under a misleading title, inserted by the Editor), several critics were convinced
that they were Umayyad. I attributed them to al-Mahdī because of
the well-known vitality and persistence of Hellenistic art in Syria,
long after its decadence elsewhere. As a result of this, motifs which
might safely be placed in a given century, if found outside Syria, may
well be a century later if found in Syria. At Qusayr 'Amra, for example, the paintings, which we have seen must date from the beginning of the eighth century, might easily have been taken as of much
earlier date, if judged on stylistic grounds, likewise many motifs in

the façade of Mshattā, if taken separately. And we now know from observations and excavations beneath the floor made during the recent rebuilding of about a third of the Aqsā Mosque in 1938–42,[1] that previous to al-Mahdī the mosque did not have a wide central aisle, so there would have been no need for the larger consoles of 60 by 110 cm. (23·6 by 43·7 in.).

The Umayyad Aqsā Mosque

It follows from the account of Muqaddasī that an earlier mosque, with arcades resting on marble columns and running from north to south, was incorporated in the mosque of al-Mahdī. Such arcades still exist to the east and west of the domed part.

When the dome was inserted it was naturally necessary to provide abutment to east and west by transverse arcades running through to the side walls, and consisting of a series of arches resting on independent supports placed on either side of the corresponding column of the longitudinal arcades, the older arcades being 'nipped' between the new transverse arches. During the works of 1938–42, when the plaster was stripped off, Hamilton was able to see that the masonry of the spandrels of the transverse arches is not bonded into the masonry of the spandrels of the first longitudinal arcade to the east of the dome.[2] This does not apply to the second arcade, for here the transverse arches spring from the same support as the arches to north and south, so I conclude that it had suffered more from the earthquake, and was rebuilt by al-Mahdī. A third arcade, partly walled-up, still exists farther east.

Here are some details of the first arcade (Plate 24). Height of columns and capitals 5 m. (16½ ft); springing of stilted arch begins at 7·23 m. (23¾ ft); height of apex 9·20 m. (30¼ ft). Above the three main arches are five arched openings with their sills 9·80 m. (32½ ft) from the floor, height of openings about 2 m. (6¼ ft); height of ceiling, about 12·40 m. (41 ft). The axis of the first, third, and fifth opening corresponds with the axis of the arch below, and the second and fourth with the column.

1. R. W. Hamilton, *The Structural History of the Aqsā Mosque*, 1949, pp. 10–15.

2. R. W. Hamilton, *op. cit.*, pp. 10–15

Another discovery was made under the pavement when part of it was removed. Part of an earlier north wall, in some places one course high, was found and traced for over 18 m. (59 ft). It was 1 m. (3¼ ft) thick and its south face was 18·40 m. (60 ft) distant from the inner face of the present north wall. Consequently the earlier mosque, presumably Umayyad, was only 50·80 m. (167 ft) from north to south, instead of 69·20 (227 ft), but its width cannot be fixed.

THE GREAT MOSQUE OF CORDOVA

A great part of Spain had been conquered by the Arabs in 711, and it was subject to the Umayyad Khalifs for twenty-nine years, so the fall of the Umayyads caused a great division of feeling there. 'Abd ar-Rahmān, the only survivor of the dethroned dynasty, after passing a few years in North Africa, landed in Spain in 755, and became Emīr of Cordova the following year.

History of the Mosque

Ibn 'Adhārī [1] and al-Maqqarī [2] say that after the conquest the Muslims acted on the precedent set by Khālid ibn al-Walīd after the capture of Damascus, and took half the largest church in Cordova and used it as a mosque. Terrasse has pointed out [3] that this story so closely resembles that of the Great Mosque at Damascus, that one is led to ask if it has not been invented afterwards by the chroniclers. I believe the truth of the matter to be that Ibn Jubayr brought the Damascus legend (above, p. 59 ff.) to Spain at the end of the twelfth century, that it became linked with the Cordova mosque shortly afterwards, then incorporated in the spurious chronicle of ar-Rāzī in circulation in the thirteenth century, and adopted by Ibn 'Adhārī and al-Maqqarī.

Be that as it may, 'Abd ar-Rahmān I began a mosque in 169 H. (785-6) and finished it a year later at a cost of 80,000 dinars, say

1. *Bayān*, II, p. 244; Fagnan's transl., II, p. 378.
2. I, p. 368, ll. 7-11; Gayangos's transl., I, pp. 217-18.
3. *L'Art hispano-mauresque*, p. 59, n. 2.

£40,000.[1] According to al-Himyarī[2] and al-Maqqarī the number of aisles was eleven. The mosque apparently had no minaret, for we are told that his successor Hishām added one 40 cubits high, and put the finishing touches to the work of 'Abd ar-Rahmān I.

'Abd ar-Rahmān II enlarged the mosque from the piers (arjul) which are between the columns (sawārī) to the qibla. Ibn 'Adhārī says that the added part was 50 cubits deep and 150 wide and comprised eighty columns.[3] We have just seen that the first part had eleven aisles, which implies ten rows of columns. The eighty added implies the addition of eight columns to each of these rows. As for the date Ibn 'Adhārī gives 218 H. (833) in one place and 234 H. (848) in another. His son Muhammad completed his work and inserted a new frame for the west door (Puerta de San Estéban), for above the horizontal arch of the doorway and round the tympanum of the horse-shoe arch above is an inscription, recording this restoration, dated 241 H. (855-6).

'Abd Allāh (275-300 H. = 888-912) constructed a covered passage from his palace (which stood on the site of the present Bishop's palace) to a door on the west side of the mosque. It crossed the street like a bridge. By this means he was able to go directly to the maqsūra (the screened-off area round the mihrāb and the pulpit) without being seen by the people.[4] This new doorway doubtless corresponded to the present Gate of San Miguel, the second entrance to the sanctuary on the west side. In spite of its Gothic frame with heraldic filling, there is no doubt that the actual horse-shoe arch of this doorway is original.

The next important work was the construction of a new minaret by 'Abd ar-Rahmān III. al-Maqqarī says that the old minaret was demolished in 340 H. (951-2), that the new one took thirteen months to build, and that it was of stone with two independent staircases, one in the eastern half and one in the western.[5] Farther on he says: '... and the height of the minaret amounts to 73 cubits, measured to the highest point of the open domed pavilion. ... On the summit of this dome are golden and silver apples. The circumference of each apple is three

1. Ibn 'Adhārī, II, p. 245; transl., II, p. 379.   2. I, p. 157.
3. II, p. 245; transl., II, p. 380.
4. Ibn Haiyān, Oxford MS. (Nicoll, 137), fol. 27a-28a.
5. I, pp. 369-70; transl., I, p. 219.

and a half spans; two were of pure gold and one of silver. Below and above each were lilies very beautifully worked, and at the end of the spar a little golden pomegranate.' [1]

We now come to the second enlargement of the mosque of which Ibn 'Adhārī gives a very full account.[2] It was begun by al-Hakam on his accession in 961. He decided to extend the mosque towards the south by adding eleven aisles, the width remaining the same as before. In doing this he demolished the covered passage of 'Abd Allāh, and replaced it by a new one at the extremity of the west wall which, according to Ambrosio de Morales,[3] likewise crossed the street on an arch, and still existed in his day (1575). The dome in front of the mihrāb was finished in June 965, and decoration in gold mosaic was then begun, craftsmen for the work being sent from Constantinople by the Byzantine Emperor at the express request of al-Hakam. It still exists, and forms a rectangular frame in which the mihrāb is set, and two similar frames for the doors of the rooms to right and left. The date is missing from the inscription which runs round the former, but the two latter are dated 364 H. (965). Four fine columns belonging to the old mihrāb were placed in the new one in the same year.

al-Maqqarī [4] says that the greatest addition ever made to the mosque was that made in the reign of Hishām II under the administration of his famous Minister al-Mansūr. The river preventing any further extension to the south, the addition was made on the east side. al-Maqqarī says that al-Mansūr added eight aisles each 10 cubits wide; the total width of the mosque then became 230 cubits and the number of its aisles nineteen. The work took two years and a half and was finished in 377 H. (987–8).

At the end of the fifteenth century a beautiful Gothic chapel was inserted in the northern part of the extension of al-Hakam. At the beginning of the sixteenth century the clergy wished to erect in the midst of the mosque a larger and more elaborate chapel for the Canons, and appointed Hernán Ruiz to draw up plans for it. They

1. I, p. 360. Nearly all this passage has been taken from al-Himyarī, *Rawd al-Mitār*, Lévi-Provençal's ed., p. 156.

2. II, pp. 249–56; transl., II, pp. 385–93.

3. *Antiguedades de las ciudades de España*, fol. 120 *b*.

4. I, pp. 360–61; transl., I, 227–8.

obtained permission from Charles V to undertake the projected work which was begun on 7 September 1523 and finished on 7 September 1607, according to two inscriptions on an arch at the southern end of the transept. It is to Charles V's credit that when he visited Cordova in 1526 and saw the vandalism that had been committed, he expressed himself as follows: 'If I had known what you wished to do, you would not have done it, because what you are carrying out there is to be found everywhere, and what you had formerly does not exist anywhere else in the world.'

The minaret of 'Abd ar-Rahmān III was badly damaged in the great storm of 1589 and a Renaissance top was constructed by Hernán Ruiz, son of the Hernán Ruiz who had built the Renaissance upper part of the Giralda at Seville. The work was finished in 1618. Shortly after 1650 the old part of the minaret showed signs of giving way under the weight put upon it, so it was given a casing of masonry 1·58 m. (5¼ ft) thick.[1] Don Félix Hernández, the architect in charge of the fabric, has penetrated to the old minaret by cutting through this casing on the west side of the vestibule, and has verified the existence of the two independent staircases.

Description and Analysis of the Building

The Great Mosque of Cordova forms a vast rectangle, free on all sides, and measuring about 178 m. (585 ft) from north to south and 125 (410 ft) from east to west, excluding the buttresses. It therefore covers an area of about 22,250 sq. m. (26,500 sq. yds), so it is the third largest mosque in the world, coming after the Great Mosque of Sāmarrā (38,000 sq. m.; 45,500 sq. yds) and Abū Dulaf (28,750 sq. m.; 34,500 sq. yds). It is set exactly north and south, although the direction of Mekka from Cordova is 10° 14′ s. of E. The walls, measured at the Puerta de San Estéban, are 10·50 m. (34½ ft) high, not including the crenellations, which add 89 cm. (35 in.).

The northern part of this area is occupied by the Patio de los Naranjos, which is of course the *sahn*; it is entered by six doors, the principal one being on the north alongside the campanile. Covered

1. See Torre y del Cerro's study, based on the archives of the Cathedral from 1533 to 1639, 'Obras en la Torre de la Catedral de Córdova', in the *Boletín de la R. Acad. de Ciencias ... de Córdoba*, No. 29 (Oct. and Dec. 1930).

porticoes surround it on every side except the southern, where there are seventeen arches,[1] once open but now in most cases walled-up, leading into the sanctuary (Plate 41a and Figure 47). The latter is a vast hall of nineteen aisles, the roof of which rests on eighteen arcades running from north to south, as in the Aqsā Mosque of al-Mahdī (above, p. 210). It could once be entered from the street by thirteen doors, six on the west side and seven on the east.

The *sahn* is surrounded by porticoes about 6 m. (19¾ ft) deep, covered by a flat ceiling resting on arcades, in which two columns alternate with every pier.

The Façade of the Sanctuary

This consists of seventeen horse-shoe arches (plus two in the side *riwāqs* or porticoes) about 4 m. (13 ft) in span and 5·90 (19½ ft) in height, which spring from engaged columns attached to massive stone piers, 2·40 m. (8 ft) in width. Each arch is set in a rectangular frame and between each of these frames is a tall, narrow panel which rises immediately over each pier (Plate 41a). Above is a bold cornice, resting on elaborate corbels placed close together, which supports a sloping awning of tiles running the whole length of the façade, except where it is cut into, over every pier, by spouts from the gutters of the roof. Above this awning the wall continues upwards for nearly 2 m. (6½ ft), and is then capped by a decorative cresting about 60 cm. (23½ in.) high.

The Sanctuary

The Sanctuary is entered by the fifth arch from the right, known to-day as the Puerta de las Palmas, which is on the axis of the Puerta del Perdón. On entering we find ourselves in a veritable hall of columns, with wonderful vistas in every direction (Plate 41b), except where the view is blocked by the great Chapel of the Canons. The arcades run perpendicular to the back wall, and are of a remarkable design. The columns, which are only about 3 m. (9¾ ft) in height, exhibit great variations of type; some are smooth, others fluted, a few even have

1. There are really nineteen in all, but the last one at each end opens into the side arcades.

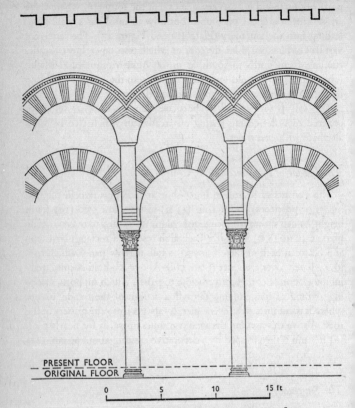

Figure 42. Cordova: The Great Mosque, construction of arcades

spiral flutings, and their diameters vary from 35–43 cm. (14–17 in.). Their bases are hidden in nearly every case, as the pavement is about 30 cm. (11¾ in.) above the original one. The capitals are very varied, being of every conceivable type of Corinthian and Composite, many of which in 1773 still bore traces of gilding.[1] On these capitals are set

1. Twiss (R.), *Travels through Portugal and Spain in 1772 and 1773*, p. 251.

impost blocks, which also vary in style and height; the horse-shoe arches which spring from them are 53 cm. (21 in.) broad and composed of white stone voussoirs alternating with composite voussoirs of four layers of red bricks set edgewise. *The present decoration is due to painted plaster*, but the actual brickwork is exposed in the fourth row from the west, second arch from the north. The bricks have been rubbed down to a wedge form, their thickness at the extrados being about 6 cm. (2¼ in.). In addition to this the impost blocks carry stone piers about a metre deep, the overhang being supported by corbels (Figure 42). These piers are about 1·75 m. (5¾ ft) in height and carry a second tier of arches, almost but not quite semicircular, and 1·07 m. (3½ ft) in span, also composed of stone and composite brick voussoirs alternately, with a covering ring of decorative brickwork. There are eight composite brick voussoirs in the arches of each tier.

By this ingenious device the required height of ceiling was obtained, in spite of the shortness of the columns, and the successive increase in the width of the arches rendered possible the establishment of the great stone gutters 47 cm. (18½ in.) wide, lined with lead, which run between each of the ridges of the roof above each row of columns, and which discharge their water by the spouts above the piers of the façade. The gutters above the enlargement of 'Abd ar-Rahmān II are a continuation of these and slope towards the *sahn* also, but those of the enlargement of al-Hakam slope south.

The Ceiling

The late Velásquez Bosco, who thoroughly investigated the roof behind the thin lath-and-plaster vaults of 1713–23 when he was architect in charge, found that there had originally been a ceiling of planks resting on strong transverse beams placed close together, above which were the gable roofs still existing to-day.[1] The thin lath-and-plaster vaults have since been removed in many places and a timber ceiling modelled on the old one re-established (Plate 41b). The height of the aisle is now 9·50 m. (31¼ ft), to which must be added 30 cm. (11¾ in.) to obtain the original height from the old floor level.

1. He never published an account of his researches, but he fortunately communicated his conclusions to Nizet, who published them in his article, 'La Mosquée de Cordova', in *L'Architecture*, XVIII, p. 446.

We now observe that there are nineteen aisles, of which the arches average 2·65 m. (8¾ ft) in span. The sixth aisle, the one by which we entered, is wider than the rest, being 7·85 m. (26 ft) instead of 6·85 (22½ ft) from centre to centre of the columns; it forms the centre aisle of the first eleven, and these eleven are divided off from the remaining eight by a wall, through which wide openings have been cut. This wall was once the eastern wall of the mosque before its third enlargement. Part of it has been stripped of plaster and it is now possible to see that it was similar to the corresponding part of the west wall. It was pierced with similar doorways, but the present openings have been cut in an arbitrary fashion, without reference to them. In some cases they are partly cut through, the part not required being walled up.

One thing is now clear: the eight aisles to the east of this wall are the eight aisles added by al-Mansūr, and therefore need no longer occupy our attention. Let us now continue our elimination a step farther. We have seen that the enlargement of al-Hakam consisted of eleven *balāt* (=aisles or bays) added to the south side. If we walk northwards from the *qibla* wall until we have passed twelve bays, we come to an arcade, resting on massive piers and running right across. This evidently marks what was the limit of the mosque before al-Hakam's addition, and further confirmation is supplied by the fact that the masonry of the western wall breaks bond immediately to the south of the point where this arcade strikes it. Ibn 'Adhārī's 'eleven *balāt*' should evidently be amended to read 'twelve'; perhaps he counted the whole *maqsūra* as one. This addition, having been completed in 966, falls, like the last, beyond the scope of this book.

Having now isolated the period which concerns us, let us attempt to fix the dividing line between period I and II. We have seen that the part added by 'Abd ar-Rahmān II comprised eighty columns, i.e. ten rows of eight each. Let us again count backwards. This, unfortunately, is possible in three rows only, on account of the Chapel of the Canons. We find that the run of these arcades is interrupted in each case by a pier. This is the very point at which we arrive if we walk backwards from the arcade on massive piers until we have passed eight columns. The part to the north of the pier must therefore represent the area of the original mosque and the part to the south the area added by 'Abd ar-Rahmān II. I must emphasize that the three piers in question are not walled-up arches; if they were they would measure at least 3·40 m. (11 ft), whereas they measure only 2·76 m. (9 ft).

I believe these piers, which are obviously 'the piers (*arjul*) between the columns (*sawārī*)' mentioned by Ibn 'Adhārī (above, p. 214), to be composed partly of a wall-pier 56 cm. (22 in.) deep (as at the north end), a fragment of the original back wall, 1·15 m. (3¾ ft) thick (like the side walls), and a buttress 1·05 m. (3½ ft) deep; total 2·76 m. (9 ft). As the walls are of ashlar, they could be cut through in this fashion without difficulty.

The North Façade of the Sanctuary

If we stand under the arches of this façade and examine the sides of the piers, it at once becomes apparent that they are composite. For example, if we stand under the second arch from the west and examine the pier to the west, we observe that there is a complete break in the masonry at the back of the shallow recess between the two engaged columns. There is a gap 22 cm. (8½ in.) wide, filled with rubble below and brick higher up, and the courses of the masonry to the south do not correspond with those of the masonry to the north. Turning now to the west face of the second pier, we find that it also is of two periods; moreover the inner arch leans forward 6 or 7 cm. (2¼ or 2¾ in.), whereas the outer is vertical. The same gap exists in the next few piers and arches and in the case of the sixth (the main entrance); the inner arch leans forward seriously and the outer slightly so. This leaning forward is of course due to the thrust of the inner arcades, which have no tie-beams and for which adequate abutment has not been provided, for the inner arcade of the façade, not counting the piers on its inner face, has a thickness of only about 1·16 m. (3¾ ft). The duplication of this façade by the addition of a second was evidently carried out to supply the necessary abutment.

The cryptic statement of Ibn 'Adhārī that an-Nāsir 'spent for the construction of the minaret, the regularization of the mosque, and *the construction of the façade of the naves to the number of eleven*, seven modi, etc.' [1] now becomes clear, likewise the significance of the inscription on the pier to the west of the central arch, which says that 'Abd ar-Rahmān [III] an-Nāsir 'has ordered the restoration of this façade

1. *Bayān*, II, p. 246.

(*wajh*) and its consolidation' and that 'the work was finished Dhu'l-Hijja 346 (February to March 958)'.[1] an-Nāsir therefore built a new façade against the old one to prevent it from being pushed still more out of the vertical, but even this has not sufficed to stop all movement, and the inclination is very noticeable towards the centre. This explains why the curious corbels (*modillons à copeaux*) of the cornice are more elaborate than those above the columns of 'Abd ar-Rahmān I's arcades; they are 170 years later.

The West Façade

Now let us leave the *sahn* and turn to the left. That part of the exterior which forms the west façade of 'Abd ar-Rahmān's sanctuary is divided into three bays by four rectangular buttresses projecting 1·35 m. (4½ ft) and measuring 3·31 (10¾ ft), 2·26 (7½ ft), 2·45 (8 ft), and 3·33 (10¾ ft) in width. The bays measure 10·34 (33¾ ft), 10·32 and 10·33 m. in width going from north to south (Plate 40*a*). The first bay is perfectly plain except for two windows with marble grilles, the second is entirely filled by the Puerta de San Estéban and its surrounding decoration; the masonry of the third has been cut away in the eighteenth century and replaced by the Capilla de San Simón.

The Puerta de San Estéban and its Decoration

We have already seen that this doorway and the rectangular frame of its arch are an insertion of 241 H. (855–6), but the ornament of the rest of the bay is most important, for it appears to be the only part of the first mosque that was decorated (Plate 40*b*). To right and left of the doorway are two bare panels with very curious decoration above them. The decorated surfaces, which are slightly oblong, are each occupied by a double staircase of three steps standing out in relief on a slightly sunk background. Both staircase and background are filled with plant ornament very coarsely executed, and a raised boss is also visible in the upper part of the sunk portion, just above the edge of the second step. Above this ornament is a smooth course of masonry. The

1. Amador de los Ríos, *Inscriptions árabes de Córdoba*, pp. 188–205; and Lévi-Provençal, *Inscriptions arabes*, pp. 8–9.

next two courses above are decorated, but the central third of the decoration has been cut away in each case to form a window, now filled with a marble grille. Over the door-frame, and at the same level as the decoration just mentioned, are four vertical strips of ornament which act as pilasters for three shallow arched panels. Five courses higher is a projecting cornice supported on nine corbels of the type called *modillons à copeaux*.

Gómez-Moreno, in 1906, suggested that this façade was actually the west façade of the church of St Vincent,[1] which is said to have occupied the site of the mosque. There are many objections to this theory. In the first place, it would be quite natural that the first work executed by the Muslims in Spain should be merely a continuation of the style in use on their arrival, as happened in Syria. Secondly the buttresses, which form one piece of masonry with the façade, being evenly spaced, would imply a church with aisles of equal width, which is scarcely thinkable. If we try to evade this difficulty by assuming five aisles – a wide central one flanked by two half the width – then we are compelled to ask: Why were only the central arcades buttressed? Then again, the curious stepped ornament suggests the Ancient East rather than Western Christendom. Finally Hernández has carried out extensive excavations under the pavement of the sanctuary of 'Abd ar-Rahmān I, and has found considerable remains of previous structures, but *none corresponding to the alignment of any part of the present structure*. So Gómez Moreno's theory must be rejected.

Were there originally Arcades round the Sahn?

This question can now be answered thanks to an interesting discovery made by Hernández. He has laid bare the east side of the tenth pier of the façade of the sanctuary and found that it is composite, as shown (Figure 43). The part *A* being due to 'Abd ar-Rahmān, had a flat face, instead of being L-shaped or T-shaped in plan. This proves that the original mosque had no lateral *riwāqs*. But at a later date this pier was made T-shaped by the addition of *B*. The finished north face of *A* runs behind *B*. Then came the addition of *C* which forms part of the reinforcing façade, which we have seen was added by an-Nāsir in

1. 'Excursion a través del arco de herradura', *Cultura Espanola*, 1906, pp. 797–8; restated in *Arquitectura*, II, p. 310.

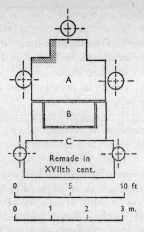

Figure 43. Cordova: The Great Mosque, construction
of tenth pier of façade of sanctuary

346 H. (958). The lateral *riwāqs* must therefore have been an innovation, introduced between the time of 'Abd ar-Rahmān I and 346 H.

The Form of the Riwāqs

It will be seen from the plan that the arcades which form the façade
of these *riwāqs* are supported by piers and columns, two columns
alternating with every pier. On the west side there are four such
groups and on the east likewise; on the north side there are seven
complete and two incomplete groups because of the projection of the
minaret. It is obvious that this scheme has been marked out on the
north side without any account having been taken of the minaret-
campanile, for the distance between the axis of the pier to the west of
the latter and the axis of the pier to the east of it is *exactly* double that
of one bay. This can only mean that the present scheme, in spite of
its Gothic dressings, goes back to a time prior to the construction of
the minaret of 340 H. (951–2). When this was built the arcade was cut
into and two bays were mutilated. We can therefore say that the *sahn*
was already surrounded by *riwāqs* in 340 H.

The Original Form of the Mosque of 'Abd ar-Rahmān in 170 H.

It follows from our analysis that the mosque originally consisted of a sanctuary 73·50 m. (241 ft) wide and 36·80 (221 ft) deep, divided into eleven aisles by ten arcades of twelve arches each, resting on

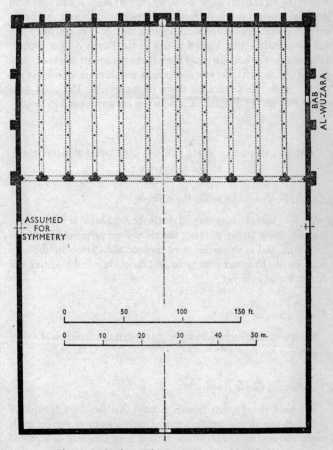

Figure 44. Cordova: The Great Mosque, original plan

marble columns and running perpendicular to the back wall. These arcades consisted of two tiers of arches, the lower of horse-shoe form, the upper slightly less than semicircles, supporting a flat ceiling 9·80 m. (32¼ ft) above the floor; above it were eleven parallel gable roofs with deep, lead-lined gutters between. The sanctuary opened on to the *sahn* by eleven horse-shoe arches resting on T-shaped piers; the *sahn* was 73·21 m. (240 ft) wide and 60·07 (197 ft) deep. It had a western door as shown, a northern door on the north–south axis, and probably an eastern door corresponding with the first. The sanctuary had one door only – that known to-day as the Puerta de San Estéban (Figure 44). The sanctuary had three buttresses to east and west, projecting 1·50 m. (5 ft), and two corner ones, and there were probably ten on the south side to take the thrust of the arcades. The walls were about 1·14 m. (3¾ ft) thick. The *sahn* was *not* surrounded by *riwāqs*.

ARCHITECTURAL ORIGINS OF THE GREAT MOSQUE OF CORDOVA

Arcades Perpendicular to the Back Wall

We have seen above (p. 207 ff.) that in the Aqsā Mosque of al-Mahdī, probably built in 163 H. (780), the aisles were perpendicular to the back wall, and in the earlier Aqsā mosque also. These are the only examples we have met with so far, so I conclude that this feature was due to Syrian influence.

The Horse-shoe Arch

We have already seen (above, pp. 74–5) that this feature is of Syrian origin.

The Parallel Gable Roofs

We have already seen (above, p. 207) that the Aqsā Mosque of al-Mahdī was almost certainly roofed with a series of parallel gable roofs. The roofing system of our mosque must therefore be regarded as of Syrian origin also.

The Scheme of the Arcades round the Sahn

The scheme, which we have seen must certainly go back to a date before 340 H. (951-2), is precisely that which we have already met with in the Great Mosque at Damascus (above, pp. 53-5). Here then we have another example of Syrian influence.

Syrians in Spain

How are we to explain these numerous indications of Syrian influence? By the fact that Andalusia was full of Syrians. 'Abd ar-Rahmān I was an Umayyad refugee from Syria where he had been born in 731, and he naturally had many Syrians round him. There is ample proof of this. For example Ibn al-Qutīya (d. 977) tells us that during the troubles in the reign of the Khalif Hishām (724-43), when there was open warfare between the Syrians on one side and the Arabs of the towns, allied to the Berbers, on the other, the Governor of Andalusia asked if the people were prepared to submit. 'We will swear obedience and fidelity to you,' cried the Berbers and the Arabs of the towns, 'but we can no longer endure in our midst *these hordes of Syrians.*' Farther on we read that Hishām decided to segregate the Syrians in the different provinces of Spain: 'Thus the people from Damascus were established at Elvira; those from the Jordan province at Ryia, those from Palestine near Sidonia, the people from Homs in the neighbourhood of Seville, those from Qinnasrīn at Jaen.' [1]

The same author tells us that after the invasion of the Normans (which took place in 844-5) the walls of Seville were rebuilt by 'Abd Allāh, a Syrian client of 'Abd ar-Rahmān II.[2]

The Double Tier of Arcades

This is the most original feature of the mosque. We have seen that there is a double tier of arches in the Great Mosque at Damascus and in the Aqsā Mosque (presumably Umayyad) which preceded the Aqsā of al-Mahdī, but the treatment is different from what we find at

1. Houdas' transl., *Recueil de textes et de traductions ... de l'École des Langues orientales vivantes*, pp. 235-6.
2. Ribera's text, p. 65; transl., p. 52.

Cordova. It has been suggested that the Cordovan scheme was in-spired by some double-tiered Roman aqueduct, such as the Acue-ducto de los Milagros at Merida, but here again the treatment is not quite the same, so we must allow considerable originality to the archi-tect of the mosque for his ingenious solution, for nothing quite like it exists elsewhere.

THE CISTERN OF RAMLA

This cistern is known locally as Bīr al-Anezīya. At the beginning of the nineteenth century, we find it attributed to St Helena, e.g. by Chateaubriand in 1806.[1] It is situated about half a mile to the north-west of Ramla, on the road from Jaffa to Jerusalem. It consists of a subterranean excavation, lined with strong retaining walls and divided into six aisles by five arcades of four arches each, running from east to west and resting on cruciform piers. It forms an irregular four-sided figure which tapers from 24 m. (78¾ ft) on the north side to about 20·50 (67¼ ft) on the south. The piers, however, are placed in a fairly regular fashion and the tapering form is partly compensated for by the diminishing projection of the wall-piers as one goes south (Figure 45). All the wall-piers are capped with inverted splay-face mouldings. The arches are all pointed and appear, on testing a num-ber of photographs with a pair of compasses, to be struck from two centres varying from one seventh to one fifth of the span apart. Wherever the plaster has fallen it can be seen that *key-stones have been adopted instead of median joints*. The height to the crown of the vault is 8 m. (26¼ ft) and the interior has a truly monumental appearance.

On the east–west arcades rest tunnel-vaults 55 cm. (21½ in.) thick, reinforced by three arcades running from north to south, which also spring from wall-piers. As these arches rise to the same level as the former there is a distance of about 2·50 m. (8 ft) between their sum-mits and the crown of the vault; the wall which fills this space and serves to reinforce the vault is lightened by arched openings, about 1·50 m. (5 ft) wide and 1·75 m. (5¾ ft) high (Plate 43). There is no bond between the filling wall and the vault above. The piers are cruciform in plan with arms averaging 31 cm. (12¼ in.) in length;

1. *Itinéraire de Paris à Jérusalem*, i, p. 131.

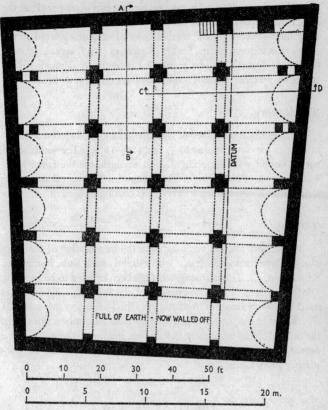

Figure 45. Ramla: The Cistern, plan

they have no mouldings, neither have the wall-piers on the north side.

A staircase 1·02 m. (3¼ ft) wide runs down the north side to the bottom of the cistern, which has a well-preserved pavement. This staircase has necessitated a slight modification of one of the arches; there being no room for a return on the north wall, it was replaced by half an arch like a flying buttress, which gives about 3 m. (9¾ ft) clearance above the staircase. A series of holes averaging 55 cm. (21½ in.) square, pierced in the vault of each bay, enabled twenty-four people at the same time to draw water by means of ropes and buckets. These holes were once covered by the marble bases of columns pierced in the centre so as to form collars, for De Monconys (1647) says: '... dans le haut de la voute il y a des trous où l'air entre, & desquels par les colomnes percées comme des ronds de puys on tiroit de l'eau.' [1]

The Masonry

The masonry is composed of well-dressed and finely jointed blocks, in courses varying from 29 to 41 cm. ($11\frac{1}{2}$–16 in.). The vaults are of rubble bound with a mortar of great strength, for the fallen south vault consists of huge blocks like monoliths. The whole of the interior walls is covered with a very solid coating of cement.

The Date

On the plaster of the vault opposite the first landing of the staircase is a large rectangular frame with a slightly sunk Kufic inscription, which runs: '... This is among what has been ordered to be made by Dīnār the client of the Commander of the Faithful. ... And it was executed by the hands of 'Abd A ... in Dhu'l-Hijja 172 (May 789).' [2] The Khalif in question was Hārūn ar-Rashīd. Not only is this cistern the only 'Abbāsid monument in Palestine, but it constitutes *the earliest known example of the systematic and exclusive employment of the free-standing pointed arch.*

THE RIBĀT OF SŪSA

The Ribāt of Sūsa on the Gulf of Gabes is known locally as Qsar ar-Ribāt. It is a square fortified building measuring roughly 39 m. (128 ft) a side without the towers, of which there are eight: one in the centre of each side and one at each corner; all are semicircular, ex-

1. *Journal de Voyages*, I, p. 300.

2. First published by van Berchem, 'Inscriptions arabes de Syrie', in *Mém. de l'Institut égyptien*, III, pp. 420–23. The above version is a new reading made by Dr L. A. Mayer, after the inscription had been cleaned a little; published in Wiet, *Répertoire d'épigraphie arabe*, V, p. 189.

cept the entrance tower and that at the south-east corner. The whole is built in masonry in courses of about 51 cm. (20 in.), and the total height of the walls above the present ground level is about 8·50 m. (28 ft).

The Interior

The entrance is in the tower in the centre of the south side, which originally only projected 3·17 m. (10¼ ft) until an addition was made to it in 1264 H. (1848), according to an inscription over the entrance. We descend about 2·80 m. (9¼ ft) by a staircase, of which nearly half belongs to the added part.

Arrived at the bottom of the staircase we enter the *ribāt* proper by a door with a lintel and semicircular relieving arch. In front of us is a passage of three bays: the first is flanked by open tunnel-vaulted rooms which may have served for the guard, whereas the second and third bays, which have transverse tunnel-vaults, are flanked by tunnel-vaulted galleries which really form one with them. The third bay opens into the courtyard between a staircase which runs up to right and left (Figure 46).

The courtyard measures 19·21 m. (63 ft) from north to south and 20·41 (67 ft) from east to west. On the east, north, and west sides are vaulted porticoes which open on to it by arches resting on piers, five to east and west and six on the north. The east and north arcades have been reconstructed, but the west *riwāq*, which has arches more or less hemispherical, may be original although the masonry is concealed by plaster. This is rendered still more probable by the fact that each bay is covered by a tunnel-vault perpendicular to the façade, whereas the bays of the north and east *riwāqs* are covered by cross vaults.

Behind these porticoes are twenty-six tunnel-vaulted rooms without windows, all of which open into the porticoes by a single door, except those in the corners which open into the room next to them. These rooms vary in depth from 3·50 to 3·60 m. (11½–11¾ ft), except on the east side where they are 3 m. (9¾ ft) only. On the south side there are five similar rooms and the two corner rooms, all being 3·85 m. (12½ ft) deep. Above these rooms on the east, north, and west is a series of similar rooms to which the vaulted porticoes form a terrace, 5·30 m. (17½ ft) above the level of the court.

The Mosque

On the south side these rooms are replaced by a mosque, divided into eleven aisles by ten arcades of two arches each, placed perpendicular to the *qibla* wall. The semicircular arches spring from low cruciform piers without mouldings. On these arcades rest tunnel vaults reinforced by an arcade running from east to west. In other words, we have here exactly the same vaulting system as that we have just seen in the Cistern of Ramla, and exactly as we shall find later in the Mosque of Bū Fatātā and the Great Mosque of Sūsa.

The roof of the mosque being on the same level as the rooms of the upper storey, the whole forms a terrace 9·90 m. (32½ ft) above the level of the court, which goes all round like a rampart walk although there are no crenellations to-day, but only a low parapet. The staircase to this upper terrace is in the south-west corner.

The Manār

The Manār at the south-east corner, is a circular tower 4·72 m. (15½ ft) in diameter and 15·38 (50½ ft) high to the floor of the gallery at the top. Over the entrance is a marble slab with a Kufic inscription saying that 'this is one of the things which have been built by Ziyādat Allāh the son of Ibrāhīm ... in the year 206 (821–2)'.[1] Ziyādat Allāh was the third ruler of the Aghlabid Dynasty.

Function of a Ribāt

A *ribāt* was a small fortified barracks built on the frontier of Muslim territory and garrisoned with volunteers. Those anxious to acquire merit by taking part in the holy war could offer their services and pass some time in a *ribāt*, giving themselves up to religious devotion in the intervals of warfare.

1. Houdas and Basset, *Épigraphie tunisienne*, in the *Bull. de Correspondance africaine*, IV, pp. 168–70.

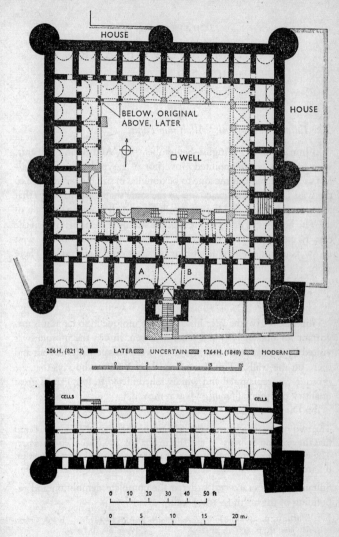

Figure 46. Sūsa: The Ribāt, plan

CHAPTER 12

THE MOSQUE OF ʿAMR
IN 212 H. (827)

The Enlargement of ʿAbd Allāh ibn Ṭāhir

In Jumādā II, 212 (August–September 827) ʿAbd Allāh ibn Ṭāhir, who had just been appointed Governor of Egypt by the Khalif al-Maʾmūn, ordered this mosque to be doubled in size by the addition to the west (= sw.) of its exact area in the same shape. Maqrīzī says that the part added included the great miḥrāb, and all that is to the west of it.[1] The number of doors in the mosque was now thirteen: five on the east (= NE.) three on the north (= NW.) side, four on the west (= sw.), and one for the Khaṭīb or preacher on the qibla side.[2] There were 378 columns.

Later History of the Mosque

I must now give the later history of the mosque in so far as it is important for our analysis and reconstruction. In 985 the mosque was visited by Muqaddasī, who says there were mosaic patterns here and there on the walls.[3] This is confirmed by Yāqūt, who says that the mosque was replastered and whitewashed in 387 H. (997) and a great quantity of mosaic (fusaifisā) was removed.[4]

Ibn Duqmāq says:

The two riwāqs which are in the ṣaḥn of the mosque. al-Ḥākim ordered that they should be built ... and this in Shaʿbān 406 (Jan.–Feb. 1016)....
These two complete the number of riwāqs which still exist: seven on the front, seven on the back, five to the east, and five to the west.[5]

Sultan Baybars (1260–77) ordered the complete demolition and rebuilding of the north (= NW.) wall.[6]

1. Khitat, II, p. 249, ll. 33–6. 2. Ibid., II, p. 253, ll. 22–3. 3. pp. 198–9.
4. Muʿjam, III, p. 899, ll. 21–2. 5. IV, p. 68, ll. 14–20.
6. Ibn Duqmāq, IV, p. 69, l. 22 to p. 70, l. 14; Maqrīzī, II, p. 251, l. 39 to p. 252, l. 13.

Maqrīzī says that the mosque was once more in a ruinous state, that 'its arches were out of the perpendicular, and that it was on the point of collapsing, while the great ones of the realm after the death of Sultan Barqūq (1399) had too much other business and pleasure to attend to'. A certain Burhān ad-Dīn, Chief of the merchants, took up the matter and resolved to restore the mosque at his own expense and that of his fellows. The whole *qibla* side of the mosque was demolished (*hadm*) and rebuilt '*in its whole length and breadth, from the great mihrāb to the sahn*', the breaches or weak points in the wall were all repaired, and the whole mosque was plastered 'so that it became new again, after it had been on the point of collapsing'. This restoration was completed in 804 H. (1401–2).[1]

This restoration is a fact of vital importance which cannot be emphasized too much, for the idea that the sanctuary of the Mosque of ‘Amr is an authentic document of the first few centuries of Islam was very widespread. We shall see that the present sanctuary does not even go back to the reign of Barqūq.

Pococke's Plan

We now come to the oldest existing plan of the mosque, made by Pococke in 1737. It is of the first importance, as very far-reaching changes in the structure were to be made before the end of the century. It shows a mosque with *riwāqs* of unusual depth, there being seven rows of columns on the side of the *qibla*, seven on the opposite side, and six in the lateral *riwāqs*.[2]

Murād Bey's Restoration

An account of Murād Bey's work has been given by a contemporary, al-Jabartī, who says that the mosque was in a ruinous state, the roof and columns having fallen, and the right-hand half (i.e. the sw. *riwāq*) being out of the perpendicular, had fallen likewise. He says that Murād Bey was persuaded to undertake the restoration, and that he expended large sums, that 'he set up its corners and strengthened its construction, and arranged its columns, and perfected its decoration, and built two minarets to it, and restored the whole roof with

1. II, p. 253, ll. 10–18.   2. *Description of the East*, i, p. 28 and pl. XI.

sound wood, and plastered the whole of it ... and an assembly was held in it on the last Friday of Ramadān 1212 (18 March 1798).' [1]

What modification did Murād Bey make? Our next plan – that made by Pascal Coste between 1818 and 1826 – must give the answer. Here we see the NW. *riwāq* reduced to a single aisle, the NE. to three, the SW. to two, and the sanctuary to six. A mausoleum appears in the east corner for the first time, likewise a fountain in the *sahn*, which is readily recognized as the present one. Nevertheless, although so soon after Murād Bey's restoration, Coste says: 'A l'époque actuelle, la mosquée d'Amrou est presque abandonnée, plusieurs parties tombent en ruine, faute d'entretien.' [2]

Muhammad 'Alī apparently took it in hand for Orlebar, writing in 1845, says: 'By order of the present pasha, it is undergoing repair. which are entirely revolutionizing it.' [3] Girault de Prangey, speaking of these works, says: '... en 1843, j'ai vu les deux tiers en reconstruction, du sol jusqu'aux toits.' A little farther on he says, speaking of the sanctuary: 'De ce côté, dans la direction de l'Est à l'Ouest, regnent six rangs de nefs, *malheureusement reconstruites tout récemment.*'[4] It must have been during these works that the façade of the sanctuary took its present form, as may be seen from Teynard's photograph taken in 1851.[5] Here the alternation of square piers between two pairs of columns, a feature not shown on Coste's plan, appears for the first time, and these piers have pilasters which terminate in a moulding typical of the period of Muhammad 'Alī.

DESCRIPTION AND ANALYSIS

The present Mosque of 'Amr is a vast enclosure measuring 109·05 m. (358 ft) internally on the south-east side, 105·28 m. (345 ft) on the north-west, 120·55 (395 ft) on the north-east, and 117·28 (384 ft) on the south-west, that is to say the south-east side is 3·50 (11½ ft), and

1. *'Ajā'ib al-Āthār*, III, p. 170.

2. *Architecture arabe, ou monuments du Kaire*, p. 31.

3 'Mohamedan Architecture in Cairo', *Journ. Bombay Branch, Roy. Asiatic Socy*, II, p. 123.

4. *Monuments arabes d'Égypte, de Syrie et d'Asie-Mineure*, pp. 2–3.

5. *Égypte et Nubie*, I, pl. 5.

the north-east 2·72 m. (9 ft) longer than the side opposite. In addition to this it is 7·60 m. (25 ft) askew. The walls, which are a patchwork of various periods, vary from 1 to 2 m. (3¼–6½ ft) in thickness.

The North-West Façade

This is about 9·40 m. (30¾ ft) in height, and there are still three entrances in it as in Ibn Tāhir's day. The central part for about 55 m. (180 ft) is about 2 m. (6½ ft) thick. Seven windows still exist in this part, similar to the five in the thick part of the south-west wall (north end). A small column is set on each side of the opening, and a beam 2 m. (6½ ft) long is placed transversely on it. The window arch is sprung from this beam. Above these beams is another one parallel to the wall face, which cuts off the tympanum from the lower part of the window, each part being filled by a stucco grille. These windows are obviously late copies, made when these two lengths of wall were rebuilt, probably after the great earthquake of 1303, of the windows in Ibn Tāhir's work which we shall study presently, except that they lack the little brick colonnettes at their inner and outer corners.

The South-West Façade

For the first 34 m. (111 ft), measured from the left, this façade has an appearance of age. There are six windows, of which the first (Plate 44) appears to have consisted of a central opening flanked by a pair of little niches (the right one has disappeared during some patching of the brickwork). The other five bear a strong resemblance to those of the north-west façade; for example, they have no engaged colonnettes at their inner and outer corners, and the misshapen form of their slightly horse-shoe arches recalls the form of those arches of the Mosque of al-Hākim which are due to the restoration of 1304. This, added to the exceptional thickness of the wall, makes it probable that this length of wall is of the same date as the thick part of the north-west wall. After these windows there is a long strip of mean brickwork which runs to a point level with the façade of the sanctuary. A good part of the wall from this point to the end appears to belong to the work of 212 H. (827) and two walled-up windows are visible on the axis of the second and fifth aisles of the sanctuary.

The South-East Façade

On turning the corner we observe that the first 34 m. is a uniform piece of brickwork; it is plain below but the upper 5 m. is occupied by a row of windows. In each a central arched opening is flanked by two narrower ones on either side. They average 3·30 m. (10¾ ft) in width over all, and there is about 2·25 m. (7½ ft) of plain brickwork between them, so that the pitch, or distance from centre to centre, is about 5·25 m. (17¼ ft). After this part the qibla wall is a mean patchwork of many periods with timber incorporated in some places; there are four clumsy buttresses and the projecting back part of two mihrābs. The east corner is formed by a domed mausoleum certainly not earlier than the nineteenth century.

The North-East Façade

At a distance of 28 m. (92 ft) from the corner we observe two windows, the arches of which must clearly have rested on engaged columns. Beams have been let into the wall at the springing of these arches and also lower down. The springing of the arch of a third window has been preserved. The present façade of the sanctuary cuts right into the second window. During the works carried out in 1932 the lower part of this wall, which was badly eaten away, was hacked out to a depth of nearly a metre in some places and new brickwork inserted. This resulted in the discovery, in the heart of the wall, of five entrances with part of the plaster lining of their door-jambs intact. These openings averaged 2·70 m. (8¾ ft) in width and are very evenly spaced. The southernmost was found to have a marble sill 85 cm. (33½ in.) below the present floor of the sanctuary.

The Interior

On entering one of the doors in the north-west façade, we find ourselves in the north-west riwāq. The sahn is little better than a piece of waste ground, covered by earth and sand. The bases of three rows of columns which once formed the north-east riwāq still exist almost complete. The arches ran perpendicular to the sahn, and the springing of many can still be seen on the wall. Nothing remains of the south-western *riwāq*.

On the far side is the sanctuary which opens on to the *sahn* by twenty arches resting on piers and coupled columns. Internally it is divided into twenty aisles by nineteen arcades, each of six arches braced by wooden tie-beams, running perpendicular to the back wall. The flat wooden roof dates from the end of the nineteenth century. There are two mihrābs in the tenth and fifteenth aisles counting from the west, dated 1212 and 1211 H. respectively, the former date being the year in which Murād Bey's work was completed.

The only part that shows any signs of early date is the right side where there are six wall-piers, each with a column standing about a metre from it and joined to it by wooden architraves, some of which are carved with a late Hellenistic composition (Plate 45*a*), unlike any-thing else to be found in the Muslim Architecture of Egypt. It is ob-viously a descendant of the Syrian friezes mentioned above (pp. 38–9) in connexion with the cornices of the dome piers in the Dome of the Rock. For this reason they must be put as far back as possible, for nothing of the sort is known in Tūlūnid work. But, on the other hand, we cannot put them farther back than 212 H. (827), for the mosque did not extend so far before that date. Here, therefore, we have without a doubt, a genuine portion of the work of 'Abd Allāh ibn Tāhir, a fixed point on which our analysis must be pivoted. But these six wall-piers tell us more; the only possible interpretation to which they lend themselves revolutionizes an idea hitherto accepted without question, viz., that the arcades of the sanctuary always ran perpendicular to the back wall. In the example illustrated (Plate 45*a*) the broken-off end of a tie-beam can be seen. These engaged columns, now functionless, can only have served for the springing of the arches of six arcades running parallel to the *qibla* wall. An engaged column, with remains of the upper half of a similar carved wooden entablature, has recently been exposed between the fifth and sixth windows from the north, and a column-base in the next pier to the north, so this system must have prevailed in the north-west *riwāq* also. If any doubt still remains as to the age of the present arcades, it may be pointed out that they cut into the seven blocked-up windows still existing in the back wall. We have seen that these windows average 3·30 m. (10¾ ft) in width and the spaces between them 2·25 m. (7¼ ft). The wall space at the end of

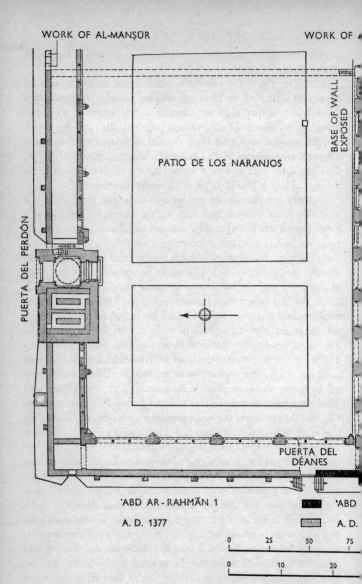

WORK OF AL-MANṢŪR   WORK OF A

BASE OF WALL
EXPOSED

PATIO DE LOS NARANJOS

PUERTA DEL PERDÓN

PUERTA DEL
DÉANES

'ABD AR-RAHMĀN 1   'ABD

A. D. 1377   A. D.

0   25   50   75

0   10   20

Figure 47. Cordova: The Gre

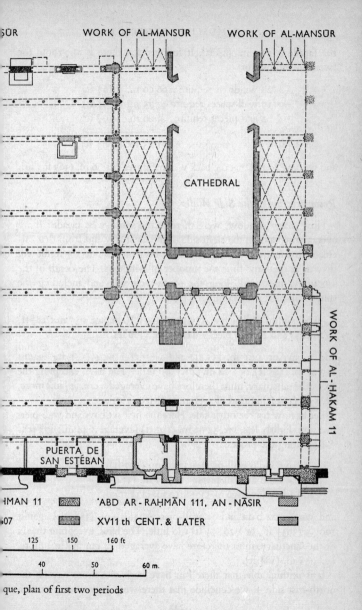

CATHEDRAL

WORK OF AL-HAKAM II

PUERTA DE
SAN ESTÉBAN

ḤMAN II ░░░░░ 'ABD AR-RAḤMĀN III, AN-NĀSIR

607 ▒▒▒▒▒ XVII th CENT. & LATER

125	150	160 ft
40	50	60 m.

que, plan of first two periods

the façade is 1·50 m. (4¾ ft). It follows that there is just room for twenty windows for

20 windows require   66·00 m. (216½ ft)
19 wall spaces require 42·75 m. (140½ ft)
2 end pieces require   3·00 m.   (9¾ ft)

                        111·75 m. (366¾ ft)

and we have found that the back wall measures 111·86 m. (367 ft 1 in.).

Reconstruction of the Side Walls

How many windows were there in the south-west façade? If we average the bays on the right side of the sanctuary and from that calculate how many bays there must have been on this side, the result will give us at the same time the number of windows. The depth of the sanctuary, measured along the south-west side and including the outer wall pier, is 33·43 m. (109 ft).

6 bays and 6 wall piers = 33·43 m. (109 ft) (average 5·57 m.; 18¼ ft)
20 bays and 20 wall piers = 111·43 m. (366 ft)

add 1 bay, or 4·61 m. (15 ft) and we get 116·04 (381 ft) against 117·28 m. (385 ft), or 1·24 m. (4 ft) too little. The bays, excepting the six of the sanctuary, must therefore have averaged 8 cm. (2¾ in.) more, i.e. 5·65 (18½ ft) instead of 5·57 m. (18¼ ft).

Let us now try the other side. Here the first six bays and wall-piers measure slightly less, viz. 32·62 m. (107 ft) (average 5·44 m.; 17¾ ft).

Repeating the process:

6 bays and 6 wall-piers = 32·62 m. (107 ft)
21 bays and 21 wall-piers = 114·17 m. (374¾ ft)
add 1 bay (average of 5) = 4·12 m. (13½ ft)

and we get 22 bays and 21 wall-piers = 118·29 m. (388¼ ft) against 120·55 (395¼ ft), or 2·26 (7½ ft) too little. The bays, excepting the six of the sanctuary, must therefore have averaged 14 cm (5½ in.) more, i.e. 5·58 m. (18¼ ft).

It is unthinkable that there can have been one more bay on the north-east side. If we conclude that there were only twenty-one on the north-east side, we must increase the width of those beyond the sanctuary by 41 cm. (16 in.) to 5·99 m. (19¾ ft); if we decide that there were twenty-two on the south-west side we must decrease their width by 32 cm. (12½ in.) to 5·33 m. (17½ ft). Let us choose the smaller adjustment and assume that there were twenty-two bays and twenty-one wall-piers on each side. If we now turn to Coste's plan (1818–26) we find that he too shows this number of bays and wall-piers; Pococke also, in 1737, or sixty years before Murād Bey, shows twenty-one rows of columns in this direction. Our choice, therefore, appears to be correct. Ibn Duqmāq, the only author to mention the windows, says: 'The trussed [window-]arches (hanīya al-mukandaja)[1] – which are at the top of the walls of the mosque. There are seventy-eight … seventeen on the south (= SE.) wall, and on the north (= NW.) wall, including those which are hidden by the staircase to the roof and the dīwān istifāʿ al-aḥbās, seventeen also, and on the east (= NE.) wall, including those that are hidden by the said dīwān, twenty-two. In the west (= SW.) wall twenty-two, of which some are hidden by the cage of the staircase.' Our reconstruction of the side walls is therefore correct, but how reconcile the number of windows (twenty) which we have calculated for the south-east and north-west walls with the seventeen of Ibn Duqmāq? I suggest that a window was omitted above the three miḥrābs and the three north-western doors.

The Windows

By combining what remains of the two windows on either side of the west corner (Plate 46), and another one at the south-west end of the sanctuary in the second bay from the sahn, we can reconstruct the very remarkable windows of 212 H. (827) as follows: The arched opening was flanked externally and internally by little colonnettes, built of specially shaped bricks, for which recesses were provided. A dwarf column of marble was placed on either side of the opening and partly sunk in the jamb, a hollow being expressly left in the brick-work. Three substantial pieces of wood are set on each side perpendicular to the face of the wall, partly resting on the column and partly

1. Kandaja = beam employed in vaulted construction; Kazimirski, I, p. 930a; see also Freytag, IV, p. 63, col. 1; therefore presumably the tie-beams of the arches (hanīya) of the windows.

embedded in the brickwork. Resting on them, and at right angles to them, are five similar pieces running back into the wall, of which the central one ran right across the opening like a tie-beam, and served as a support for the stucco grille about 4 cm. ($1\frac{1}{2}$ in.) thick which filled the tympanum of the arch, whilst a similar grille, rectangular in shape, filled the lower part of the window (Figure 48).

The arch is composed of four rings of bricks set as shown, the inner ring being recessed to take a *permanent* timber framework, consisting of an exterior and interior centering, each composed of three pieces of wood scarfed together, and kept a fixed distance apart by four struts mortised into them.

The woodwork was decorated as follows: The side of the beam was covered by a thin strip of wood on which was carved a flowing acanthus frieze (Plate 46) which instantly recalls a whole series of similar ornament, beginning with the sixth century at al-Barā, Mijlayya, the Golden Gate at Jerusalem, and the cornices of the dome piers in the Dome of the Rock (Plate 3) and several wall-plates of A.D. 780 in the Aqsā Mosque (Plate 42). This frieze turns into the window recesses, continues along the transverse beam, turns outwards once more and runs along until it meets the next arcade (Figure 49). Above this, in the turned-in part, is a cornice of *acanthus spinosus*, which is not carried along the wall face, but stops at about 25 cm. ($9\frac{3}{4}$ in.) from the edge of the window with a bold vertical frame.

Reconstruction of the Interior

Between 1926 and 1933 a number of trial trenches were made in the Mosque of 'Amr which have provided decisive evidence as to the number, position, and direction of the arcades of the mosque. First it was found that a line of brick foundations, 1·25 m. (4 ft) wide, ran roughly parallel to the present façade of the sanctuary, proving that it must originally have had seven aisles as I had predicted.[1] It was also found that similar rows of foundations, 1·25 m. (4 ft) wide, ran from the piers with engaged columns at the right end of the sanctuary to piers on the north-east wall, parallel to the first mentioned. It was found that the columns did not rest on these old foundations, but de-

1. In the competition held in 1927 for the reconstruction of the Mosque of 'Amr, 'à la période de sa plus grande splendeur'.

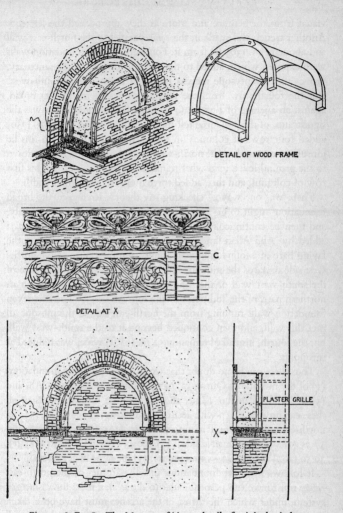

DETAIL OF WOOD FRAME

C

DETAIL AT X

PLASTER GRILLE

X→

Figure 48. Fustāt: The Mosque of 'Amr, detail of original window
of 212 H. (827)

245

viated from them more and more as they approached the left end. Another trench was made in the *sahn*, parallel to the north-east wall and about 12 m. (39½ ft) from it. Fourteen rows of foundation walls were exposed which, added to the seven belonging to the sanctuary, proves that twenty-one arcades ran from north-east to south-west. But the fourth row from the north-west was 2 m. (6½ ft) broad, against an average of 1·25 m. (4 ft) or so for the rest. What was the significance of this? Maqrīzī tell us that Sālih ibn ʿAlī in 133 H. (750) added four rows of columns on the north-west side. To do this he must have demolished the north-west wall of Qurra ibn Sharīk down to the ground level, used what remained as a foundation for his first row of columns, and then added three more of the normal width.

There was one way of checking my theory. If correct, the broad foundation ought to go as far as the centre line of the mosque only, and then be continued, with a much smaller width, across the part added by ʿAbd Allāh ibn Tāhir. Further excavations resulted in the laying bare of a foundation wall going from the centre of the north-west side towards the mihrāb. This, of course, was the foundation of the south-west wall of the mosque of Qurra ibn Sharīk and, in its northern part, of the addition of Sālih ibn ʿAlī in 750. The first seven foundation walls running from the north-east side of the mosque all met this wall, and then continued beyond it to the south-west wall, but the fourth, instead of remaining 2 m. (6½ ft) wide, was reduced at this point.

Thus there can be no doubt that we have the authentic foundations (1) of the mosque of Qurra, (2) of the addition of Sālih ibn ʿAlī, and (3) of ʿAbd Allāh ibn Tāhir, and the internal measurements of all these can now be given with accuracy as follows: (1) 98·20 m. (322 ft) north-east, 95·85 (314 ft) south-west, 50 (164 ft) north-west, and 57·55 (188 ft) on the *qibla* side; (2) 120·55 (395 ft), 117·70 (385 ft), 49·50 (162½ ft), and 57·55 m. (189 ft); (3) the same as at present.

It follows from the foundations that the arcades of the north-east *riwāq* must have run perpendicular to the *sahn*, a most unsatisfactory system, under which the thrust of the arcades must have been taken by tie-beams. But another surprise was to come. The foundation wall running parallel to the façade of the sanctuary was exposed for a considerable length, and it was found that the foundation walls of the south-west *riwāq* took off perpendicularly from it, and ran parallel to

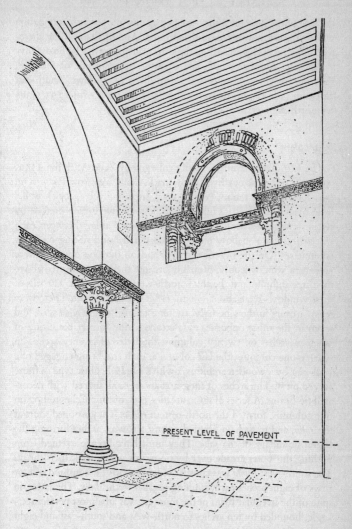

PRESENT LEVEL OF PAVEMENT

Figure 49. Fustāt: The Mosque of 'Amr, reconstruction of a bay on right side of sanctuary

the side of the *sahn* until they stopped against the seventh foundation wall on the north-west side of the mosque. 'Abd Allāh ibn Tāhir, therefore, constructed his arcades on the same principle as Ibn Tūlūn did fifty years later. Another trench laid bare the opposite side of the *sahn*, showing that its measurements had been as follows: south-east 52·15 m. (171 ft), north-west 51·58 (169 ft), north-east 42·33 (138½ ft), north-west 41·20 (142 ft).

Summary

The Mosque of 'Amr, as finally enlarged by 'Abd Allāh ibn Tāhir, consisted of a vast but irregularly marked out area, roughly 110 m. (361 ft) wide and 120 m. (394 ft) deep, surrounded by a brick wall a little over 9 m. (29½ ft) high. The side walls were each pierced by twenty-two windows lighting the twenty-two aisles; between each externally was a shallow niche with a fluted hood resting on brick colonnettes. On the side of the *qibla* and on the side opposite were seventeen windows only, probably because they were omitted above the three mihrābs and the three north-western entrances. The sills of these windows were about 5·50 m. (18 ft) from the floor. There were seven arcades in the sanctuary, running parallel to the *qibla* wall, and seven in the *riwāq* opposite, each arcade of the former consisting of nineteen arches on twenty columns, the latter of twenty arches on twenty-one columns, the last column at each end being engaged to a wall-pier by a wooden architrave, with a late Hellenistic type of frieze carved on it. The arches of these arcades were all braced with decorated tie-beams. A series of seven arcades, each of four arches resting on five columns, formed the north-eastern *riwāq*. They stopped short at the *sahn*, and must have abutted against a row of arches forming the lateral boundary of the *sahn*. They must have been prevented from pushing this outer arcade over by tie-beams which took their thrust. The south-west *riwāq* was constructed differently; it consisted of four rows of eight arches each, running parallel to the *sahn*. The latter, in spite of the irregular form of the mosque, was an almost perfect rectangle, bounded by ten arches to north-west and south-east and eight on the other two sides.

CHAPTER 13

QAIRAWĀN: I

HISTORY OF THE GREAT MOSQUE

THE mosque, as enlarged by Bishr ibn Safwān (see above, p. 110), was demolished, with the exception of the minaret and mihrāb, by Yazīd ibn Hātim in 155 H. (772) [1] and rebuilt in 157 H. (773-4).

Ziyādat Allāh, the third ruler of the Aghlabid Dynasty, demolished Yazīd's mosque and rebuilt it in 221 H. (836). al-Bakrī says that he 'had all the mosque demolished, and even ordered the mihrāb to be destroyed. People pointed out to him that all his predecessors had abstained from touching this part of the edifice, because 'Uqba ibn Nāfi' had constructed it; he persisted in his resolution, not wishing that the new building should exhibit the least trace of work that was not his. In order to turn him from his intention, one of the builders proposed that the old mihrāb should be enclosed between two walls, in such a way that no part of it was visible from the interior of the mosque. This plan was adopted, and down to our time the mosque of Qairawān has remained just as Ziyādat Allāh left it. The present mihrāb, as well as all that surrounds it, from top to bottom, is constructed of white marble open work covered with carving. Part of this decoration consists of inscriptions, the rest forms arabesques of various patterns. Round the mihrāb are extremely beautiful columns of marble. The two red columns of which we have spoken are placed in front of the mihrāb, and serve to support the [semi-]dome of which they form part. The mosque contains 414 columns, forming seventeen naves. Its length is 220 cubits, its width 150'.[2]

The Work of Abū Ibrāhīm Ahmad, 248 H. (862-3).

According to Ibn Nājī, he decorated the mihrāb with marble panels, placed faience tiles on its façade, and made the beautiful

1. al-Bakrī, p. 23; de Slane's transl., p. 59.   2. al-Bakrī, pp. 23-4.

pulpit. The date of this work, which will be discussed below (pp. 296–9), is given by Ibn 'Adhārī as 248 H. (862–3).[1]

Additions of Ibrāhīm II, son of Ahmad

al-Bakrī continues:

Ibrāhīm the son of Ahmad ... prolonged the naves of the sanctuary and constructed, at the end of the nave which leads to the mihrāb, the dome called Qubbat Bāb al-Bahū (Dome of the Gate of the Pavilion). It is surrounded by thirty-two columns of beautiful marble; its interior is covered with magnificent carved decoration and arabesques executed with wonderful sharpness; all who see it do not hesitate to declare, that it would be impossible to find a more beautiful monument elsewhere.[2]

He does not give the date of completion, but Ibrāhīm II reigned from 875 to 902.

Shortly after A.D. 1043 the Governor, al-Muʿizz ibn Bādīs openly defied the Fāṭimid Khalif of Egypt by ordering the Friday prayer to be made in the name of the Abbāsid Khalif. The Fāṭimid Khalif took a diabolical revenge by encouraging the various branches of the great Hilālī tribe of Bedawīn, at the rate of a dinar per man, to cross the Nile and establish themselves in Barqa. Eventually immense hordes of Bedawīn arrived in the neighbourhood of Qairawān, which was taken and sacked in 446 H. (1054–5) the population massacred, the houses ruined, the fruit trees cut down, and the water-courses blocked. al-Muʿizz fled and the whole province was devastated and ruined.[3] al-Marrakūshī says that the town was still in ruins when he was there in 1217.[4]

The next event concerning the mosque is the restoration effected under the Hafsid Dynasty in 693 H. (1294); it is recorded by two inscriptions, one on the Bāb Lalla Rejāna the other on the right side of a porch on the west side.

1. p. 106.   2. p. 24.
3. Ibn 'Adhārī, *Bayān*, I, p. 300.
4. Fagnan's transl., pp. 192 and 305.

DESCRIPTION AND ANALYSIS OF THE GREAT MOSQUE

The mosque consists of a great oblong enclosure with its main axis pointing approximately south-east (the true direction of Mekka is 20° 43' s. of e.). The internal measurements are: north-west 65·30 m. (214 ft), south-east 70·28 (230 ft), north-east 120·80 (396 ft), south-west 120·50 (395 ft).

The Exterior

This presents a most irregular and unsatisfactory appearance (Plates 47–8) the outline being broken by buttresses of varying size and form, irregularly spaced. The doors on the south-west side are almost invariably set between two buttresses, the space between being occupied by a porch. The whole has been covered with innumerable traces of whitewash, except the buttresses on the *qibla* side. As the ground slopes from north-west to south-east the walls vary in height from 8 (26¼ ft) to about 10 m. (32¾ ft). The only redeeming features externally are the five domes and the massive minaret.

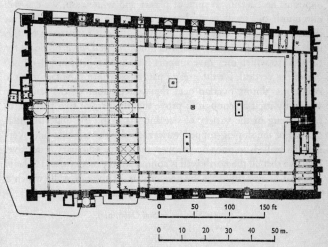

Figure 50. Qairawān: Great Mosque, plan

The only part of the whole structure that in any way approaches the monumental is the wall on the *qibla* side. Here the buttresses, although varying in size, are all of one form – a rectangular pier not bevelled off at the top. They also appear to follow a certain rhythm, two or three small ones alternating with each massive one. And here, fortunately, two massive buttresses have escaped a baptism of whitewash (Plate 47*a*) and it is possible to see that they are of the same peculiar small masonry as the minaret (Plate 25). Traces of this scheme of large and small buttresses with flat tops are visible round both flanks, as far as the northern limit of the sanctuary, after which all have sloping tops, but no two are of the same width and all vary more or less in the level at which the slope back begins.

These sloping-topped buttresses are obviously the work of many hands and denote various makeshift attempts to keep the walls from collapse. There is no possibility of confusing the two types and periods. Take, for example, the buttress to the right of the walled-up entrance on the east side of the sanctuary (Plate 47*b*) and compare it with the buttress flanking it to the left. The former is closely related to the small buttresses of the *qibla* wall, the latter to the sloping-topped buttresses on the west side. Now let us examine the walled-up door opposite; here again, in spite of plaster and whitewash, we can still distinguish the small vertical type to the left of the door, and at exactly the same distance from it. As for the other buttresses on this side, which are very deep and wide, their *raison d'être* is obvious, for the wall to which they give support is from 20 to 25 cm. (7¾–9¾ in.) out of the vertical, for the greater part of its length. The fact that the two types almost overlap near the western door of the sanctuary would by itself be enough to prove that they are of two periods, to say nothing of the variety of size and shape and the quite irregular spacing of the sloping-topped variety; finally the fact that one overlaps the walled-up door on the west side of the sanctuary is decisive. I believe that all the north wall is comparatively modern, and Saladin says that he was told that the greater part of the east wall (which is not leaning outwards) was rebuilt in the eighteenth century.[1]

1. *La Mosquée de Sidi Okba*, p. 9.

The Doorways

There are eight doorways, four on the east side and four on the west. On the east side only one has a domed porch, viz. the fourth from the north, known as the Bāb Lalla Rejāna due, according to an inscription, to Abū Hafs in 693 H. (1294). The other three are set in shallow, arched recesses of varying depth, flanked by engaged columns. The arches of the first two are exactly alike, both having a moulding which runs round, forms a loop at the apex, and is then carried round so as to form a rectangular frame, the result being a perfect replica of the arch of the Bāb Lalla Rejāna. I therefore conclude that they are of the same period. As for the third, its masonry is entirely hidden by whitewash, but its arch is of a simple pointed form which in no way resembles the arches of the early part of the mosque.

On the west side all the doors are preceded by little porches, of which I and 4 are domed, one is cross-vaulted and one has a mean roof of rafters. The only door partly free from plaster and whitewash is the main entrance to the sanctuary (known as Bāb as-Sultān) opposite the Bāb Lalla Rejāna. Here we have the same moulding framing the arch and forming a loop at the apex, so it is probably of the same date except its mean cresting, which is on a par with the architecture of a village *welī*. The same remark applies to the first door from the north. As for the second and third they are meaner still.

The two Original Doors

To the south of the third door on the west side is a curious recess slightly overlapped by a buttress. At first sight it looks like a walled-up window. At the same spot on the opposite side is another recess, 2·75 m. (9 ft) wide, covered by a round horse-shoe arch; it is clearly a walled-up entrance (Plate 47*b*). An examination of the wall surface on the inner side of the other recess showed the line of filling distinctly visible.

These two entrances must have exactly flanked the old façade of the sanctuary as we have seen at Damascus, Cordova, etc., until the portico was formed by prolonging the naves of the sanctuary, in the reign of Ibrāhīm II, at some date after 875, when I conclude that fresh doorways were made on the site of the present third entrance from the north, to flank the new façade. Now, let it be especially noted, these two walled-up entrances are merely plain openings flush with the wall, just as mosque entrances *always were until the beginning of the tenth century*. Here is the series: Great Mosque of Wāsiṭ, Mosque at Quṣayr al-Ḥallābāt, Ḥarrān, Cordova, Mosque of 'Amr, Sūsa (below, pp. 269–73), Sāmarrā, Abū Dulaf, and the Mosque of Ibn Ṭūlūn. Then comes the first monumental entrance, the Great Mosque of Mahdīya, finished about 308 H. (921).[1]

So I regard these two walled-up entrances as the only two that date from the time of Ziyādat Allāh.

The Saḥn and the Riwāqs

Let us now enter the mosque by the door in daily use – the third from the north on the west side. The *saḥn*, like the mosque, is trapezoidal in shape and entirely paved with marble (Figure 50 and Plate 49). Its east side measures 67·18 m. (220½ ft), the west side 66·98 (219¾ ft); its width next the sanctuary is 52·46 m. (172 ft) but on the side of the minaret 50·23 (164½ ft) only.

All the north façade, as Saladin remarks,[2] has certainly been reconstructed at various times (Plate 50a). The façades on the *saḥn* are all more or less equal in height, except the southern one, which is higher, measuring 8·80 m. (29 ft) to the top of the parapet. The arcades on the north side rest on columns, but the others rest on more or less uniform supports, consisting of rectangular piers with two free-standing columns attached to their front face; the latter are invariably surmounted by a pulvin of several courses of small masonry which serves for both columns. When we examine the *riwāqs* further we find still more differences between them. For example, the inner arches of the southern portico, of a slightly pointed and slightly horse-shoe form, are quite different in shape, both from those of the façade and from those of the sanctuary itself of which they are a prolongation, those which duplicate the central aisle excepted. The eastern *riwāq* differs internally from the western, for in the former an arcade of columns grouped in pairs runs down the centre, whereas in the latter, an arcade on single columns is crossed by transverse arcades which start from a column placed behind each pier of the façade and run back to

1. See my *Muslim Architecture of Egypt*, I, p. 3.   2. *Mosquée*, p. 81.

the outer wall, where there is a narrow wall-pier with an engaged column to receive them.

We have seen that Ibrāhīm II, the son of Ahmad, extended the aisles of the sanctuary towards the north, so the inner (i.e. perpendicular) arcades of the south *riwāq* cannot be earlier than his reign (875–902). This suits the form of the arches very well, for their slightly pointed, slightly horseshoe form is just what we find in the dome-bearing arches in front of the mihrāb, which we shall see must date from 248 H. (862–3), those of the inner arcades of the central aisle, which must be of the same date (below, p. 257), and those of the Jāmi' Tlēta Bibān dated 252 H.(866).

But what are we to think of the transverse arcade next the *sahn*, not only here but on all four sides? Each arch is surrounded by a narrow moulding which forms a loop at the apex, continues to right and left and forms a frame as in some of the doorways on the eastern side. The above treatment cannot possibly date from the ninth century, to which these *riwāqs* are generally supposed to belong. There is not a single example of this treatment in Egypt until after 1300, and in North Africa the earliest example appears to be the Bāb Lalla Rejāna, on the east side of the mosque, built by Abū Hafs in 693 H. (1294). Even in the Great Mosque of Tunis the arcades on the east side of the *sahn*, dated 648 H. (1250–51), lack this feature.

It would therefore appear that the arcades bordering the *sahn* are part of the work of restoration carried out by Abū Hafs, after Qairawān had been a ruined city for over two centuries, as a result of the devastations of the Hilālī Bedawīn in 446 H. (1054–5).

The south *riwāq* consists of seventeen aisles formed by sixteen arcades, all of two arches, except the lateral supports of the dome which are of one arch only. All these arcades abut against an inner transverse arcade of seventeen arches resting on columns. These arches all have outer mouldings which are cut into and partly hidden by the masonry which fills the spandrels of the arcades of the portico. This shows that the portico has been constructed later, i.e. it can be none other than the part added by Ibrāhīm II, who 'prolonged the naves of the sanctuary'. Before this the old façade of the sanctuary must have run *with an unbroken face from* one side of the mosque to the other. This proves that originally there were no side *riwāqs*, as in the Great Mosque of Cordova of 'Abd ar-Rahmān I, and as later in the

Great Mosque of Tunis when rebuilt in 250 H. (864). The arches of this portico, as already mentioned, are of the pointed horse-shoe form, which is quite in keeping with 261–89 H. (875–902).

The Sanctuary

This is a veritable hall of columns (Plate 50b). It is divided into seventeen aisles by sixteen arcades running perpendicular to the back wall, but without reaching it, for a transverse arcade runs at a distance of about 6 m. (19¾ ft) from it, and it is against this arcade that the sixteen arcades abut. Each of these arcades consists of seven arches, and they are braced by two transverse arcades which run across between the first and second and the fourth and fifth arches from the original façade on the *sahn*; the latter arcade, however, does not cross the central aisle. The columns average about 3·55 m. (11½ ft) in height and their diameters vary from 34 to 44 cm. (13½–17¼ in.) The capitals are of the most varied type; many columns have bases but most have not. The columns of the 'lining arcade' of the central aisle average 4·23 m. (13¾ ft) in height and those carrying the dome are taller still, ranging from 4·68 to 4·86 m. (15¼–16 ft). The latter are the finest in the sanctuary, some being of beautifully coloured marble and some of granite and porphyry.

The arches of all these arcades, including the transverse arcades, are all of the round horse-shoe type with a very slight return, except the arches of the inner arcades of the central aisle, and the dome-bearing arches which are of the pointed horse-shoe form. An old photograph in my collection, taken perhaps sixty years ago, shows that all these arcades were braced longitudinally and transversely by wooden tie-beams, since replaced by iron rods, except those between the transverse arcade and the *qibla* wall.

The Original Ceiling

Some of the composite beams of the ceiling of the transverse aisle were taken down in 1935. They consisted of trunks of trees, almost cylindrical, boxed in on three sides with planks of cypress wood. Some bore eleventh-century painted decoration on their outer face, but six were older planks which had been reversed, and which had an earlier painted decoration, presumably due to Ziyādat Allāh. They have been published by Marçais.[1]

The Central Aisle

This is wider than the rest and is flanked by two arcades in contact. The arches of these double arcades are separated by a gap of several centimetres, roughly filled in with cement. They cannot have been constructed simultaneously for the following reasons. The arches of the outer arcade on each side are of the same shape as the rest, but those of the inner arcade are of a pointed horse-shoe form with slightly more return than the former. In addition to this, the pulvins of the two arcades are independent and of different sizes, those of the 'lining arcade' being wider and sometimes higher; had these two arcades been constructed simultaneously, it is difficult to believe that the builders would not have bound the pairs of columns more securely together by making one block of stone to form a common pulvin for each pair, or that they would at least have built them of one piece of coursed masonry, as they have done over the pairs of columns in the back row. Moreover, had these double arcades been built simultaneously, it is impossible to believe that the builders would not have constructed each pair of arches as one arch over one centering, instead of using two centerings of quite different outline. One is inevitably forced to conclude that the inner arcade is a lining, added to a pre-existing and slightly wider central aisle at a later date.

If this conclusion is correct, what consequences follow from it? One very important one – the dome-bearing arches cannot have been constructed until the arcades of the central aisle had been duplicated, for the two columns from which the eastern and western dome-bearing arches spring are each placed exactly centrally with regard to these double arcades, so that the thrust of the great arch is taken equally by each half of the double arcades. And what is still more vital, it also follows that the frontal arch of the dome must likewise have been constructed when the central aisle was lined. The three dome-bearing arches, as well as the wall arch, have the same pointed form as the inner arches of the central aisle.

1. 'Plafonds peints du IXe siècle à la Grande Mosquée de Kairouan', in the *Revue des Arts asiatiques*, IX, pp. 1–8.

The Mihrāb and the Dome in front of it

As all these date from 248 H. (862–3), they will be described and discussed later on (below, pp. 298–9).

Conclusions

The mosque as rebuilt by Ziyādat Allāh in 221 H. (836) was the same in size and shape as the present structure. The walls were flanked, not by a number of buttresses of every size and shape, as at present, but by a regular scheme. On the *qibla* side two or three buttresses, about a metre square, alternated with a large one, and there was a very massive one at each corner; all these buttresses were flat-topped. The east and west sides of the mosque were apparently flanked by buttresses of the smaller type only, and the north side was probably treated in the same way. The sanctuary consisted of sixteen arcades of seven arches each, resting on marble columns and running perpendicular to the back wall but ending, before reaching it, against a transverse arcade. Seventeen aisles were thus formed, but the central one was not flanked, as at present, by a pair of double arcades, but by single ones only; it was therefore 1·20 m. (4 ft) wider than at present. The façade of the sanctuary was formed by the transverse arcade, which now runs from one side of the mosque to the other behind the south portico. As in the Great Mosque of Cordova of 'Abd ar-Rahmān I, there were no arcades round the *sahn*.

Except for the outer decorative moulding of the arches which formed the façade of the sanctuary and the painted beams of the ceiling, the whole mosque internally and externally, including the entrances, appears to have been absolutely plain.

CHAPTER 14

SĀMARRĀ: I

HISTORICAL INTRODUCTION

HĀRŪN AR-RASHĪD during his lifetime had nominated al-Amīn, his son by Zubayda the grand-daughter of al-Mansūr, as Heir-Apparent, at the expense of al-Ma'mūn who, although several months older, was the son of a Persian slave-girl. Hārūn died in 809, and by 813 al-Ma'mūn had taken Baghdād, where enormous damage was done to the Round City, and put al-Amīn to death.

al-Ma'mūn carried on campaigns against the Byzantine Empire and for this purpose he imported several thousand Turks every year from Central Asia. Ya'qūbī says:

Ja'far al-Khushshakī related to me the following: al-Mu'tasim used to send me, in the reign of al-Ma'mūn, to Nūh ibn Asad at Samarqand to purchase Turks, and each year I would bring him a number, so that during the reign of al-Ma'mūn he accumulated upwards of 3000 youths. When he succeeded to the Khalifate he maintained his search for them. When these alien Turks went out riding, they would gallop and collide with people to right and left. ...[1]

The disorders caused by these Turkish troops caused al-Mu'tasim to leave Baghdād and found a new capital higher up the Tigris. In 221 H. (836) he fixed on the site of Sāmarrā.

As at Baghdād one of the first things that had to be done was to write 'for workmen, masons, and artificers, such as smiths, carpenters, and all other craftsmen to be sent, and for teak and other kinds of wood, and for palm-trunks to be brought from Basra ... and for marble workers and men experienced in marble paving to be brought. And the workshops for working marble were established in Latakia and elsewhere'.[2]

And al-Mu'tasim not only gathered together craftsmen from all parts of the empire, but he brought material also, at least from Egypt, for

1. Ya'qūbī, *Geography*, pp. 255–6.   2. *Ibid.*, p. 258.

Severus ibn al-Muqaffa' says that he sent men to Egypt with orders that the columns and the marble should be taken from the churches in every place, and after they had pillaged the churches of Alexandria, they went out to the Church of St Menas, at Maryūt to the west of Alexandria, and 'set to work to rob the church of its coloured marbles and its unequalled pavement, which was composed of all colours and had no equal'.[1] Nor was this all; al-Mu'tasim captured Ammurīya (Amorium in Phrygia) in 838, and took the city gate to Sāmarrā.[2]

THE JAUSAQ AL-KHĀQĀNĪ, OR PALACE OF AL-MU'TASIM

The ruins of this immense structure were investigated by Viollet in 1907. He only made a few trial excavations, but, shortly after, very extensive excavations were carried out by a German expedition under Sarre and Herzfeld.

There was first a great basin, 127 m. (417 ft) square, in the low-lying ground close to the Tigris. From this a great flight of steps (or a ramp)[3] 60 m. (197 ft) broad ascended to the higher ground in front of the Bāb al-'Āmma.

The Bāb al-'Āmma

This, the best preserved part of the Palace, consists of a great triple-arched façade, nearly 12 m. (39½ ft) high, formed by three parallel tunnel-vaulted rooms overlooking the Tigris (Plate 51). The central one forms a great līwān, 7·86 m. (26 ft) broad, 17·50 (57½ ft) deep, and 11·10 (36½ ft) high opening for its whole breadth on to the ledge above the Tigris, except in so far as it is reduced by two pilasters which carry the frontal arch. This arch has the same form as that of the Baghdād Gate of Raqqa. At the back of this līwān is a doorway, 4 m. (13 ft) wide and 7·10 (23¼ ft) high, with a window above.

1. See Evetts' text and translation, *Patrologia orientalis*, x, pp. 512–14; or Seybold's ed., pp. 286–7.

2. Ibn ash-Shihna, Sauvaget's transl., p. 32.

3. Ross, when he was here in 1834, saw 'an inclined platform resting on arches' leading down to the lower ground; *Journal Roy. Geographical Socy*, xi, p. 129.

The two lateral līwāns are only 4·11 m. (13½ ft) deep, and the part behind the frontal arch is covered by a semi-dome on squinches. They consist of a low semi-cylinder, surmounted by a semi-dome, the former being constructed of bricks in horizontal courses, but the semi-dome is built of rubble on account of the difficulty of constructing such a small curved surface with flat square bricks. These lateral līwāns each form monumental entrances to a tunnel-vaulted room of the same width, lying behind. They are not in communication with

Figure 51. Sāmarrā: The Bāb al-'Āmma, ornament on
intrados of frontal arch

the great līwān and can only be entered from in front. Herzfeld concludes they were intended for the guard during public audiences held in the great līwān.

The interior of the līwāns was decorated with stucco ornament; part is still *in situ*, and part was found by Viollet, and later by Herzfeld, in the débris on the floor. The intrados of the frontal arch of the great līwān was decorated with a broad central strip and two much narrower borders, 32·5 cm. (12¾ in.) wide. The latter were composed of ascending vine stalks forming a double row of loops, each containing a vine-leaf with lobes separated by drill-holes, like eyes, surrounded by concentric grooves. The central strip, 95 cm. (37¼ in.) broad, was occupied by a series of eight-lobed rosettes, apparently knotted at their points of contact (Figure 51).

Within the great līwān was a dado which Herzfeld,[1] with extra-ordinary ingenuity, has reconstructed as shown (Figure 52) from fragments of stucco, part of which had already been found by Viol-let.[2] As he remarks, it is closely related to the famous façade of Mshattā, but I cannot help thinking that the pieces from which he composed the squares really belong to the soffit of the arch, in which case his design must be modified so that a six-lobed rosette comes be-tween each triangle. This could make the resemblance to Mshattā still closer.

The top of the wall, immediately below the offset of the vault, was decorated with a fine frieze in high relief, composed of a larger and

Figure 52. Sāmarrā: The Bāb al-'Āmma, stucco dado

smaller motif set alternately. The larger was a fluted chalice filled with a three-petalled flower, somewhat like a *fleur de lys*.

The doorway at the back of the great līwān opens into six trans-verse halls, 'which must be regarded as a series of antichambers. ... After this comes a square court with a fountain, symmetrically bounded on each side by three rooms in which the stream of visitors was divided. To the north one reached the rooms of the Khalif which are grouped round three courts. On the south lay the Harīm, en-larged by a southern annexe and much more divided up, and directly on the court was the great bath. Going directly forward, however, one passed through a further forehall into an oblong Court of Honour, which had plain walls to north and south, whereas on the

1. *Der Wandschmuck*, pp. 217–22 and Abb. 310.

2. 'Un Palais musulman', in the *Mém. de l'Acad. des Inscr.*, XII, pp. 707–8 and pl. XXI.

east side appeared the front of the Throne-Room with its three door-ways. …' [1]

The Throne-Room

This consisted of a square central hall, which was almost certainly covered by a dome, with four halls, each built like a three-aisled basilica radiating from it, therefore somewhat like the Throne-Room at Mshattā, four times repeated. Herzfeld remarks that the reason why these four halls were built like basilicas was the need for obtaining light by means of clerestorys. Fragments of a fine marble frieze were found in the square central hall. Between the arms of the cross were smaller halls with dadoes of marble tiles, also a mosque-room for the Khalif with a mihrāb and a stucco dado (Plate 52a).

The Harīm

A transverse axis runs through the central room and the T-shaped rooms to north and south. Only the southern continuation has been excavated. In front of the southern hall 'lies first of all a broad hall the full width of the Harīm court. The west and east sides of the court are occupied by small, repeatedly modified living rooms, all provided with a water supply, partly in great lead pipes, partly in blue glazed, partly in rough clay pipes, also washing rooms and latrines. Opposite to the Throne-Room, on the south side of the court, and again occupying its full width, is a peculiar square room. There is first of all a surrounding corridor, 21 m. (69 ft) long, on all four sides, then a square room with four wide doorways in the axes, and in it four marble columns at the corners of the basin. The room was decorated all over with paintings of figures.' [2]

The Great Esplanade

In front of the eastern basilica-like hall of the Throne-Room group is another great hall, about 38 m. (125 ft) wide and 10·40 m. (34 ft)

1. Herzfeld, 'Mitteilungen über die Arbeiten der Zweiten Kampagne von Samarra', in Der Islam, v, p. 200.
2. Ibid., v, pp. 200–1.

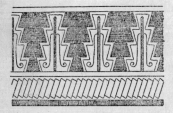

Figure 53. Sāmarrā: cresting of Great Esplanade (bottom right, compared with other types, Ming Oi (top) and Turfan (bottom left)

deep, which opens on to the Great Esplanade by five doors. This is a great open court measuring about 350 by 180 m. (1,150 by 590 ft), which is divided by a canal into a paved western part, with two fountains, and an unpaved eastern part intersected by little canals. Its panelled enclosing walls were capped with the cresting shown in Figure 53.

The Little Serdāb

If one walks eastwards from the Great Esplanade one comes to the Little Serdāb in the main axis of the Palace. The entrance forms a square room, on the walls of which is a frieze of double-humped camels walking along, executed in painted stucco, with a circular fountain. The entrance staircases of the *serdāb* are on the west side of the upper building. The *serdāb* itself is a cavity cut in the rock, 21 m. (69 ft) a side and about 8 m. (26¼ ft) deep. In each wall of the pit are three grottoes, connected together by corridors. On its floor was a water basin. A court is attached to the east of the square surrounding building. The whole *serdāb*-complex separates two somewhat similar courts, a pavilion with T-shaped hall lying on their north and south sides. The *serdāb* was completely enclosed by long parallel rows of rooms, to be taken for stables.[1]

1. Herzfeld, *loc. cit.*, v, p. 201.

The Polo-Ground

In the middle of the east court is a lodge, from which one overlooks a wide transverse enclosure over 180 m. (590 ft) long and about 65 m. (213 ft) broad. ... It is to be recognized as the polo-ground, the stables are those of the polo-ponies, and the lodge is for the spectators. With this we have reached the east edge of the Palace, which touched the Game Preserve. Opposite the lodge, on the main axis of the Palace, rises a great high pavilion, overlooking both the polo-ground and the race-course of the game preserve (ḥair) whose track, about 5 km. (3 miles) long, loses itself in the distance. The middle axis of the Palace, from the pavilion on the Tigris, across the basin, the monumental staircase, the Bāb al-'Āmma, the kernel of the Palace, the Great Esplanade, and the little Serdāb, to the pavilion on the race-course measures 1,400 m. (4,600 ft).[1]

The Great Serdāb

This is a separate walled square of 180 m. (590 ft) a side, and touches the north-east corner of the kernel of the Palace, with its south side lying on the north wall of the Great Esplanade. It consists of a deep, square cavity of 80 m. (262½ ft) a side, hewn in the rock, with cruciform extensions on its axes measuring about 115 m. (377 ft). In the floor of this pit is a second circular hollow of 70 m. (230 ft) diameter. This hollow must have been a basin, for a deep underground canal leads to it. On the upper platform many small irregular rooms are set round the inner side of the walls. A number of them are roofed with intersecting vaults. ... To the east various groups of buildings are set along the north wall, amongst which one rises above the rest. The usual T-formed reception hall has a rotunda in the place of the transverse arm.[2]

Herzfeld concludes:

The magnificence of the decoration of the Palace was in keeping with this composition, the like of which certainly existed nowhere else. The dadoes of the walls were everywhere decorated with stucco ornament. ... In the throne-rooms the stucco dadoes are replaced by similar ones of carved marble. In the rooms between the arms of the cross, the dado bears a facing of marble tiles. The upper part of the walls of the Harīm were decorated with fresco paintings of living forms, of which important remains have come to light. ... All woodwork, doors, beams,

1. Herzfeld, *loc. cit.*, v, pp. 201-2.   2. *Ibid.*, v, p. 201.

and ceilings were of teak-wood, carved and painted, or only painted and partly gilded. Delicately wrought nails of gilt bronze heightened the effect. ... Amongst the epigraphic finds must be mentioned remains of inscriptions on teak beams, many craftsmen's signatures in Greek, Syriac, and Arabic. ...[1]

Figure 54. Sāmarrā: painting decorating domed hall of the Harīm

The Wall-Paintings

The great acanthus scrolls, composed as they are of calices set one within the other, immediately recall some of the great acanthus scrolls in the Dome of the Rock, except that the calices are here treated like the cornucopias in the same building, even down to the transverse band of white dots, obviously a painted reproduction of the disks of mother-of-pearl (Figure 54).

1. Herzfeld, *loc. cit.*, v, p. 202.

CHAPTER 15

SŪSA

THE MOSQUE OF BŪ FATĀTĀ

IF one enters the south gate of Sūsa (on the Gulf of Gabes) and proceeds north, one soon comes to this little known mosque (Figure 55). On entering a door (*A*) in a modern wall, one immediately has a view of the north façade (*B*) crowned by the Kufic inscription of Aghlab ibn Ibrāhīm, who reigned from 223 to 226 H. (838–41).[1] Stumpy piers, only 90 cm. (35½ in.) high, including their splay-face mouldings, support three horse-shoe arches, the springing of which is almost exactly one-third of the radius below their centre. At a height of 3·34 m. (11 ft) the façade is set forward about 10 cm. (4 in.). The total height of the façade is only 4·87 m. (16 ft), and along its summit runs a Kufic inscription in a frame 48 cm. (19 in.) broad, bordered above and below by a splay-face moulding 18 cm. (7 in.) high.

The Interior

The arches open into a tunnel-vaulted portico (*C*) 2·24 m. (7¼ ft) wide, the right half of which is occupied by a mass of masonry intended to reinforce the vault when the comparatively modern minaret was built. A doorway with lintel and round relieving arch, at the back of this portico, leads into the sanctuary, which is only 7·71 m. (25¼ ft) wide and 7·86 m. (25¾ ft) deep. It consists of three aisles, formed by two arcades running from north to south, each divided into three bays by two other arcades running from east to west. These arcades spring from eight wall-piers and four low cruciform piers placed at their points of intersection. The lateral arches have a slight return, whereas the transverse arches are stilted semicircles; the former are about 3·15 m. (10¼ ft) in height, the latter about 3·65

1. Houdas and Basset, 'Épigraphie tunisienne', in the *Bulletin de correspondance africaine*, fasc. IV, p. 171.

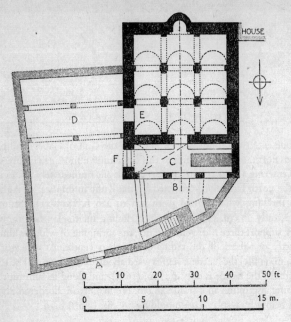

Figure 55. Sūsa: Bū Fatātā Mosque, plan

(12 ft). The transverse arches serve as reinforcements for the tunnel-vaults. The courses of the masonry are 50 cm. (19¾ in.) high.

The vaulting system of this mosque is the third example of its kind in Islam, the first being the Cistern of Ramla 172 H. (789), the second the mosque on the upper floor of the Ribāt of Sūsa, 206 H. (821–2), and we shall see that it was employed again, some ten years later, in the next monument which we are going to study.

This mosque is also important (1) because it is the second oldest in North Africa, (2) because it is the first monument (after the Dome of the Rock) with a monumental inscription forming one with the architecture and the decoration, and (3) because it is the only example of a mosque with what may be described as a *portico in antis*, with the solitary exception of the Mosque of as-Sālih Talā'i' at Cairo, built in 555 H. (1160).

THE GREAT MOSQUE OF SŪSA

The Great Mosque of Sūsa (Plate 54) occupies an island site quite near the Bāb al-Bahr, at the north-east corner of the town. It forms an irregular polygon, measuring about 60 by 90 m. (197 by 295 ft). On closer examination, however, the mosque proper turns out to consist of a perfectly regular rectangle measuring 49·39 by 57·16 m. (162 by 187 ft) internally, with irregular annexes to right and left (Figure 56).

The two entrances in daily use open into the Western Annexe, which consists of a court, nearly 8 m. (26¼ ft) wide and over 43 m. (141 ft) long, to which we descend about a metre. On the east side are three doors, with lintels and horse-shoe relieving arches, leading into the west *riwāq* of the mosque. The *sahn* measures roughly 41 by 22·25 m. (135 by 73 ft), and is surrounded on three sides by low arcades of slightly horse-shoe form, resting on squat T-shaped piers.

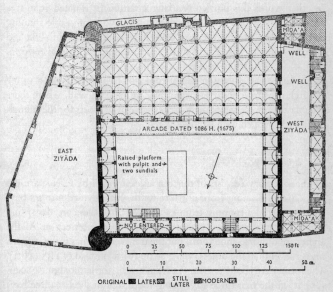

Figure 56. Sūsa: The Great Mosque, plan

There are six arches to east and west and eleven to north and south, but those on the south side are pointed and rest on columns. The rest are exactly like those in the Mosque of Bū Fatātā.

The height of the façade, measured at the north and south ends of the western side, is 6·48 (21¼ ft) and 6·60 m. (21½ ft) respectively. As in the Mosque of Bū Fatātā, it is crowned by a fine inscription frieze in simple undecorated Kufic. The maximum height of the characters is 28 cm. (11 in.); the band, 68 cm. (26¾ in.) broad, on which they are carved is curved forward to the extent of 10 cm. (4 in.) to compensate for foreshortening and thus help the observer at ground level. This is the earliest example of this device known to me; the Fātimids introduced it into Egypt, where it appears for the first time in the stucco friezes below the dome of the Mosque of al-Ḥākim, 380–403 H. (990–1013). This inscription runs round the whole *sahn*, except on the south side, where we have seen that the arches rest on columns. But a further examination shows that the inscription runs along the back wall of the portico formed by this arcade, and across its two ends. In other words this portico is a later insertion (it is dated 1086 H = 1675), before which the Kufic frieze must have been visible running all round. At that time the *sahn* must have been bounded to east and west by seven arches instead of six, and measured a little over 26 m. (85¼ ft) from north to south.

The three *riwāqs* vary in depth from 4·08 to 4·27 m. (13¼ to 14 ft) An arch runs from each T-shaped pier to the back wall, where there is a pilaster to receive it; these arches serve as supports for the tunnel-vaults with which each bay is covered.

The Sanctuary

The sanctuary consists of thirteen aisles, formed by twelve arcades of six arches running from north to south, each divided into six bays by other arcades running from east to west. All these arcades spring from low cruciform piers placed at their points of intersection. All the arches are of horse-shoe form, but the transverse arches spring from a higher level than the others, viz. 2·82 m. (9¼ ft) instead of 1·35 (4½ ft). The former are about 3·70 m. (12 ft) in height, the latter about 4·80 m. (15¾ ft) in the first three bays going south, but in the last three bays both lateral and transverse arches are of the same height, say about

5·93 m. (19½ ft). The first three bays going south are covered by tunnel-vaults springing from the low lateral arcades and are reinforced by the higher transverse arches, exactly as we have observed in the Mosque of Bū Fatātā, in the mosque on the upper floor of the Ribāt close by and, earlier still, in the Cistern of Ramla (Plate 43).

The only exception is the third bay in the central aisle which is treated differently: the wall above the low lateral arches is carried up about 55 cm. (21½ in.) to a simple cornice which forms the bottom edge of a pointed-arched panel adorned with squares, like tiles, set lozenge-wise and decorated with crudely executed motifs – rosettes in eight-pointed frames formed by the outline of two crossed squares, floral designs vaguely recalling classical forms, etc., a sort of rustic version of earlier types (Plate 53). Above this panel is a simple moulding at a height of 6·51 m. (6½ ft) forming the lower border of a plain Kufic inscription, which runs round all four sides. Immediately above this inscription are eight brackets, two on each side, and above this, at 7·23 m. (23¾ ft) is a seventeenth-century wooden ceiling. Above this ceiling is a dome, as may be seen in Plate 54. On the analogy of the Great Mosque of Qairawān (Plate 63) we can be quite sure that eight colonnettes, carrying four squinch arches, rest on these brackets.

The next three bays going south are covered by cross-vaults at a slightly higher level than the tunnel-vaults. Here again the third bay of the central aisle – that is to say the bay in front of the mihrāb – is likewise covered by a dome, the interior of which, until recently, was also hidden by a wooden ceiling.

It is obvious that the mosque has been extended towards the south, that the first three bays are the original portion, of which the first dome marks the bay in front of the original mihrāb, that the old back wall has been cut through as at Cordova, and that the sanctuary has been extended three more bays towards the south. There must consequently be a break in the masonry of the side walls at the junction of the third and fourth bays going south, but owing to plaster and whitewash it is impossible to distinguish anything.

To the right of the mihrāb is a door. I had it opened and, to my amazement, saw a small room 1·13 m. (3¾ ft) wide and 2·90 m. (9½ ft) deep, filled by a *pulpit on wheels*, light enough for one man to be able to pull it forth. Although the pulpit was not very old, I was immediately reminded of the 'silla (chair) del rey Almáçor' at Cordova, mentioned by Ambrosio de Morales in 1575,[1] of the very old pulpit on wheels in the Great Mosque of Tunis, and of another dated 490 H. (1082) in the Great Mosque of Algiers.[2] Evidently we have here something specially Maghrebin. Can it be that the old throne idea survived longer in conservative Western Islam than elsewhere, and the *minbar* being regarded as a symbol of royalty and authority, it was considered advisable to keep it safely locked up until required for official use?

The Tower or Bastion

At the north-eastern corner of the mosque proper is a round tower which forms a salient on the north and east façades (Plate 54 to left). On this tower a little octagonal domed pavilion has been constructed, which must be of more recent date, to which two staircases ascend from the roofs of the north and east *riwāqs*. Below this pavilion is another chamber in the top of the tower itself, which is entered directly from the roof. Before the upper part was added, the top of the tower must have formed an open platform, presumably for the call to prayer.

There is a similar tower at the south-east corner of the part that has been added to the sanctuary. It has not been crowned by a domed pavilion, but remains in a state resembling what I believe to have been the original state of the other.

The Cresting

At the summit of the east wall, close to the tower, can still be seen from the Eastern Annexe the outline of three round-topped crenellations, embedded in the masonry of the staircase to the domed pavilion.

The Date

The Kufic inscription, which runs round three sides of the *sahn* and continues behind the added portico on the south side, ends: '...the Emīr Abu'l-'Abbās, son of al-[Aghlab]...in the year 236 H. (850–51).'

1. *Antiguedades de Córdoba* (1575), fol. 124a.
2. Published by Marçais in *Hespéris*, II, pp. 359–85.

Summary

The Great Mosque of Sūsa formed a rectangle measuring about 57 m. (187 ft) in width and 50 m. (164 ft) in depth. The *sahn*, roughly 41 m. (134 ft) wide and 22·25 (73 ft) deep, was bordered by eleven horse-shoe arches to north and south and eight to east and west, resting on squat T-shaped piers and crowned above by a Kufic inscription which ran all round and ended with the date. Behind these arcades, on three sides of the court, were *riwāqs* one bay deep, each bay being covered by a tunnel-vault perpendicular to the *sahn*. On the south side was the sanctuary, consisting of twelve arcades of three horse-shoe arches, running from north to south and forming thirteen aisles, covered by tunnel-vaults which were strengthened by two transverse arcades. The piers were cruciform in plan. The central aisle was slightly wider than the rest and the bay in front of the mihrāb was covered by a dome on squinch-arches supported by eight colonnettes resting on little brackets. There were three entrances on the west side, one on the east, and probably one on the north. A round bastion at the north-east corner served as minaret.

CHAPTER 16

SĀMARRĀ: II

THE GREAT MOSQUE OF SĀMARRĀ

THE Khalif al-Muʻtasim died in 227 H. (842) and Hārūn al-Wāthiq succeeded him. The latter died in 832 H. (847) and was succeeded by al-Mutawakkil, who built the Great Mosque.

The Outer Walls

The Great Mosque (Plate 55) forms an immense rectangle with bastioned walls of burnt brick, measuring about 240 by 156 m. (784 by 512 ft) internally (proportion approximately as 3 : 2); its area, therefore, is nearly 38·000 sq. m. (45,500 sq. yds). It is consequently the largest mosque in the world, being half as large again, without its *ziyādas*, as Ibn Tūlūn is with them (26,000 sq. m.; 31,000 sq. yds). Only its enclosing walls have been preserved, the roof and the supports on which it rested having disappeared. These walls, which are 2·65 m. (8¾ ft) thick, are of light red bricks 25–27 cm. (9¾–10½ in.) square and 7 cm. (2¾ in.) thick. The bastions are nearly semi-circular in plan, averaging 3·60 m. (11¾ ft) in diameter with a projection of 2·15 m. (7 ft). The curtain walls between them average 15 m. (49¼ ft) in length. There are four corner towers, twelve intermediate towers to east and west, and eight to north and south, making forty-four in all (Figure 57). These towers stood on rectangular bases of two or three courses of brick.

The Doorways

There were sixteen doors, their widths varying considerably. In every case, except in the centre of the north side, the brickwork above the doors has fallen,[1] but it would appear from an examination of the

1. This was already the case as long ago as 1834; see Ross, in the *Journ. Roy. Geog. Socy*, XI, p. 128.

best-preserved jambs, that the opening was covered by wooden beams with a brick relieving arch above. But above this, in the southernmost doorway on the west side, is a strip of perfectly smooth brickwork, slightly in advance of the side of the doorway below,

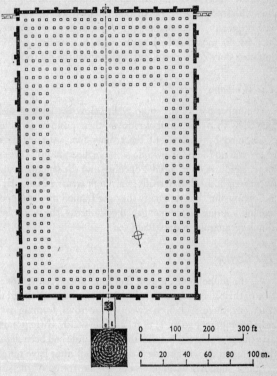

Figure 57. Sāmarrā: The Great Mosque, plan

which goes right through the wall. In the corresponding door on the opposite side we can see the springing of a very small arch which formed part of a vault going right through the wall. This can only mean that there were several little arched windows (probably three) above each door.

The Frieze

The towers are perfectly plain, but each curtain wall is decorated with a frieze of six recessed squares with bevelled edges, except the southernmost on each side where there are only five. In each square is a shallow saucer, about 25 cm. (10 inches) deep, still covered in a few cases with stucco (this shows that the brickwork of the mosque was not bare originally). The total height of the walls is now about 10·50 m. (34½ ft). In most of the curtain walls is a vertical groove, which doubtless once contained a gutter pipe from the flat roof.

The Windows

The upper part of the south wall, below the level of the frieze, is pierced with twenty-four windows, their position obviously being determined by the axes of the twenty-five aisles of the sanctuary (there was no room for a window above the mihrāb). There were two more windows on each side, opening into the sanctuary and making twenty-eight in all. Externally, they are narrow rectangular openings like arrow-slits, but internally they are framed by a scalloped arch of five lobes springing from engaged colonnettes, the whole being set in a sunk rectangular frame (Plate 56a).

The Interior

All the supports of the roof had long since been removed for the sake of their material, but it was clear from the trenches left that in the sanctuary there had been twenty-four rows forming twenty-five aisles averaging 4·20 m. (13¾ ft) in clear width, corresponding to the axes of the windows, and that the central aisle had been slightly wider than the rest. It was also clear that the roof must have rested directly on these supports without arches, for no traces of the springing o arches are visible on any of the walls.

Herzfeld excavations confirmed that there had been twenty-four rows of nine supports each in the sanctuary, and the same number of three supports each in the north riwāq. The side riwāqs each consisted of twenty-two rows of four supports, running parallel to the sahn. There were thus 464 supports in all.[1]

1. *Erster vorläufiger Bericht*, pp. 6–7.

Just sufficient vestiges remained of the piers for it to be possible to fix their form. The bases were squares of 2·07 m. (6½ ft) a side. On them stood an octagonal brick pier with marble columns at the four corners. As these columns were only 2 m. (6½ ft) long, three superimposed ones were required in each case, joined by metal pegs and lead, as in the Great Mosques of Kūfa and Wāsit (above, pp. 13 and 41–2). The brick core was plastered over and coloured to imitate marble. The clear height to the beams of the ceiling was 10·35 m. (34 ft).

The Mihrāb

An opening in the centre of the south wall turned out to be a broken-through mihrāb. It was not round but rectangular in plan, as we have seen at Ukhaidir, and as was the rule in early times in 'Irāq and Persia, being 2·59 m. (8½ ft) broad and 1·75 m. (5¾ ft) deep. It had been flanked by two pairs of columns of rose-coloured marble from 'Aintāb, with clock-formed bases and capitals, on which rested two concentric arches set in a rectangular frame, nearly as high as the clear height of the mosque. There were traces of gold mosaic in the spandrels.

The Decoration

Muqaddasī says that the mosque rivalled that of Damascus and that its walls were decorated with minā.[1] Herzfeld suggested that this word meant mosaic, and his excavations confirmed this, for extensive remains of glass mosaic were found.[2]

The Ziyāda

It is clear that a wall took off from the southern end of the two side walls, and the springing of a shallow vault can only mean that this wall was decorated with blind arcades, like the Court of Honour at Ukhaidir. Air photographs show that these walls formed part of a great enclosure which surrounded the mosque on the east, north, and west. This great rectangle is placed in a still greater one which surrounded it on all four sides, so as to leave three great open areas on the

1. p. 122.   2. *Erster vorläufiger Bericht*, p. 8.

east, south, and west, and a much narrower one on the north. The walls of these *ziyādas* were of bricks, the greater part of which have been carried away. This outer enclosure measured 376 by 444 m. (1,230 by 1,455 ft). The total area of the mosque and its *ziyādas* therefore amounted to almost 17 hectares or 41 acres.[1]

On the analogy of the Mosque of Ibn Tūlūn at Cairo, one would expect to find buildings containing latrines and places for ablution in these *ziyādas*; unfortunately Sarre and Herzfeld did not have time to excavate here.

The Minaret

This, known as the *Manāret al-Malwīya*, or *Malwīya* (= spiral), stands free at a distance of 27·25 m. (89 ft) from the north wall of the mosque, and exactly on its middle axis. The square socle, which measures nearly 33 m. (108 ft) a side, is connected with the mosque by a ridge 25 m. (82 ft) long and over 12 m. (39½ ft) wide – the remains of a ramp, ending in a little bridge and leading up to the top of the socle, in a manner closely resembling the approach to the Zikkurat at Babylon.[2] On this socle, which is about 3 m. (10 ft) high, rests a great helicoidal tower with a ramp about 2·30 m. (7½ ft) in width, which begins in the centre of the south side and winds round in an anti-clockwise direction until it has made five complete turns (Plate 56*b*). At the summit of this part is a cylindrical storey, decorated with eight similar pointed-arched recesses, each set in a shallow pointed-arched frame resting on a pair of brick columns. The southern niche forms a doorway, at which the ramp ends; it opens on to a steep staircase, at first straight and then spiral, leading to the top platform, which is exactly 50 m. (164 ft) above the socle.[3] Eight holes are to be seen on this platform, from which Herzfeld concluded that there was once a little pavilion here, resting on eight wooden columns.

The ramp becomes steeper and steeper as it rises, the reason being the desire to have each storey of the same height. As the circumference of each complete turn becomes less with the diminishing diameter, the steepness had to be increased to get the same rise per revolution as in the preceding one.

1. Herzfeld in *Der Islam*, v, p. 204.   2. The comparison is Herzfeld's.
3. *Erster vorläufiger Bericht*, pp. 12–13.

ath-Th'ālibī says that 'al-Mutawakkil used to mount the minaret of Sāmarrā on a donkey from Upper Egypt, and the steps of this minaret were on the outside. Its height is 99 cubits.' [1]

ARCHITECTURAL ORIGINS OF THE GREAT MOSQUE

The Minaret

That the helicoidal staircase principle, embodied in the minarets of Sāmarrā and Abū Dulaf, is derived from the Babylonian *zikkurat*, or Tower of Babel, is generally admitted. But *zikkurats* were not of one type only. The more usual type consisted of a staged tower, composed of receding storeys with vertical faces, the summit of the lowest storey being reached by a steep free-standing staircase running up at right angles in the centre of the south or south-east side. The higher storeys were reached by a continuation of this staircase. It is not this type which has been the parent of the Malwīya tower, but another type, square in plan with a gentle staircase or ramp running round it and making a number of complete revolutions until it reaches the top. Curiously enough, only one certain example of this type has been found – the *Zikkurat* of Khorsābād, excavated a hundred years ago by Place, who found three storeys intact and the remains of a fourth. He says that instead of the circular building which he expected, he found a perfect square of 43·10 m. (141 ft) a side. A very gentle staircase began at the south corner, continued the whole length of one side, turned the corner, and, always rising, passed all the corners in succession until the excavators found themselves back at their point of departure, but 6·10 m. (20 ft) higher. The staircase continued to go round the tower in an anti-clockwise fashion, as at Sāmarrā. Three storeys, each 6·10 m. (20 ft) in height, were found to exist, and the remains of a fourth. [2]

Basing himself on the description which Herodotus gives of the *zikkurat* of the temple of Bel at Babylon, he concluded that the tower once consisted of seven storeys which, at 6·10 m. (20 ft) each, give 42·70 m. (140 ft) as the total height. Although no other example of this type of *zikkurat* has been discovered, the description given by

1. *Latā'if*, p. 97. I owe this reference to Dr Adolf Grohmann.
2. Place, *Ninive*, I, pp. 137–48 and pl. 36–7.

Herodotus is conclusive as to the existence of towers with spiral-stair-cases. Here is Rawlinson's rendering:

'In the middle of the precinct there was a tower of solid masonry, a furlong in length and breadth, upon which was raised a second tower, and on that a third, and so on up to eight. The ascent to the top is on the outside, by a path which *winds round* all the towers.' [1]

It will be noted that Herodotus says that there were eight stages, whereas Place in his restoration of the *Zikkurat* of Khorsabad gives seven only. However, the Esagila tablet, found by G. Smith, contains a description of the same *Zikkurat* of Bel, with the dimensions of each receding storey of which there were seven.[2]

Finally, it cannot be maintained that no model for the Malwīya existed in 'Irāq in the ninth century A.D., for this *zikkurat* of Babylon was seen as late as the second half of the twelfth century by Benjamin of Tudela, who expressly mentions the staircase going round and round it.[3] This point being established, it is clear that the only innova-tion made by the architects of al-Mutawakkil was to carry out the idea on a circular instead of a square basis.

The Clock-formed Capitals

The earliest examples of this feature known to me are the capitals of the engaged shafts at the corners of the Sasanian monument of Paikuli, due to Narsé in the third century A.D.[4]

THE MOSQUE OF ABŪ DULAF

Historical Introduction

Some years after he had built the Great Mosque of Sāmarrā, al-Mutawakkil decided to build a new city to the north of Sāmarrā, and chose for its site a place called al-Mahūsa. Work was begun in 245 H.

1. *The History of Herodotus*, I, p. 318.
2. Scheil and Dieulafoy, 'Esagil ou le temple de Bèl-Marduk', in *Mém. de l'Institut national de France*, XXXIX, pp. 293–372.
3. Asher's text, p. 65; transl., p. 107; or Adler's transl., in the *Jewish Quarterly Review*, XVII, p. 537.
4. Herzfeld, 'Reisebericht', *Zeitschr. der Deutschen Morgenländischen Gesell-schaft*, LXX, pp. 227–8.

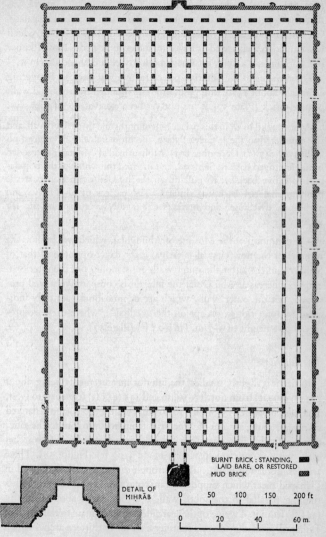

DETAIL OF
MIḤRĀB

BURNT BRICK : STANDING,
LAID BARE, OR RESTORED
MUD BRICK

0   50   100   150   200 ft

0   20   40   60 m.

Figure 58. Sāmarrā: Mosque of Abū Dulaf, plan

281

(859–60), and the Shari' al-A'zam, or Great Street, of Sāmarrā was therefore lengthened by about three *farsakhs* so that it reached his palace. On 1 Muharram 247 (17 March 861) he moved to his new city, which was named Ja'farīya, and as he sat in audience he said: 'Now I know that I am indeed a king, for I have built myself a city and live in it.' [1]

The remains of the Ja'farīya palace form a vast enclosure covering an area of about 1¼ sq. km. (½ sq. mile) surrounded by bastioned walls of mud-brick (Plate 57). It has not yet been excavated. Ya'qūbī says:

'al-Mutawakkil lived in this palace nine months and three days in all, and was murdered in the Ja'farīya Palace, the most unlucky of palaces, on 3 Shauwāl 247 (11 December 861). Muhammad al-Muntasir succeeded him. He moved back to Sāmarrā, and ordered the whole of the population to move back ... to pull down the buildings and transport the building material back to Sāmarrā. The palaces of al-Ja'farīya and its houses, dwellings, and markets fell rapidly to ruin. The site lay waste. ... [2]

The condition of the Mosque of Abū Dulaf, which was built as the mosque of the new city, al-Ja'farīya, is the exact opposite of that of Sāmarrā; in the latter the outer walls are standing but the interior is empty, whereas at Abū Dulaf the interior is comparatively well preserved, but the outer walls, which are of mud-brick, are only indicated by long ridges, except on the north side, where they are preserved to a height of 5–7 m. (16½–23 ft) (Plate 57).

The Interior

In size it is slightly smaller, the interior measurements being about 213 m. (699 ft) from north to south and 135 (443 ft) from east to west. The *sahn* measures 155·80 by 103·93 m. (511 by 340 ft) and is flanked by *riwāqs*, all the arcades of which run from north to south. The sanctuary is divided into seventeen aisles by sixteen arcades of five arches each, with an average span of 3·13 m. (10¼ ft) (Figure 58). These arcades, instead of being carried through to the south wall, all end in T-shaped piers which support a transverse arcade of seventeen arches running parallel to the south wall, at a distance of about 10·45 m. (34¼ ft) from it. Twelve of these arcades also terminate to the north in T-shaped piers, they carry a transverse arcade of thirteen arches which

1. Ya'qūbī, *Geography*, pp. 266–7.   2. *Op. cit.*, p. 267.

forms the south façade of the *sahn*. The latter average 4·16 m. (13¾ ft) in span except the middle one, which measures 5·19 m. (17ft). The depth of the sanctuary, including the transverse arcades, is 29·20 m. (96 ft). If we add 10·45 m. (34 ft) to this we get 39·65 m. (130 ft) as the total depth of the sanctuary. At one time this transverse aisle presented a problem, but the discovery by excavation of two oblong piers measuring 3·80 by 1·55 m. (12½ by 5 ft) has shown that there was a transverse arcade which divided this great aisle into two parts, each about 4·50 m. (14¾ ft) in width.

The two arcades at either end are carried right through to the north wall of the mosque, forming side *riwāqs* 14 m. (46 ft) in depth. Nineteen of these arches face the *sahn*; they average 4·15 m. (13½ ft) in span (like those of the façade of the sanctuary) except the central one of the west side (the opposite one has gone) which measures 4·91 m. (16 ft). The piers which carry the arcades of the side *riwāqs* are oblong, averaging 4·03 by 1·57 m. (13¼ by 5¼ ft), whereas those of the sanctuary and the northern *riwāq* are more nearly square, averaging 2·10 by 1·73 and 2·18 by 1·52 m. (7 by 5½ ft and 7¼ by 5 ft) respectively. All the piers are of burnt brick.

In the north *riwāq* there are, of course, sixteen arcades, as in the sanctuary, but of only three arches each, averaging 3·10 m. (10¼ ft) in span. They end against the *sahn* in T-shaped piers, but to the north they end in simple wall-piers, also of burnt brick, which are bonded into the mud-brick wall to a depth of 25 cm. (10 in.). The central aisle of the sanctuary is wider than the rest, being 7·30 m. (24 ft) against an average of 6·20 (20½ ft) for the rest, and the central aisle of the north *riwāq* is treated in the same way.

All the piers which face the *sahn* have the upper half of their face decorated with a recessed panel containing a narrow, arched recess. The arches have all been constructed of two rings of square bricks, those of the inner ring being set face outwards and those of the outer ring edgewise, as in the Baghdād Gate of Raqqa (Plate 33), except that each ring is only a brick and a half, instead of two bricks thick.

The brickwork is inferior to that of the Great Mosque of Sāmarrā; the bricks vary in size from 25 to 29 cm. (10–11½ in.) square and 7 cm. (3 in.) thick.

The mosque must obviously have had a flat roof like that of Sāmarrā, apparently not more than about 8 m. (26¼ ft) high.

The Outer Walls

The walls, where best preserved, are about 1·60 m. (5¼ ft) thick. A direct measurement can be obtained at the north end of the third aisle from the east, where the mud brick wall with a thick coating of plaster on each face, has been exposed.[1] As at Sāmarrā, they were strengthened by half-round bastions, three of which can still be seen on the south side. They are about 3 m. (10 ft) in breadth, project about 1·20 (4 ft), and were faced with burnt bricks, as at Raqqa. There were four corner towers, eleven intermediate ones to east and west, eight on the north side, and an uncertain number, probably six, on the south, making thirty-eight in all. The curtain walls average 14 m. (46 ft) in length. In some places on the north wall, grooves for drain-pipes, 20 cm. (8 in.) deep and 18 (7 in.) wide, similar to those in the Great Mosque at Sāmarrā, can still be distinguished.

There were six doors to east and west and three on the north side, making fifteen; they had jambs of burnt brick, some of which have been preserved. They were placed so as to come on the same axes as the corresponding arches of the *riwaqs*, and no attempt was made to place them in the centre of the curtain walls.

The Ziyādas

The mosque proper is surrounded by an open area 108 paces wide, and this area is surrounded by halls 42 paces deep, built of mud brick and only approximately traceable. The excavations of Sarre and Herzfeld in 1912–13 gave more exact measurements, and the dimensions of the whole complex were found to be 350 by 362 m. (1,150 by 1,117½ ft).[2] Unfortunately we still await the publication of the plan made at the time.

---

1. For protection against rain. As Petrie says: 'A wall of mud brick exposed to rain will soak it in, for a foot or two from the top, with little harm. But if water runs down in a stream, however small, it will rapidly cut through the bricks. The wall requires a firm face for its protection'. *Egyptian Architecture*, pp. 6–7.

2. See *Der Islam*, v, p. 204.

The Minaret

This, which has been well described by Ross as a Malwīya in miniature,[1] is placed in the northern *ziyāda*, on the north–south axis, at a distance of 9·60 m. (31½ ft) from the north wall of the mosque. The base, which is about 2·50 m. (8¼ ft) high and 11·20 m. (36¾ ft) square, was decorated with a row of thirteen or fourteen little niches on the north, east, and west sides, but on the south side there are only ten on account of the entrance to the ramp. Above this base rises the spiral part; the entrance, which is 1·17 m. (3¾ ft) in width, is in the centre of the plinth. The passage turns to the right immediately and begins its spiral path, the first quarter revolution being cut through the brickwork of the plinth. The ramp is so badly damaged that it soon becomes unclimbable; it attains a height of about 16 m. (52½ ft) and apparently made three complete turns in an anti-clockwise direction.

The Date

We have seen that al-Mutawakkil began his new city in March 860 and entered it in March 861. The mosque therefore must have been built between these two dates and abandoned for ever on 17 December of that year.

THE HOUSES OF SĀMARRĀ

According to Herzfeld:

The houses of Sāmarrā are built after a fixed scheme. A covered entrance leads from the street or lane into a roomy rectangular court, for which the proportion 3 : 2 is preferred. At its end lies a ⅃-shaped main hall with two smaller rooms in the corners. This grouping of rooms is occasionally repeated in a second court, and we must then regard the two similar lay-outs as serai and *harīm*, but when they are repeated on opposite sides of the same court they indicate summer and winter dwellings. The rest of the court is surrounded by rows of rectangular dwelling and store-rooms. In most houses a number of small side courts with store-rooms are to be found. The houses always have baths and canalization and not seldom wells; in one case an installation came to light

1. *Journ. Roy. Geographical Socy*, XI, p. 129.

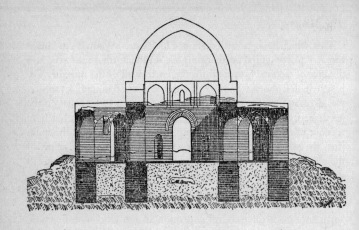

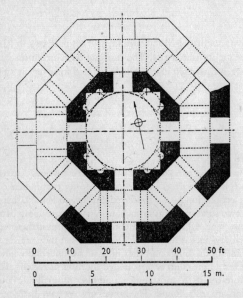

Figure 59. Sāmarrā: Qubbat as-Sulaibīya, plan and section

which certainly is not to be taken for anything but a place for making coffee. Occasionally open halls on columns occur, and underground dwelling-rooms with ventilating arrangements (*serdāb*); one house possesses a long row of separate shops on the main street, not unlike the plan of Pompeian houses. All houses were of one storey. ... The number of rooms in a house reaches as many as 50. The building material is generally unburnt brick, frequently only mud *pisé*. Burnt brick, on the contrary, is only employed for water and drain pipes and, in the form of great tiles (up to 50 cm.; $19\frac{1}{2}$ ins. square), for the pavements of courts and rooms. The roofs were without exception flat timber roofs; the doors are nearly always covered horizontally, only rarely with pointed arches. Windows occur which were filled with great coloured bulging disks of glass of 20–50 cm. (8–$19\frac{1}{2}$ in.) diameter. In some houses the ⊥-shaped halls and a few special rooms, in others nearly all the rooms, are decorated. The courts on the contrary only bear decoration exceptionally and the outer walls never. The dadoes of the rooms are decorated to a height of 1 m. ($3\frac{1}{4}$ ft), i.e. a double cubit, also the door-frames, the upper edge of the walls, and occasionally the intrados of arched doorways. ... Over the dadoes, sometimes even in the dadoes themselves, are very often small niches, mostly shaped and framed in a very baroque fashion, as usual in modern houses in the East, and which are called *tāqchah* in Persian. The material of the dado decoration is fairly pure gypsum with a slight mixture of earth. ...' [1]

THE QUBBAT AS-SULAIBĪYA

On the west bank of the Tigris, on the top of a hill about a mile south of the Qasr al-'Āshiq, are the ruins of an octagonal building. It consists of an inner octagon of which all the sides are intact, and an outer octagon of which more than half has collapsed. Between the two is an ambulatory 2·62 m. ($8\frac{1}{2}$ ft) in width, which must have been covered by a tunnel-vault, for the springing of the sixteen transverse arches on which the vault rested are to be observed, two at the ends of each side of the inner octagon. There is an arched entrance 2·13 m. (7 ft) wide in each remaining face of the outer octagon, but only four, 1·60 m. ($5\frac{1}{4}$ ft) in width, in those sides of the inner octagon which face the four cardinal points. On passing into the interior one is surprised to find

1. *Erster vorläufiger Bericht*, pp. 14–15.

that the central chamber, instead of being octagonal also, is a square averaging 6·31 m. (20¾ ft) a side. The four corners of the square almost penetrate to the faces of the octagon, thereby seriously weakening it (Figure 59). Each doorway is flanked by a semicircular niche 63 cm. (25 in.) wide. Just enough remains of the zone of transition at the south-east corner to show that the square was converted into an octagon by squinches, from which we may safely conclude that it was covered by a dome. The whole building is constructed of a kind of artificial stone in the form of bricks, measuring 32–33 cm. (12½– 13 in.) square and 10 cm. (4 in.) thick; they are mainly composed of clay, but with a strong admixture of quartz. It is as hard as stone.

Identification and Date

The building, by its construction and material, obviously belongs to the same period as the other ruins at Sāmarrā, and the curious sort of artificial stone employed shows that it belongs to the later period, for this material is used for the Qasr al-'Āshiq, but not for the earlier buildings. Let us see whether any of the known facts concerning the burial of any of the Khalifs who lived at Sāmarrā fit it. The first, al-Mu'tasim, was buried in the Jausaq al-Khāqānī, al-Wāthiq in the Hārūnī Palace, the mother of al-Mutawakkil in the Great Mosque of al-Ja'farīya (i.e. the Mosque of Abū Dulaf), al-Mutawakkil himself in the Ja'fari Palace. al-Muntasir was the first 'Abbasid Khalif whose grave was generally known, for his Greek mother requested, and obtained, permission to erect a mausoleum for him. It lay in the neighbourhood of the Qasr as-Sawāmi' and the Khalifs al-Mu'tazz and al-Muhtadī were subsequently buried in it also. Herzfeld, on the strength of these facts, suggested that the Qubbat as-Sulaibīya was possibly the mausoleum of these three Khalifs.[1] In December 1911 he excavated under the pavement and found three Muslim tombs.[2] This may be taken as a striking confirmation of his brilliant suggestion that this mausoleum is the one erected by the mother of al-Muntasir after his death in June 862. It is therefore not only the earliest existing mausoleum in Islam but probably the first ever built.

Although other octagonal mausoleums are known, there is no

1. *Archäologische Reise*, II, p. 86.
2. *Erster vorläufiger Bericht*, p. 30.

other example of a mausoleum with an octagonal ambulatory throughout the Middle East. The only country where such a type at one time enjoyed a certain amount of popularity is India.

THE ORNAMENT OF SĀMARRĀ

The ornament of Sāmarrā when first discovered, was divided into these groups, which were called the First, Second, and Third Style. It now appears probable that, if there was any chronological priority in their evolution, it was in the inverse order, so I propose to call Herzfeld's Third Style – Style A; his Second Style – Style B; and his First Style – Style C.

Style A

The distinguishing feature of Style A is the vine ornament, which we have already met with in the Dome of the Rock and Mshattā. But a change has taken place in the vine-leaves, which generally remain five-lobed as before (or occasionally three-lobed), but which have now four bold 'eyes' between the lobes with concentric ridges round them. It is tempting to believe that this new feature was evolved when the 'eyes' were made by thrusting a peg into the still plastic stucco, which might cause one concentric ridge at least. Two other changes must be mentioned: (1) the three grapes superimposed on the leaf at its junction with the stalk do not appear any more, and (2) the increase in the density of the background filling (Plate 58b). This style appears already fully developed in the Bāb al-'Āmma, the earliest building at Sāmarrā.

Style B (Plate 58a)

Central plant compositions are richly developed in this style, e.g. rosettes formed of buds, but there is no arabesque and above all no stalks. There is therefore no plant *growth*, each member being independent and having a separate termination. With the tip of each member, with the circumference of the tree, all growth ends. We find the palmette tree reduced to the tree-top and the upper branches only. In other words, the character of the style is mainly anti-naturalistic. Spirally rolled-up lines play a great part in it. One of the most attractive features of Styles A and B is that they lend themselves to the formation of large circular or lobed rosette compositions and to the filling of compartments of various shapes – square, octagonal, etc.

Style C

The patterns of this group, except for a few of the simplest borders, were made with moulds.

The relief is always a shallow cutting resembling chip-carving. It is so slight and shallow that there are no cast shadows but only shade, except in quite vertical light which, practically speaking, does not occur.

The pitch of the pattern is always very small in relation to the height, the elements are repeated quickly after each other, like a row of small planks ... one first of all cut a model out of a wooden plank, from that took off a form in clay, baked this clay, and from it cast the stucco ornament.[1] The use of moulds was a procedure which made possible the decoration of large surfaces with great speed. The elements are very varied: bottle-shaped motifs, trefoils, arabesque palmettes, spirals, etc. The design is dominated by the idea of absolute surface filling, the complete *horror vacui*. No trace of ornamental background is left. Lines in the geometrical sense, that of single-dimensioned surface borders, divide each design from the other. The work is therefore limited to the construction of these border lines instead of the surfaces. This is such a labour-saving device that one cannot avoid the thought that this principle has, for that reason, gained such power on account of the economy of labour required for the almost unheard of and almost insoluble problem of the construction of Sāmarrā.[2]

1. Herzfeld, *Der Wandschmuck*, p. 10.
2. *Ibid.*

CHAPTER 17

QAIRAWĀN: II

THE CISTERNS OF QAIRAWĀN

ABOUT a kilometre from the north gate of Qairawān, known as the
Bāb Tunis, are two large circular cisterns (Plate 59). The smaller one
receives the water of the Wādī Merj al-Līl when it is in flood, the rim
of the basin being below the level of the bed of the wādī. This cistern,
although practically circular, is really polygonal, being composed of
seventeen straight sides, averaging 6·25 m. (20½ ft) in length. Each
corner is strengthened, externally and internally, by a round buttress.
This cistern is the basin of decantation, where the mud settles. One of
its sides is in contact with one of the sides of a much larger basin, to
which there is a circular channel of communication in the partition
wall, several metres above the bottom. This larger cistern has forty-
eight sides, with a rounded buttress at each corner internally and externally and, in addition, an intermediate buttress externally in the
centre of each side. The total depth is perhaps about 8 m. (26¼ ft). The
interior diameter is just under 130 m. (427 ft), of the lesser cistern
37·40 m. (123 ft). The masonry is of rubble covered with a very hard
coating of cement. These two cisterns have a truly monumental
aspect. On the side opposite the smaller basin are two oblong covered
cisterns into which the water passes from the great cistern by openings
several metres from the bottom, being thus decanted for a second
time.

Identification and Date

al-Bakrī writes:

Outside the city of Qairawān are fifteen cisterns (*majel*) ... and the most
important and grand was the cistern of Abū Ibrāhīm Ahmad ... at Bāb
Tunis, which is round and extremely large ... and joined to this cistern
on the qibla side are [two] long arched vaults. ... North of the cistern is

a smaller one joined to it, known as al-Fisqīya, into which the water falls ... and it enters from this cistern into the great one, when the level of the water is two fathoms (*qāma*), by an opening between the two cisterns.[1]

As for the actual date it is provided by Ibn 'Adhārī, who says that it was excavated in 246 H. (860–61) and finished 248 H. (862–3).[2]

THE NILOMETER ON RŌDA ISLAND

The famous Nilometer at the southern end of Rōda Island consists of a tall graduated octagonal column, which serves as a measuring gauge, standing in a stone-lined pit, roughly 6·20 m. (20¼ ft) square, with a staircase running down to the bottom (Plate 60). Connexion is made with the Nile by three tunnels, all opening into the east side. The staircase begins at the south end of the east side. We descend twenty-four steps to a landing in the south-west corner, turn to the right and, after four more steps, arrive at a ledge which occupies the rest of the west side. Two more flights of eight and five steps respectively, bring us to a landing in the north-east corner. After two more steps on the east side, the square part of the pit comes to an end and a circular pit begins; it is 4·35 m. (14¼ ft) in diameter and 2·09 m. (6¾ ft) deep. Eight steps, leading to the bottom, are cut in the south-eastern sector.[3]

The four sides of the pit are relieved by arched recesses at the same level as the landing on the west side; each recess is covered by a pointed-arched vault resting on a pair of engaged colonnettes with clock-formed capitals and bases. On the east side of the pit, and at the same level, is a ledge 49 cm. (19¼ in.) wide, with a recess like that opposite, 1·84 m. (6 ft) wide and 85 cm. (33½ in.) deep. At the back is the opening of the tunnel from the Nile. Careful measurements show that the pointed arches of these recesses have been struck from two centres one-third of the span apart. That is to say these arches are what

1. p. 26.   2. *Bayān*, I, p. 106.

3. Until 1925, the Nilometer was full of clay-like mud to nearly a metre above the landing on the west side. The above description, based on a thorough examination of the whole structure, has only been rendered possible by the complete clearance of the pit, begun in 1925 at my request by Mr Tottenham, then Under-Secretary of State for Public Works.

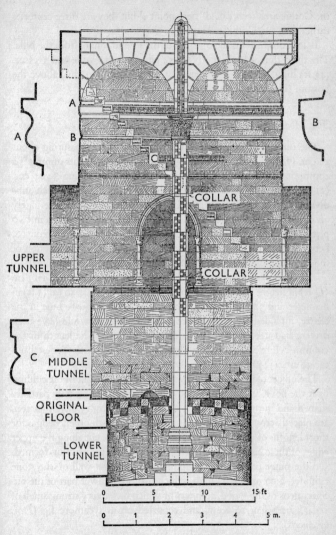

Figure 60. Cairo: The Nilometer, section

293

the Gothic architects called 'tiers-point',[1] but they are three centuries earlier than any Gothic example.

Below this recess is the opening of the second tunnel from the Nile. The third tunnel from the Nile, 52 cm. (20½ in.) wide and 1·35 m. (4½ ft) high, opens into the circular part, 26 cm. (10¼ in.) above the bottom (Figure 60).

The Measuring Column and its Subdivisions

The measuring column is a tall octagonal shaft measuring about 18 cm. (7 in.) a side and 48 cm. (19 in.) in diameter. At its summit is a composite capital. It is divided into 16 cubits averaging 54·04 cm. (21¼ in.) by transverse lines, and the ten uppermost are each sub-divided into 24 qirāt by 24 divisions, grouped four by four alternately on either side of a vertical line. The column has been broken in two places, (1) in the twelfth cubit, the length of which has been reduced, between 1798 and 1853 to 22·5 cm. (9 in.), and (2) at the junction of the 16th and 17th, the length of the cubits remaining unchanged.

The column rests on a pedestal 83 cm. (32½ in.) square and 1·17 m. (3¾ ft) in height and this rests on a granite mill-stone, 1·50 m. (5 ft) in diameter and 32 cm. (12½ in.) thick, which has a square hole in the centre, intended for the wooden axle by which it would have been driven, had it been used for its original purpose. The length of the column before it was broken, plus 1·17 m. (3¾ ft) for the pedestal and the 32 cm. (12½ in.) of the mill-stone, makes 19 cubits.

The object of this mill-stone was to spread the weight of the column over the floor, which is of wood. Two pairs of trunks, only partially shaped and measuring about 65 by 33 cm. (25½ by 13 in.) in section, are placed across each other and morticed into each other. Ledges for short lengths of planking, 7 cm. (2¾ in.) thick, are cut along the upper edges of these beams; a level floor, circular in shape, was thus formed. On the outer edge of this planking was built the wall of the stone cylinder, 2·09 m. (6¾ ft) high, which forms the lower part of the pit. Specimens of the wood, splinters of which had a very strong smell of cedar, were sent to Kew, and reported on as sycamore fig (*Ficus sycamoris*).

1. See Viollet-le-Duc, *Dictionnaire de l'architecture*, I, pp. 45–6.

The Beam

The function of keeping the column in a truly vertical position was originally performed by a beam, which was seen in position by Four-mont (1747–51), who says: 'Sur l'épaisseur de cette poutre, & de deux côtés, il y a une inscription en langue Arabe. ... On y lit que ce Bâti-ment fut élevé l'an de l'Hégire 247, de J.C. 862.' [1]

Ibn Khallikān's Account

Ibn Khallikān, in his *Biographical Dictionary*, gives an account of Abu'r-Raddād, which is of vital importance for the dating of the pre-sent structure. He says that he was in charge of 'the New Miqyās of the Nile', and adds that 'it was founded by Ahmad ibn Muhammad al-Hāsib by order of al-Mutawakkil'. The Khalif al-Mutawakkil wrote to say that verses of the Qurān and phrases appropriate to the Nilometer should be inscribed on it, and the name of the Khalif. Then follow the inscriptions which were carved on the Nilometer. The most impor-tant one, which ran round the four sides of the pit near the top, began with Qurān, XIV, 37 and ended: 'Nilometer of happiness, grace, and salvation, the construction of which has been ordered by 'Abd Allāh Ja'far al-Imām al-Mutawakkil ... by the hands of Muhammad al-Hāsib in the year 247 (861–2).' [2] The Nilometer, therefore, was once definitely dated 247 H. (861–2) by an inscription on the beam, and by an inscription which ran all round the four sides of the pit. The latter has been tampered with, for although the first part is still to be seen on the east and north sides of the pit, the historical part has been re-moved and replaced by verses from the Qurān. As the Kufic charac-ters of this part are very similar to the rest, but not so carefully carved, it is probable that it is not much later, and as Ibn Tūlūn is known to have carried out works on the Nilometer in 259 H. (872–3), and as he repudiated the authority of the Khalif and became independent ruler of Egypt just about this time, I suggest that the removal of the his-torical part of the inscription and the Khalif's name is most probably due to him.

Needless to say, this Nilometer had nothing to do with the Nilo-

1. *Description des plaines d'Héliopolis et de Memphis*, pp. 136–7.
2. *Wafayāt al-A'yān*, Būlāq ed. of 1273 H., I, pp. 382–4.

meter erected by Usāma in the time of al-Walīd, i.e. before A.D. 715, for Eutychius, who wrote in 939, calls it 'the New Nilometer, the *old one* having ceased to be used', [1] likewise Ibn ad-Dāya,[2] Yāqūt,[3] etc., and Maqrīzī; the latter adds, 'as for that which was erected by Usāma, *it had been carried away by the water*'.[4]

THE GREAT MOSQUE OF QAIRAWĀN

The Work of Abū Ibrāhīm Ahmad in 248 H. (862-3)

We must now study that part of the mosque which I attributed above (p. 258) to 248 H. viz. the mihrāb and the dome in front of it.

The Mihrāb (Plate 61)

This is a recess, 1·98 m. (6½ ft) wide and 1·58 (5¼ ft) deep, and horse-shoe in plan, flanked by a fine pair of orange-red marble columns. Its frontal arch is of a stilted and very slightly pointed horse-shoe form, which springs at a height of 2·93 m. (9½ ft) and rises to 4·56 m. (15 ft). Its decoration, both within and without, is truly remarkable and in some respects unique.

Let us begin with the recess, which is lined with a series of marble panels (some of openwork) assembled in four registers totalling 2·72 m. (9 ft) in height (Plate 62b). There are seven main panels to each register, divided by six vertical strips 11 cm. (4 in.) wide, and bordered to left and right, next the flanking columns, by strips 23 cm. (9 in.) wide. There are therefore twenty-eight main panels, each about 4 cm. (1½ in.) thick, which are *not* set at a distance of a few centimetres from the curved back of a previous mihrāb, as al-Bakrī's story would lead one to believe. Actually a hollow space has been intentionally excavated behind those places where there is an openwork panel, in order to enhance its effect. At the edges of such panels, however, the brickwork behind is actually in contact with the marble lining. If, therefore, the marble were taken away, we would find a curved surface corresponding to it, with patches hollowed out to a depth of

1. Pococke's ed., II, pp. 446-9.   2. *al-Mukāfa'a*, p. 110.
3. *Mu'jam*, IV, p. 610.   4. *Khitat*, I, p. 58, l. 8.

about 15 cm. (6 in.) at those places that correspond with an open-work panel.

People evidently were gradually led to conclude that this old wall behind was a more ancient mihrāb so that, as Marçais puts it,[1] the old wall 'which one perceived in the darkness without being able to reach it, became a sacred wall, and the legend of the mihrāb of 'Uqba formed by a process almost banal', and gave rise to al-Bakrī's story (above, p. 249). It is, moreover, incredible that 'Uqba's mosque of 50 H. (670) can have had a concave mihrāb (see above, p. 44).

The semi-dome has a wooden lining covered with a coating of some sort, to which is applied the painted decoration, consisting of vine scrolls forming loops, filled in most cases by a five-lobed vine leaf and a bunch of grapes, which at once recalls Mshattā. In its present state the design stands out in yellowish brown on a very dark background.

The Lustre Tiles

The face of the mihrāb arch and a rectangular surface surrounding it, measuring about 6·5 m. (21¼ ft) in width and 1·70 (5½ ft) in height, are decorated with lustre tiles of a fine yellowish-white clay measuring 21·1 cm. (8¼ in.) square and about 1 cm. (½ in.) thick. There are 139 complete tiles and about 16 fragments. Those forming the frame are placed lozenge-wise, so as to form a chess-board pattern set obliquely, but those decorating the face of the arch are set irregularly. Many are placed upside down, and it is obvious that they were not intended to be set as they now are, nor made for the place which they now occupy.

They belong to two distinct types, one which may almost be described as polychrome, the other as monochrome. Now and then we meet with motifs recalling Sāmarrā ornament.

It is Marçais who has finally settled the disputed question of their date.[2] He points out that the *Ma'ālim al-Imān* of Ibn Nājī (d. 1433) cites at Tujībī, who died in 1031, as follows:

[The Emīr] made the mihrāb; They [had] imported for him these precious tiles for a reception hall which he wished to construct, and they [had] imported for him from Baghdād teak wood to be made into

1. *Manuel d'art musulman*, I, p. 22.
2. *Les Faïences de la Grande Mosquée de Kairouan*, pp. 9–10.

lutes, which he made into a pulpit for the Great Mosque. And he had the mihrāb brought from 'Irāq in the form of panels of marble; he constructed this mihrāb in the Great Mosque of Qairawān, and placed these faience tiles (qarāmīd) on the face of the mihrāb. ...1

The Emīr of whom he is speaking is Abū Ibrāhīm Ahmad (856–63). We have seen from Ibn 'Adhārī (above, pp. 249–50) that Ahmad completed his work on the mosque in the year 248 H. (862–3). This, therefore, may definitely be taken as a safe date for the decoration of the mihrāb with the marble panels and lustre tiles, and for the date of the pulpit also. The tiles thus take their place as *the earliest known examples of lustre pottery of certain date*.

The Dome in Front of the Mihrāb

This rests on three free-standing arches and one wall arch (Plate 64); they spring at a height of 5·77 m. (19 ft) and rise to 9·15 (30 ft). The square thus formed is terminated by a cornice, the top edge of which is 10·83 m. (35½ ft) from the ground. The dome-bearing arches are slightly pointed and slightly horse-shoe in form, with a maximum span of 4·95 m. (16¼ ft) contracting to 4·87 (15¾ ft) at the springing. Each spandrel is filled by an arched niche, elaborately decorated, and two saucers diminishing in size as the spandrel tapers. Above is a wooden frieze, 15 cm. (6 in.) broad, decorated with a Kufic inscription in red paint.

The octagonal zone of transition, 2·51 m. (8¼ ft) in height, is formed by eight semicircular arches springing from engaged colonnettes, which rest on little corbels inserted in the cornice (Plate 63). The octagon thus formed is brought forward still nearer to the circle by eight little embryo squinches. The eight arches form shallow panels, and the four which come above the corners are pierced by shell-like squinches of nine lobes, and their nine-lobed outline is repeated in the four panels which alternate with them, and in each frame so produced is a six-lobed window.

The drum, which is 1·19 m. (4 ft) in height, is composed of eight arched windows 97 cm. (38 in.) high, and sixteen arched panels of the same height arranged in pairs between each window. This zone is terminated by a cornice at a height of 14·53 m. (47½ ft) from the ground.

1. Ma'ālim, II, p. 97.

The dome is 5·80 m. (19 ft) in diameter; it has been constructed with twenty-four ribs, each springing from a little corbel. Between the ribs are concave segments, no less than 30 cm. (12 in.) deep at the base, diminishing to nothing at the apex. Externally the zone of transition is set in a rectangle of masonry 7·62 m. (25 ft) square and 2·95 m. (9½ ft) in height, its sides being relieved by four shallow panels with horse-shoe heads. Above this block is the drum which, instead of being circular, is treated as an octagon with slightly concave sides, as at Sūsa twelve years earlier. The dome is treated externally like a Cantaloup melon with twenty-four very bold convex ribs (corresponding to the concave flutes of the interior) which taper away to nothing at the apex.

The Date

We have already seen (above, p. 257) that the dome in front of the mihrāb must be of the same date as the 'lining' arcades of the central aisle. The facts which Marçais cites in support of an attribution to Ziyādat Allāh in 221 H. (836) all speak against it. He says:

Le style est bien celui des sculptures sur marbre de la niche du mihrâb [we have seen that these panels came from 'Irāq in 248 H. (862–3)], *des sculptures sur pierre des sommiers et des corniches, qui figurent dans la galerie sud de la cour* [we have seen that the aisles of the sanctuary were prolonged by Ibrāhīm II after 261 H. (875)], *et il est encore celui qui règne sur la façade de la Mosquée des Trois Portes.*[1]

The latter is dated 252 H. (866). Thus the three facts cited by Marçais all speak for a date later than 221 H. and point to Abū Ibrāhīm Ahmad in 248 H. (862–3).

THE MOSQUE OF THE THREE DOORS, AT QAIRAWĀN

About half-way between the south gate of Qairawān and the Great Mosque is a little chapel, known as the Jāmi' Tleta Bibān, or Mosque of the Three Doors, on account of its façade, which consists of three arches framing three doorways, opening directly on the street (Plate 65). The height of this façade is 6·90 m. (22½ ft); it is at the same time

1. *Coupole et plafonds*, p. 8.

the façade of the mosque and the façade of the sanctuary, for there is no *sahn*. The arches are composed of long, narrow voussoirs, which radiate from a point below the centre. They spring at a height of 2·78 m. (9 ft) from four engaged columns surmounted by impost blocks with splay-face mouldings above and below, recalling those in the sanctuary of the Great Mosque. The arches are of a slightly pointed, slightly horseshoe-form, like the dome-bearing arches of the Great Mosque, and those which line the central aisle.

The spandrels are filled with palmette-like leaves set in loops formed by tendrils, but the top edge of this ornament has obviously been mutilated. As Marçais points out,[1] its upper part has been cut away to make room for an inscription dated 844 H. (1440–41) which runs right across. Above this are three bands of decoration, set between four mouldings, the first and third being occupied by the Kufic dating inscription of 252 H. (866). The whole is crowned by a cornice resting on twenty-five corbels, recalling those over the lateral doorways of the Great Mosque of Sūsa.

But if we stand back and view the façade as a whole, we observe that it has been subjected to a still greater disturbance, for, as Marçais has pointed out, the whole of the decoration described above must have been displaced to the right when the minaret was built.

The interior is without character and apparently modern; when Marçais wrote it had a wooden roof, but it is now vaulted with brick.

1. *Manuel*, I, p. 67.

CHAPTER 18

THE WORKS OF AHMAD IBN TŪLŪN

TŪLŪN, the father of Ahmad, was a Turki slave, who had been sent by the Governor of Bukhārā to the Khalif al-Ma'mūn in 200 H. (815–16). His son Ahmad, who was born in 835, received an education quite exceptional for one in his position, and had many favours conferred on him by the Khalif. He was sent from Sāmarrā to Egypt by his step-father in 868, with authority over the capital Fustāt, but not over the provinces. In 869 the Governorship of the whole of Egypt was conferred upon him.

Foundation of al-Qatā'i'

Ahmad, who had resided hitherto in the Dār al-Imāra of al-'Askar, now found Fustāt and al-'Askar too small for the vast number of his troops and followers, so he proceeded to found a new suburb in 256 H. (870). The area covered by it corresponded roughly to the area at present bounded on the east by the Citadel, on the north by the Shāri' as-Salība, which runs from the Citadel to Sayyida Zaynab, on the west by the Qal'at al-Kabsh, and on the south by a line drawn from east to west a little to the north of the Great Aqueduct.[1]

The Palace of al-Maydān

Ibn Tūlūn at the same time had a palace built which, together with the hippodrome where polo-matches took place, went by the name of al-Maydān. Its position, according to Ibn Duqmāq and Maqrīzī, corresponded to what is now the Maydān Rumayla, under the rock on which the Citadel was subsequently built. In front of it was a great Maydān extending as far as the mosque which he began a few years later. There were nine gates to the palace, one of which, called Bāb as-Salāt, or Gate of Prayer, opened on to a very wide road leading to

1. Maqrīzī, Khitat, i, p. 313, ll. 18–28, and p. 315, l. 15 to end.

Ibn Ṭūlūn's Mosque, about 600 m. (1,970 ft) away. There was also a triple gate called Bāb al-Maydān, and when the army marched out Ibn Ṭūlūn, mounted on horseback, left alone by the middle arch and the army by the two side ones.

Ibn Ṭūlūn, in 259 H. (872–3), founded and endowed a hospital intended solely for civilians,[1] and built an Aqueduct,[2] which still exists, its great brick intake tower being at Basātīn, a village about two miles south of the Citadel. It is a hollow block of brickwork, measuring 20·50 m. (67 ft) from east to west, 10·24 (33½ ft) from north to south, and about 10·50 m. (34½ ft) in height (proportions therefore a double cube). The central pit measures 4·74 by 4·07 m. (15½ by 13¼ ft) and the platform provided a place for two oxen working two *sāqiyas*. The aqueduct which takes off towards the north is in a very bad state.

THE MOSQUE OF AL-MAYDĀN

This famous mosque, the greatest work of Ibn Ṭūlūn, still stands to-day in a remarkable state of preservation. At one time we were almost entirely dependent on Maqrīzī (1424), and to a much lesser extent on Ibn Duqmāq for its history, but we now have a much earlier source, al-Balawī's *Sirāt Aḥmad ibn Ṭūlūn*, written early in the eleventh century, and published at Damascus by the late Kurd ʿAlī in 1939.

History

The people having complained that there was not enough room 'in the Old Mosque', i.e. the Mosque of ʿAmr, on Fridays, Ibn Ṭūlūn decided to build a new one, and chose an outcrop of rock called Jabal Yashkur as the site. The fact that the mosque was built with piers was such a novelty that two explanations were current. Ibn Duqmāq and Maqrīzī give one, according to which it was built of bricks because columns of marble cannot withstand fire. al-Balawī, however, says that Ibn Ṭūlūn was told that the mosque would need 300 columns and 'that he would not find them unless he sent to churches in the rural

1. al-Kindī, p. 216, ll. 11–13; Ibn Duqmāq, IV, p. 99; Maqrīzī, *Khitat*, I, p. 304, l. 32.

2. Ibn Duqmāq, IV, p. 57; Maqrīzī, *op. cit.*, II, pp. 457–8.

districts or in desolate parts. ... He thought this wrong and would not do so. ... The news reached the Christian, who was then in the dungeon', and he wrote that he could build it for the Prince as he would like and choose without any columns except the two for the mihrāb. Ahmad had him brought and said: 'Come, what is it you say about building the mosque?' The Christian replied: 'I will draw it out for the Prince, for him to see with his eyes, without a column but the two for the mihrāb.' Ahmad ordered skins to be brought to him ... and he drew the mosque. al-Balawī goes on to say that Ibn Tūlūn was so pleased that he set him free and entrusted him with the work.[1]

This story has all the appearance of a legend invented to explain the use of piers which were an innovation in Egypt, whereas their use is perfectly well explained by the fact that Ibn Tūlūn came from Sāmarrā, where we have seen that two immense mosques had been built on piers only a few years previously.

The Fauwāra

In the middle of the *sahn* was a fountain which Ibn Duqmāq describes as follows:

... The *fauwāra* was in the middle of the *sahn* and had windows on all sides, and over it was a gilt dome on ten marble columns, and round it were sixteen marble columns with a marble pavement. And under the dome was a great basin (*qus'a*) of marble 4 cubits in diameter with a jet of marble in the centre ... and on the roof was a sun-dial. The roof had a railing round it of teakwood.[2]

This *fauwāra* was burnt in 376 H. (986). It would appear from the above description that there was a wooden dome resting on a circle of ten columns, with a flat roof extending all round it and resting on an outer circle of sixteen columns.

The Mīda'a

'At the back of the mosque', i.e. on the north-west side, 'Ibn Tūlūn made a *mīda'a* (place for ablution)'.[3] The people apparently com-

1. Kurd 'Alī's ed., p. 182, ll. 4–15. The Christian in question was the architect who had built the Aqueduct of Basātīn; Ibn Tūlūn being dissatisfied with his work had imprisoned him.
2. IV, p. 123, ll. 6–9.   3. Ibn Duqmāq, IV, p. 123, ll. 2–3.

plained of its position, outside the mosque proper, but Ibn Tūlūn said he had placed it there on purpose, so that the mosque should be kept unsoiled. This information shows that the *Fauwāra* was meant, not for ablution as might have been imagined, but for aesthetic purposes.

The Dār al-Imāra

Maqrīzī says:

There was alongside the mosque of Ibn Tūlūn a *dār*, founded by him during the construction of the mosque. It was on the south (=SE.) side and it had a door in the wall of the mosque by which one could go to the *Maqṣūra* next the mihrāb and the pulpit [this door still exists]. In this *dār* was all that was necessary of floor coverings, curtains, and utensils, and he used to stop in this *dār* when he went to the Friday prayer. ... He would repose there, repeat his ablutions and change his garments. It was called Dār al-Imāra.[1]

The Date

The mosque appears to have been begun in 263 H. (876–7), although there are other versions, but there is no doubt about the date of its completion, for this is given by the foundation inscription as Ramadān 265 (April–May 879).[2]

Later History

By the second half of the twelfth century the mosque became completely neglected and served as a camping place for North African pilgrims on their way to Mekka.[3] In 1296, when Lājīn killed Sultan al-Ashraf, he fled and hid in the mosque for a year. Maqrīzī says that the mosque at that time was 'entirely abandoned. At night only a single lamp was lit and no one ascended the minaret to make the call to prayer. A man only stood at the door to make it'.[4] Ibn Duqmāq

1. *Khitat*, II, p. 269, ll. 22–33.
2. Van Berchem, *Corpus Inscriptionum Arabicarum – Égypte*, I, p. 29.
3. Mentioned by Ibn Jubayr, de Goeje's ed., p. 52, ll. 5–10.
4. *Sulūk*, Ziāda's ed., I, p. 827, ll. 3–11.

says Lājīn whilst hiding there 'vowed that if God favoured him and gave him power and wealth he would restore this mosque and endow it with a large *waqf*. When God gave him the throne, he kept his vow and restored it'.[1]

General Description

The Mosque of Ibn Tūlūn impresses one by its great size and by the noble simplicity of its plan. One mounts a slope to reach its doors, a few steps to enter the *ziyāda*, and from the *ziyāda* by another flight of steps to the mosque proper. This successive rise in levels recalls the Palace of Balkuwāra at Sāmarrā.

On entering one is struck by its air of peace and serenity, completely cut off as it is from the noise of the street, by its chaste ornament and devotional atmosphere. And the window grilles which, in the shadow of the porticoes, stand out against the sky like delicate lacework add greatly to the charm. The scheme of the mosque can be seen from the plan (Figure 61), and the general view (Plate 66) taken from the minaret of the Madrasa of the Emīr Sarghitmish. It consists of a *sahn* about 92 m. (302 ft) square surrounded by *riwāqs*, five aisles deep on the *qibla* side and two aisles on the other three sides. This part – the mosque proper – is enclosed by an outer wall with a remarkable cresting, and forms a great rectangle measuring 122·26 m. (401 ft) in width and 140·33 (460 ft) in depth. It is surrounded by a great outer court or *ziyāda*, except on the south-east side, which, as we have seen, was occupied by the Dār al-Imāra. This outer *ziyāda* is roughly 19 m. (62 ft) broad, and its outer walls are lower than those of the mosque proper. The whole forms a great rectangle, almost exactly square, measuring 162 m. (531 ft) in depth and 162·46 (532½ ft) in width. Its area, therefore, is 26,318 sq. m. (31,500 sq. yds), or about 6½ acres.

Material

The whole mosque is constructed of excellent red bricks measuring 18–19 by 8–8½ by 4–4½ cm. (7–7½ by 3–3¼ by 1½–1¾ in.), with joints about 2½ cm. (1 inch) thick, the whole being coated with a fine and very hard white stucco in which the ornament is cut. The bond is that

1. IV, p. 124, ll. 11–18.

known to English architects as 'English bond', i.e. courses of headers alternate with courses of stretchers.

The Ziyādas

Each length of the great outer court of the mosque proper is known as a *ziyāda*, or extension; it serves to shelter the mosque proper from immediate contact with the secular buildings of the town. As we have seen, they once contained latrines, ablution places, etc., but at present the only structure in them is the remarkable minaret. The outer walls are about 8 m. (26¼ ft) in height and 1·32 m. (4½ ft) thick. One remarkable feature must be mentioned; the central part of the wall of the north-west *ziyāda*, which corresponds with the mosque proper, is 1·13 m. (3¾ ft) higher than the rest (Plate 66).

These *ziyādas* must be regarded as corresponding to the outer *temenos* (or sacred enclosure) of a Semitic sanctuary, such as the Arab conquerors met with when they captured Damascus (above, pp. 45–7). The object of such an outer *temenos* was doubtless to separate the sanctuary proper from the secular buildings of the town. The arrangement of the Hellenistic cities of Syria generally was that the four streets placed at the cardinal points, struck the centre of the four sides of the *temenos*. Similarly, in the earliest mosques of Islam, e.g. at Kūfa, the main streets converged on the three sides of the mosque, the *qibla* side, of course, being occupied by the Dār al-Imāra. The same conditions held good for the mosque of 'Amr, and it is clear from the names of its doors (e.g. Gate of the Syrup Sellers, Gate of the Confectioners, Gate of the Spinners Bazaar, Gate of the Shroud Makers) that these doors were at the ends of bazaars.

One must therefore conclude that the outer doors of the Mosque of Ibn Tūlūn likewise marked the ends of bazaars converging perpendicularly on its outer walls, and that the *ziyādas* served to isolate the mosque proper from contact with them. It follows that the clearing, some thirty years ago, of a large area round the mosque at enormous expense, so that the walls of the *ziyādas* are also isolated, is based on a misconception and in no way represents the original condition.

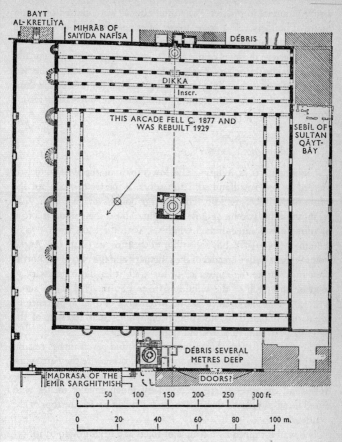

Figure 61. Cairo: The Mosque of Ibn Tūlūn, plan

The Outer Doorways

These are merely rectangular openings in the wall, for monumental entrances for mosques had not yet been evolved. These outer
walls are absolutely plain except for a couple of fillets surmounted by

307

a row of circles in squares. When the *ziyādas* were cleared of over a metre of builders' refuse some thirty years ago, it was found that the sills of the doors of the mosque proper were from 1·46 to 1·80 m. (4¾–6 ft) above the level of the *ziyāda*, and that they were originally approached by semicircular flights of steps, for the remains of the two lowest steps of such a flight were still preserved in front of the third door from the left. Most of the staircases have since been reconstructed accordingly.

The Façade of the Mosque Proper

The scheme is as follows. The lower part of the wall, which is pierced by one small and six large doors, is perfectly plain, for the jambs of the doors are flush. The six large doors average 3·20 m. (10½ ft) in width by 4·20 m. (13¾ ft) in height. Above these doors is a row of thirty-one pointed-arched windows, with their sills from 5·70 to 5·86 m. (18¾–19¼ ft) above the floor of the mosque (Plate 67). At the point where the five arcades of the sanctuary and the two of the northwest *riwāq* strike the inner face of the wall, it has been necessary to increase the pitch of the windows from 3·80 m. (12½ ft) to about 6·60 (21½ ft). The balance has been restored, and an appearance of regularity obtained by inserting plain semicircular recesses, of the same shape as the windows, but slightly smaller.

The arches of these thirty-one windows and seven niches rest on stumpy engaged columns without capitals, otherwise they are without any moulding or decorative border. The spaces between the windows and the recesses are occupied by much smaller niches with fluted hoods, so placed that their tops are in a line with the tops of the windows.

The wall is capped by a couple of fillets at a height of 10·03 m. (33 ft), above which is a row of pierced circles in squares, exactly as is the case with the outer wall. This band with its mouldings measures 1 m. (3¼ ft) in height; it is crowned by a curious open-work cresting which adds another 2 m. (6½ ft), giving a total height of 13·03 m. (42¾ ft), above the sills of the doorways. It would seem that the architect set out his design by bisecting the façade as regards its height, and then took this median line for the level of the window sills.

The Doorways

Those of the mosque proper are perfectly plain, like those of the outer wall. There were seven in the north-east and south-west sides and five in the north-west, making nineteen in all, so placed that all except the small ones at each end of the back aisle of the sanctuary correspond to a door in the outer wall. The opening is spanned by a row of palm-trunks, sawn down the centre and laid with their round side uppermost. They have then been boxed in by planking, plain at the sides but with carved ornament underneath. The original carved soffits have been preserved in four places only, viz. at the first and second large doors at each end of the sanctuary (Plate 68).[1] Above this composite lintel is a brick relieving arch, as at Sāmarrā. There are also four doors in the *qibla* wall.

The Interior

This comprises a *sahn* roughly 92 m. (302 ft) square, with thirteen pointed arches on each side (Plate 69). The sanctuary is formed by five arcades of seventeen arches each, which are carried right through to the enclosing walls, and the *riwāq* opposite of two only.

The arcades of the lateral *riwāqs*, however, abut against the outer arcades of the sanctuary and the north-west *riwāq*, and consequently consist of thirteen arches only. The arches rest on piers 2·46 m. (8 ft) wide and 1·27 (4½ ft) deep, placed about 4·60 m. (15 ft) apart; those of the sanctuary are a little over 4·40 m. (14½ ft) in height, but the rest are about half a metre less. Dovetailed wooden plates are used round the tops of these piers to strengthen them. The rise of the pointed arches, which have a slight return, is 3·70 m. (12 ft).

The Pier Capitals

These, with one exception, only differ in unimportant details. They are clearly derived from late Corinthian capitals, the two tiers of acanthus being replaced by conventionalized Sāmarrā vine-leaves. The volutes are replaced by a three-lobed leaf (Plate 72a).

1. Compare this with a strikingly similar piece (Plate 52b) from the Throne Room in the Jausaq al-Khāqānī at Sāmarrā.

The Unit of Measurement Employed

I have found that the unit employed by the architect of Ibn Ṭūlūn in setting out the mosque was the Nilometric cubit of 54·04 cm. (21¼ in.), for the principal dimensions are almost exact multiples of it, as under:

	Cubits	Should be	Actual measurement	Difference
NE. side	300	162·12 m.	162·00 m.	12 cm.
NE. side of mosque proper	260	140·50 m.	140·33 m.	17 cm.
Mosque proper, from E. to W.	225	121·59 m.	121·64 m.	5 cm.
Sahn, NE. side	170	91·87 m.	91·86 m.	1 cm.
Sahn, SW. side	170	91·87 m.	91·87 m.	NIL
Average depth of *ziyādas*	35	18·91 m.	19·06 m.	15 cm.
Average span of arches	8½	4·58 m.	4·61 m.	3 cm.
Average width of piers	4½	2·42 m.	2·46 m.	4 cm.
Average thickness of wall of *ziyāda*	2½	1·35 m.	1·32 m.	3 cm.
Average thickness of wall of mosque	3	1·62 m.	1·61 m.	1 cm.

The Form of the Arches

The arches are all pointed and stilted, and the stilted part generally has a very slight return, nevertheless it would be misleading to describe them as of horse-shoe form. Using an enlarged photograph, I found that the arches conform very closely to the outline formed by striking the two halves from centres one-fourth of the span apart, these centres, of course, being on the line of springing, which is about one-fifth of the total rise above the piers.

The Decoration of the Façades of the Sahn

The arches are surrounded by a continuous band of ornament, which turns at right angles at the springing, runs across the top of the pier, and then turns at right-angles again to run round the next arch. The wall above each pier is pierced by a small pointed arch, resting on engaged colonnettes of brick. In the spandrels between these arches and the great arches are sunk rosettes with eight lobes (Plate 69).

Above the whole runs a broad frieze of stucco rosettes, each in an octagonal frame. Old photographs show that above this frieze was a cresting.

The Decoration of the Soffits

The soffits of the arches are decorated with bands of ornament, of which ten fairly well-preserved strips exist on the outer arches of the south-west *riwāq*, and a few others elsewhere. All these bands consist of a very broad central strip enclosed between narrow borders (Plate 71). The main strip, in every case, consists of a geometrical framework, the interstices of which are filled with various elements belonging to the Style B of Sāmarrā, which suffices to prove that this decoration dates from the foundation of the mosque. This framework consists in south-west 4 and south-west 5 of quite different designs, both set out on a network of squares placed at an angle of 45°. South-west 8, south-west 9, and south-west 10 show entirely different designs, all set out on a network of equilateral triangles (Figure 62). The variety of designs, some composed of straight lines, some of interlacing circles, that can be set out on the same network is extraordinary; one of the window-grilles at Damascus (Plate 16*a* and Figure 12) has been set out on this network. In fact one may speak of two big groups of 45° and 60° patterns.

Figure 62. Cairo: The Mosque of Ibn Tūlūn, soffits of arches

The Decoration of the Inner Arcades

This is somewhat different (Plate 72*a*); there are the same arched openings above the piers, but the rosettes in the spandrels are omitted. The arches on both faces have a continuous band of ornament, 46 cm. (18 in.) wide, which turns at right angles at the springing, runs across the top of the pier, and then turns at right angles to run round the next arch. A guilloche border runs along the outer edge only. The frieze proper is a reciprocal, formed by two short undulating stems with their upper ends in contact. The cells formed thereby are filled alternately as follows: (i) In the centre is a pointed leaf from the tip of which develops a trefoil; two stalks rise from beneath the former, curl over, and form loops within each of which is a vine leaf with a prominent middle rib, its articulations indicated by drill-holes; the space left beneath is filled by a bunch of grapes. (ii) A pointed leaf stands up in the centre on a tall stalk, which divides below, curls round, and ends in the well-known Sāmarrā type of cornucopia with a pitted surface. We thus have here a mixture of Style A and B.

Figure 63. Cairo: The Mosque of Inb Tūlūn, stucco frieze round arches, diagonal treatment at springing

As a rule these friezes stop dead against each other at the corners, but on the innermost arcade of the sanctuary, which was evidently executed by picked men, for the execution is better than elsewhere, there are eight instances where this abruptness is avoided by a diagonal composition (Figure 63).

The frieze is totally different. It consists of a band of stucco ornament, which runs along just above the tops of the bands of ornament

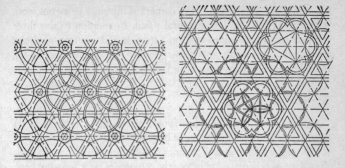

Figure 64. Cairo: The Mosque of Ibn Tūlūn, analysis of window-grilles

which run round all the arches (Plate 72b). About 20 cm. (8 in.) above this is the famous Kufic inscription on wood over 2 km. (1¼ miles) in length, which runs some 30 cm. (12 in.) below the ceilings.

The Windows

These, which stand out against the sky like delicate lacework, form one of the most beautiful features of the mosque. There are 128 in all, and their sills are from 5·70 to 5·86 m. (18¾–19¼ ft) from the floor. They average 1·80 m. (6 ft) in width and 2·30 m. (7½ ft) in height. I have shown elsewhere that only three, or at most four of the present window grilles are original. These stand out absolutely distinct from the rest by the fact that they are mainly composed of compass work, i.e. circles and segments of circles. They have all been set out by a method similar to that employed for one of the original marble grilles in the Great Mosque at Damascus (above, p. 77 and Plate 16b). As this kind of work is never found after the tenth century, there can be no doubt that these grilles date from the foundation of the mosque.

To set them out we must first construct our familiar mesh of equilateral triangles, by grouping six of which we can form hexagons wherever necessary. In south-east 6 we form hexagons in contact by their points, as shown (Figure 64); then from the corners of every hexagon we draw a circle, and in the centre of every alternate one a small circle tangential to the former. South-east 5 is more elaborate. Here we must employ concentric hexagons, but merely to give us the centres of the circles required, for the inner hexagons do not appear in the completed composition. The corners of the inner hexagons serve as centres for the six-lobed central motif. In addition to this three alternate centres are joined to form a triangle, and segments of circles are also struck from them, as shown (Figure 64). The corners of the outer hexagon serve as centres for the outer circles.

The Roof

This was composed of palm-trunks, placed about 1·25 m. (4 ft) from centre to centre and boxed in by wooden panels, panelled beams 50 cm. (19½ in.) broad and 38 cm. (15 in.) deep being thus formed. Very little of this remained before the recent works; it has now been entirely replaced by an imitation.

The Fauwāra

We have seen above that a *fauwāra*, or fountain, stood in the middle of the *sahn*, and that it was burnt in 376 H. (986). This first *fauwāra* cannot have been an ablution place, for when the mosque was first opened the people complained of the absence of any place for ablution. As for the present domed edifice in the centre of the *sahn*, it is dated 696 H. (1296) so it does not concern us.

The Minaret (Plate 66)

This is built of limestone. It is divided into four storeys of which the lowest is approximately square in plan and 21·35 m. (70 ft) in height; it has a staircase on the outside which makes one complete turn in an anti-clockwise direction. Above this is another storey, circular in plan, and 8·82 m. (29 ft) in height including the parapet (69 cm.; 27 in.), with an outside staircase which makes a little more than half a turn round it. Above this is a little octagonal kiosk of two storeys, the top of the finial being 40·44 m. (133 ft) above the ground. The second landing of the staircase is connected with the roof of the mosque by a stone bridge, borne on two parallel horse-shoe arches, 4·04 m. (13¼ ft) in span. These arches are joined by a tunnel-vault. This bridge abuts against the mosque in an absolutely inorganic fashion, its width extending from the middle of the twelfth to the middle of the thirteenth window from the right.

The four faces of the lowest storey are each decorated at the same level with a blind window divided by a column, which serves as a central support for a pair of round horse-shoe arches, set in a rectangular frame moulded in plaster. High up in the south-eastern face is another blind window.

Muqaddasī, writing in 985, says that 'its minaret of stone is small and its staircase is on the outside'; [1] and al-Qudā'ī, writing in the following century, says that it was copied from the minaret of Sāmarrā. Moreover Ibn Duqmāq [2] and Maqrīzī [3] repeat a little fable to the effect that Ibn Tūlūn, toying one day with a piece of paper and rolling it round his finger, produced a spiral and then ordered his architect to take it as a model for his minaret. This story goes back to the ninth century, for it is to be found among the fragments of Ya'qūbī printed at the end of de Goeje's edition of his *Geography*.[4]

Now this does not fit Ibn Tūlūn's minaret in its present form, so the question arises: has this minaret undergone alterations? To begin with, we have seen that the bridge must be of more recent date than the mosque, and the minaret also, for its masonry forms one with the bridge. Can it date from the period of Lājīn? Two distinctive features at once present themselves as a basis for argument, viz. the two round horse-shoe arches of the bridge and the five pairs of blind horse-shoe arches set in the faces of the minaret. Such arches appear in Egypt for the first time in the Madrasa-Mausoleum of Sultan Qalā'un, 683–4 H. (1284–5) and a few years later in the Madrasa-Mausoleum of Salār and Sangar al-Gawlī, 703 H. (1303–4). Thus we can assume that extensive alterations to the minaret formed part of the works known to have been carried out in the mosque by Lājīn in 696 H. (1296).

This is the point at which I had arrived in 1919 [5] and I still clung to the idea that the round second storey was part of an original helicoidal minaret copied from the Malwīya of Sāmarrā, and that it formed a core running right down to the ground; that its lower part had become ruined and that the present square storey was merely a new casing due to Lājīn, the bridge having been built at the same time.

---

1. p. 199.   2. IV, p. 124.
3. II, p. 267 (numbered as 268), ll. 33–5.
4. p. 371: Wiet's transl., p. 243.
5. 'A Brief Chronology of the Muslim Monuments of Egypt', *Bull. de l'Institut Français d'Archéologie Orientale*, XVI, pp. 47–8.

In 1920 Patricolo, then Chief Architect to the Comité de Conservation, decided to test this theory. He began work at the back of the recess on the south-western side and cut a horizontal shaft in the masonry, about 1·80 m. (6 ft) wide, 90 cm. (35½ in.) high, and 2·25 m. (7½ ft) deep, to which must be added the depth of the recess – 60 cm. (23½ in.). The masonry proved to be coursed; no sign of a junction circular in plan was found, or indeed any break in the masonry, although a point was reached not only well within the point above which the outer edge of the spiral staircase would have passed, had it descended to the ground, but at least half a metre within the outline of the round core embraced by the staircase of the present upper storey. This discovery is of fundamental importance; it shows that the lower part is not merely a casing, but that it forms one with the whole minaret which, on account of the features discussed above, can only have been built by Lājīn.

ARCHITECTURAL ORIGINS OF THE MOSQUE

The Design

The words of al-Qudā'ī, quoted by Ibn Duqmāq and Maqrīzī, that the Mosque of Ibn Tūlūn was built after the style of the Mosque of Sāmarrā is certainly not correct, for it does not in the least resemble either of the two mosques of Sāmarrā except in the fact that all three are surrounded by *ziyādas*. It differs from the Great Mosque of Sāmarrā in the number of its aisles – 5, 2, 2, 2, instead of 9, 4, 4, 3. As for the Mosque of Abū Dulaf, its aisles run perpendicular to the *qibla* wall instead of parallel to it. The Mosque of Ibn Tūlūn also differs from the Great Mosque of Sāmarrā in that its roof rests on arcades, instead of directly on the piers without the intermediary of arches. Its piers alone recall those of Sāmarrā, but whereas those of the former are square and have engaged marble columns at the corners, those of Ibn Tūlūn are oblong and the corner columns are only counterfeited in the brickwork.

On the other hand, its square plan repeats that of the Great Mosques at Basra, Kūfa, Wāsit, and Baghdād.

The Scheme of the Façade of the Mosque Proper

This does not recall either of the mosques of Sāmarrā, for it has no bastions. The sole feature that recalls Sāmarrā is the row of circles in squares below the cresting. Its windows in no way resemble those of the Great Mosque, which have lobed arches internally and are treated externally like arrow-slits. Ibn Tūlūn's windows, with pairs of engaged columns on both their inner and outer faces, on the contrary resemble those of the Mosque of 'Amr, minus the transverse beam and the woodwork. In other words, our façade is closely related to that of the Mosque of 'Amr as it was in 212 H. (827).

The Ornament

It is now universally agreed that the ornament of Ibn Tūlūn's Mosque is entirely derived from Sāmarrā, but whereas at Sāmarrā the three styles – A, B, and C – occur separately, in the Mosque of Ibn Tūlūn they are combined and mixed, and the vine-leaf with plastic middle rib alone is found, and not the type with sharply-cut concentric ridges.

It is principally in respect of its ornament and its piers that the Mosque of Ibn Tūlūn is a foreign, 'Irāqī building planted down on the soil of Egypt, and a large number of 'Irāqī craftsmen must have been employed for its ornament in wood and stucco. This is not surprising, for Ibn Tūlūn had come from Sāmarrā, and thousands of 'Irāqīs doubtless followed him when they heard that he had risen to power. But many were already there, for Ibn ad-Dāya tells us that in about 247 H. (861) a partisan of al-Mustansir, who had fled to Egypt in disguise, found so many people of Baghdād in Fustāt that he did not feel safe from being detected.[1]

The ornament of the Mosque of Ibn Tūlūn (and of the Dayr as-Suryānī (A.D. 914) in the Wādī Natrūn) are the two most westerly examples of the art of the 'Abbāsid Empire, which prevailed over an immense area, from Afrāsiyāb (near Samarqand) to Nīshāpūr and Bahrain.

1. al-Mukāfa'a, p. 362, quoted by Guest, in the E. G. Browne Memorial Volume, p. 171.

CHAPTER 19

CONCLUSION TO PART TWO

WITH the fall of the Umayyad dynasty, the seat of the Khalifate changed from Damascus to Baghdād. The effect was similar to the change which took place when the capital of the Roman Empire was transferred from Rome to Constantinople; in both cases the centre of gravity of the empire was changed and the mental and artistic atmosphere became more oriental. In the case of Islam the Hellenistic influences of Syria were replaced by the still-surviving influences of Sasanian Persia and 'Irāq, which profoundly modified the art and architecture, and this gave birth to the art of Sāmarrā, the influence of which extended in one direction to Egypt, where the Mosque of Ahmad ibn Tūlūn bears witness to it, and in the opposite direction to Bahrain, and to Nīshāpūr and Afrasiyāb (near Samarqand), where stucco ornament in Samarrā style has been found by excavation.

The mosques of this period vary widely in design, even in 'Irāq. The *apadāna* type – i.e. the type in which the roof rests directly on piers or wooden columns, without the intermediary of arches – was widely spread (e.g. Kūfa, Wāsit, Baghdād, Sāmarrā, etc.), nevertheless mosques with the roof resting on arcades appear at Raqqa and Ja'farīya (Mosque of Abū Dulaf), and in Egypt (Mosque of 'Amr of 827, and the Mosque of Ibn Tūlūn). The square plan of early 'Irāqī mosques (Kūfa, Wāsit, Baghdād, etc.) is departed from in the two great mosques of Sāmarrā, nevertheless it was brought to Egypt by Ibn Tūlūn. We also have vaulted mosques: the palace mosque at Ukhaidir, the Tārīk Khāna at Dāmghān, the Mosque in the Ribāt of Sūsa, the Bū Fatātā Mosque at Sūsa, and the Great Mosque at Sūsa. Mosques with a dome in front of the mirhāb can scarcely have been a feature of 'Irāqī–Persian origin, for the only examples we have, during the period covered by this work, are the Great Mosque at Damascus, 705–15; the Aqsā Mosque of 780; the Great Mosque of Sūsa, 850; the Great Mosque of Qairawān, as altered in 862–3; and the Great

318

Mosque of Tunis, 864. It must be emphasized that this feature does not occur in the mosque known as the Tārīk Khāna at Dāmghān, nor at Raqqa nor Sāmarrā. The dome over the mihrāb in the Mosque of Ibn Tūlūn dates from the end of the thirteenth century. Another important point: in three early mosques – at Cordova in 787, Qairawān in 836, and Tunis in 864 – the *sahn*, except for the sanctuary on the *qibla* side, was not surrounded by *riwāqs*.

Two other features must also be mentioned (1) arcades perpendicular to the *qibla* wall – a peculiarity first found in Syria in the Aqsā Mosque of al-Mahdī (*c.* A.D. 780), then in the Great Mosque of Cordova in 787, and then in the Great Mosque of Qairawān, as rebuilt by Ziyādat Allāh in 836; and (2) the square form of the minaret, a type derived from the church towers of pre-Muslim Syria, which remained the fixed type of the Syrian minaret until the early part of the thirteenth century. This type was carried to Qairawān and Cordova, and became the standard type in Western Islam until modern times.

In Palace architecture there were marked differences between that of the Umayyads and 'Abbāsids, partly due to the difference in court ceremonial which, under the former, was still informal and governed by Bedawīn ideas of equality, whereas under the latter, Persian influences predominated and the Khalif adopted the ceremonial of the ancient Persian court, which almost deified the king. Hence elaborate throne-rooms, generally domed, for private audience, preceded by a vaulted līwān (or four radiating līwāns) for public audience.

The *bayts* also were different, following the type of Qasr-i-Shīrīn, and not the Syrian type of Mshattā and Qasr at-Tūba.

The scale was immense; at Ukhaidir the palace complex measures 112 by 87 m. (367 by 285 ft), whilst the Khalif al-Mu'tasim's palace at Sāmarrā, with its great and lesser *Serdab*, garden court, and polo ground, measures about 1,400 m. (4,600 ft) along its main axis. Axial planning is a marked feature in the palaces of this period (e.g. Merv, Ukhaidir, Sāmarrā).

These immense palaces, which had to be run up like lightning at the caprice of an all-powerful Khalif, could not be built with the care and finish to which we have been accustomed in Syria, neither was the splendid stone of Syria available. The best material available was burnt brick, of a quality very inferior to that used later in the twelfth and thirteenth centuries. But a great part of the palaces of Sāmarrā are built of that basest of material – mud brick – hidden by thick coats of stucco. Herzfeld calls these palaces 'immense improvisations', and he is doubtless right when he points out that the 'Schragschnitt' style (my Style C) was due to the great economy of labour, and the vast surfaces which could be decorated with it in a short space of time.

In these palaces the decoration is usually confined to the stucco dadoes and door-jambs, the wooden door-soffits and the ceilings. Glass mosaic (*fusaifisā*), of which such great use was made during the Umayyad period, was sometimes employed, e.g. in the Great Mosque of Sāmarrā and the Palace of Balkuwārā and also in the Mosque at Madīna.

Of mausoleums two only have come down to us. This is doubtless due to the fact that Muslims, at this time, do not appear to have been as anxious as they were later to have buildings above their graves. Moreover, in view of the unsettled nature of the times, many 'Abbāsid Khalifs did not wish the site of their graves to be generally known, for example, when al-Mansūr died a hundred graves were dug. al-Muntasir was the first whose grave was generally known, for his Greek mother obtained permission to erect a mausoleum (the Qubbat as-Sulaibīya) for him. This is perhaps the explanation of its octagonal form and domed tomb chamber, nevertheless it is difficult to give a really satisfactory explanation of its architectural peculiarities. It had no descendants, except in India. The other, the Mausoleum of Ismā'il the Samānid, appears to have been based on a type of building which had been used in Sasanian times for temples of fire. It was an epoch-making building, and fixed the general form of Muslim mausoleums for many centuries to come.

Geometrical ornament in this early period of Islam was not the prominent feature it became in later times. It was mainly called into use for window grilles, although geometrical networks, filled with arabesque, were sparingly used at Sāmarrā (mostly octagons in contact by their sides), but more so in the Mosque of Ibn Tūlūn. When employed for window grilles it was mainly or entirely composed of interlacing circles, which were struck from the corners of a mesh of hexagons, as we have seen above (p. 313). This very beautiful type of grille is not found after the tenth century. Grilles entirely composed of interlacing straight lines, so universal later on, do not appear to have been employed at this period.

A new type of pointed arch appears, the four-centred arch. This type, although it is usually called Persian, first appears at Raqqa in 772; this fact must be emphasized, especially in view of the unscientific attempts made in recent years to claim a Persian origin for the pointed arch. Only two Persian buildings are known dating from the first three centuries of Islam, (1) the Tārīk Khāna at Dāmghān, end of eighth century, and (2) the Mausoleum of Ismā'īl the Samānid at Bukhārā, before 907. In the former most of the arches are elliptical, and only a few have a slight tendency to a pointed form; in the latter the arches are of the two-centred type, already known in Syria, in 564 (Qasr Ibn Wardān), 705–15 (Great Mosque at Damascus), 712–15 (Qusayr 'Amra), etc.

The earliest existing squinches in Islam, a feature borrowed from Sasanian Persia, date from this period, e.g. Ukhaidir, 778; Sāmarrā, 836; Great Mosque of Sūsa, 850; Great Mosque of Qairawān, as altered in 862–3; and the Great Mosque of Tunis, 864.

One of the most important innovations was the introduction of lustre tiles, which were first made in 'Irāq, the earliest definitely datable examples of this technique, which was destined to have a wonderful future, being the lustre tiles brought from 'Irāq in 248 H. (862–3), which now surround the mihrāb of the Great Mosque of Qairawān.

Bands of inscription were usually made to stand out by giving them a blue background, e.g. the Nilometer in 861, and the Mosque of Ibn Tūlūn in 879; and the frieze on which they were carved was sometimes made to curve forward to correct foreshortening, e.g. the Great Mosque of Sūsa in 850–51.

In fortification a marked advance on Umayyad practice was made at Baghdād and Raqqa; both these cities had double walls flanked by half-round towers, and the four gates of the former were bent entrances, a device unknown to the Romans or to the Byzantines before that date. At Ukhaidir a further advance was made, in the provision for a downward fire from the gallery in the wall, throughout almost the whole circuit of the enclosure; also in the elaborately defended gateways, with outer portcullis and slits in the vault above the entrance passage; unlike the bent entrance, this type of gateway had been known to the Romans. In North Africa and Spain fortification was still strongly influenced by previous Byzantine practice, e.g. the

Citadel of Merida and the Walls of Sūsa, where all the towers are square, although the Ribāt of Sūsa is an exception.

But the influence of this imperial art of the 'Abbāsid Empire, although widespread, did not extend over the whole of Islam. Umayyad art was still full of life in Syria, as is proved by the wooden panels of the Aqsā Mosque, and the style of that structure as rebuilt by al-Mahdī about A.D. 780. Moreover, Umayyad art had a new career in Spain, whither it was taken by 'Abd ar-Rahmān, the last Umayyad, and the 'hordes of Syrians' who emigrated to that country.

This same Syrian Umayyad influence also manifested itself in Tunisia, e.g. the vaulting system in the Ribāt of Sūsa and in the Great Mosque of Sūsa (which recalls that of the Cistern of Ramla) and also in the decoration of the tympanums below the dome of the latter.

Five interesting Public Works have come down to us from this period, viz. the famous Cistern of Ramla, with its tunnel-vaults resting on thirty-eight pointed arches; the Manār, or Lighthouse of Sūsa; the monumental Aghlabid cisterns of Qairawān; the Nilometer, with its fine mouldings and splendid Kufic frieze; and the Aqueduct of Basātīn.

BIBLIOGRAPHY

BELL (G. L.), *Ukhaidir*, Oxford, 1914.

BRÜNNOW and VON DOMASZEWSKI, *Die Provincia Arabia*, Strassburg, 1905. (See II, pp. 105–76 for Mshattā.)

CRESWELL (K. A. C.), *Early Muslim Architecture*, 2 vols., Oxford, 1932–40.

FLURY (S.), 'Samarra und die Ornamentik der Moschee des Ibn Tūlūn', in *Der Islam*, IV, pp. 421–32.

FUAD SAFAR, *Wāsit*, Cairo, 1945.

GABRIEL (Albert), 'Kasr el-Heir', in *Syria*, VIII, pp. 302–29.

HAMILTON (R. W.), *The Structural History of the Aqsa Mosque*, Oxford, 1949.

HERZFELD (Ernst), *Samarra: Aufnahmen und Untersuchungen*, Berlin, 1907.

Erster vorläufiger Bericht über die Ausgrabungen von Samarra, Berlin, 1912.

'Die Genesis der islamischen Kunst und das Mshatta-Problem', in *Der Islam*, I, pp. 27–63 and 105–44.

'Mitteilung über die Arbeiten der Zweiten Kampagne von Samarra', in *Der Islam*, V, pp. 196–204.

Der Wandschmuck der Bauten von Samarra und seine Ornai Berlin, 1923.

Die Malerei von Samarra, Berlin, 1927.

Geschichte der Stadt Samarra, Hamburg, 1948.

JAUSSEN and SAVIGNAC, *Les Châteaux arabes de Qeseir 'Amra, Harâneh et Tûba*, 2 vols., Paris, 1922.

KÜHNEL (Ernst), 'Mschatta'. (*Bilderhefte der Islamischen Kunstabteilung*, Heft 2), Berlin, 1933.

'Samarra'. (*Bilderhefte der Islamischen Kunstabteilung*, Heft 5), Berlin, 1939.

ARÇAIS (Georges), *Coupole et plafonds de la Grande Mosquée de Kairouan*. Tunis & Paris, 1925.

afonds peints du IXe. siècle à la Grande Mosquée de Kairouan', the *Revue des Arts asiatiques*, IX, pp. 1–8.

(Alois), 'Kusejr 'Amra und andere Schlösser östlich von Moab'. zungs-Berichte der philos.-hist. Classe der K. Akad. der Wissenaften, Wien, CXLIV, Abh, VII. 8vo., Vienna, 1902.

'Amra, fol., 2 vols., Vienna, 1907.

Puttrich-Reignard (O.), 'Die Palastanlage von Chirbet el Minje'. *Palästina-Hefte des Deutschen Vereins vom Heiligen Lande*, Cologne, 1939.

Reuther (Oscar), *Ocheïdir*, Leipzig, 1912.

Richmond (E. T.), *Moslem Architecture*, London, 1926.

Rivoira (G. T.), *Architettura musulmana*, Milan, 1914. English transl., Oxford, 1918.

Saladin (Henri), *La Mosquée de Sidi Okba à Kairouan*, Paris, 1899.

Sarre and Herzfeld, *Archäologische Reise im Euphrat- und Tigris-Gebiet*, fol., 4 vols., Berlin, 1911-20.

Schulz and Strzygowski, 'Mschatta', in the *Jahrbuch der Kgl. Preuszischen Kunstsammlungen*, xxv, pp. 205-373.

Viollet (H.), 'Description du palais de al-Moutasim à Samarra', in *Mémoires de l'Acad. des Inscr. et Belles-Lettres*, xii, pp. 577-94.

'Un Palais musulman du IXᵉ siècle', *Ibid.*, xii, pp. 685-717.

de Vogüé (Melchior), *Le Temple de Jérusalem*, Paris, 1864.

INDEX

*The following pages describe
other Penguin and Pelican
publications*

THE KORAN

Translated by N. J. Dawood

L 52

The Koran is the earliest and by far the finest work of classical Arabic prose. It is regarded by Muslims as the infallible word of God, a transcript of a tablet preserved in heaven, revealed to the Prophet Mohammed by the Angel Gabriel. It is the foundation scripture of Islam and one of the three monotheistic scriptures of the world. It preaches the oneness of God and emphasizes his divine mercy and wisdom. Mr Dawood has made the first modern translation into contemporary idiom without losing the poetry and historical grandeur of the original, in his belief that the Koran is not only one of the greatest books of prophetic literature but also a literary masterpiece of surpassing elegance. The traditional arrangement of the chapters of the Koran has always followed the plan of having the longest first, with the shorter ones last. This was instituted merely as a matter of convenience and the translator has abandoned this, commencing with the shorter and more beautiful revelations and ending with the longer and more difficult ones.

LANDSCAPE INTO ART

Kenneth Clark

A369

Sir Kenneth Clark has shown the belief that art is part of our general consciousness and gives a special value to all our experiences. In this book, which is based on his first course of lectures as Slade Professor at Oxford, he is concerned with man's relation to nature as reflected in the history of landscape painting. In the first part he considers the acceptance of descriptive symbols, the curiosity about facts, the creation of fantasy to relieve his fears, and a belief in a Golden Age of order. The great landscape painters of the nineteenth century, Constable and Corot, Turner and Van Gogh, Cézanne and Seurat, are treated in detail. Finally he considers the future of landscape painting at a time when the more vital artists have turned away from nature.

'The importance of this book to art criticism and to the history of art can scarcely be exaggerated. Ruskin and others have written notable pages on the art of landscape painting, but no such complete work on it as a separate branch of art has appeared in English.' – *Cambridge Review*

THE AESTHETIC ADVENTURE

William Gaunt

A386

The Aesthetic Adventure is an account of the aesthetic movement in Victorian England and the part played in it by
Rossetti, Ruskin, Swinburne, Pater, Whistler, Wilde, and
many others. The personalities of the artists and writers are
depicted with such reality that we almost feel ourselves
taking part in their quarrels and law-suits and being involved for or against 'art for art's sake', especially as their
cutting witty words are often quoted. The social climate
in which they lived is brought to life so well that we come
to feel at home in it.

'Of all that has been written about the nineties no book
has set forth that distinctive period in art so comprehen-
sively and so wittily as *The Aesthetic Adventure*.
'All the familiar names from Baudelaire to Sickert come
under review – with the amusing things they said and the
extraordinary things they did – in a book which is emi-
nently sane and entertaining.' – *Daily Telegraph*

THE PELICAN HISTORY OF ART

Edited by Nikolaus Pevsner

The Art and Architecture of India:
Hindu, Buddhist, Jain
BENJAMIN ROWLAND

Architecture in Britain 1530–1830
JOHN SUMMERSON

Art and Architecture in France 1500–1700
ANTHONY BLUNT

Painting in Britain: The Middle Ages
MARGARET RICKERT

The Art and Architecture of Russia
GEORGE HEARD HAMILTON

The Art and Architecture of the Ancient Orient
HENRI FRANKFORT

The Art and Architecture of Japan
ROBERT TREAT PAINE AND ALEXANDER SOPER

Sculpture in Britain: The Middle Ages
LAWRENCE STONE

The Art and Architecture of China
LAURENCE SICKMAN AND ALEXANDER SOPER

Architecture in Britain: The Middle Ages
GEOFFREY WEBB

Greek Architecture
A. W. LAWRENCE